Why Black Lives Matter

African American Thriving for the Twenty-First Century

EDITED BY

Anthony B. Bradley

CASCADE *Books* · Eugene, Oregon

Cascade Books
An Imprint of Wipf and Stock Publishers
199 W. 8th Ave., Suite 3
Eugene, OR 97401

www.wipfandstock.com

PAPERBACK ISBN: 978-1-7252-5211-0
HARDCOVER ISBN: 978-1-7252-5212-7
EBOOK ISBN: 978-1-7252-5213-4

Cataloguing-in-Publication data:

Names: Bradley, Anthony B., editor.

Title: Why black lives matter : African American thriving for the twenty-first century / edited by Anthony B. Bradley.

Description: Eugene, OR: Cascade Books, 2020 | Includes bibliographical references.

Identifiers: ISBN 978-1-7252-5211-0 (paperback) | ISBN 978-1-7252-5212-7 (hardcover) | ISBN 978-1-7252-5213-4 (ebook)

Subjects: LCSH: African Americans—Social conditions. | African Americans—Conduct of life. | African Americans—Religious life.

Classification: E185.625 .W60 2020 (print) | E185.625 (ebook)

Manufactured in the U.S.A.   10/19/20

To the Rev. Dr. Frank J. Blackshear (1941–2019), former pastor of Greater Zion Hill Baptist Church (New York, NY), and the entire Greater Zion Hill Baptist Church family for preaching the word and celebrating the gospel in Harlem.

Contents

Acknowledgments

T he contributors and I have worked on this book for a long time and we are grateful to have the project in print. This project would not be possible were it not for the great team at Wipf and Stock, including Matthew Wimer, George Callihan, and others, who were willing to take the risk of publishing forward-thinking and controversial topics that tackle important issues of this generation.

I am very thankful for Marvin Olasky, when he was Provost at the King's College (2007–2011), for providing office space and resources to initially bring this project to a close during my year as a visiting professor of theology. Additionally, I'd like to thank Brigadier General Tim Gibson, USAF, Ret., President of the King's College, for his support of faculty publishing and to current provost Mark Hijleh for encouraging faculty to lead with our scholarship. My thanks is also extended to the King's College student editorial team of Matthew Rosenbaum and Daniel Hay who both did superb jobs with the initial copying editing of the first edition. Finally, I am greatly indebted to Phillip Reeves for managing the entire process of making this updated edition possible. Without him, none of this would have happened.

Contributors

Vincent Bacote, PhD, is an Associate Professor of Theology and the Director of the Center for Applied Christian Ethics at Wheaton College in Wheaton, Illinois. Dr. Bacote believes that doctrine is central to the life of the church. He is the author of *The Political Disciple: A Theology of Public Life* and *The Spirit in Public Theology: Appropriating the Legacy of Abraham Kuyper*. Dr. Bacote has contributed to books including *Black Scholars in White Space: New Vistas in African American Studies from the Christian Academy; On Kuyper; Aliens in the Promised Land: Why Minority Leadership Is Overlooked in White Christian Churches and Institutions; Keep Your Head Up*; and *Prophetic Evangelicals*. He is a regular columnist for *Comment* and has had articles appear in magazines such as *Books and Culture, Christianity Today, Think Christian* and *re:generation quarterly*, and journals such as *Christian Scholars Review, Urban Mission*, and *The Journal for Christian Theological Research*.

Anthony Bradley, PhD, is a professor of religious studies, chair of the program in Religious and Theological Studies, and director of the Center for the Study of Human Flourishing at the King's College in New York City. Dr. Bradley lectures at colleges, universities, business organizations, conferences, and churches throughout the US and abroad. His writings on religious and cultural issues have been published in a variety of journals, including *The Philadelphia Inquirer, The Washington Examiner, The Atlanta Journal-Constitution, The Detroit News, Christianity Today*, and *World Magazine*. Dr. Bradley is called upon by members of the broadcast media for comment on current issues and has appeared on C-SPAN, NPR, CNN/Headline News, and Fox News, among others. He studies and writes on issues of race in America, mass incarceration and overcriminalization, youth and family, welfare, education, and ethics. His books include: *Liberating Black Theology, Black and Tired, The Political Economy of Liberation, Keep Your Head Up, Aliens in the Promised Land, John Rawls and Christian Social Engagement, Black Scholars in White Spaces, Something Seems Strange, Ending Overcriminalization and Mass Incarceration*, and *Faith in Society: 13 Profiles of Christians Adding Value to the Modern World*.

Rev. Howard Brown is Senior Pastor of Christ Central Church in Charlotte, North Carolina. Rev. Brown is the founding Senior Pastor of Christ Central Church. He holds a Master of Divinity degree from Covenant Theological Seminary and an English degree from Clemson University. Before coming to Charlotte, he ministered and led churches in Atlanta and Baltimore. Pastor Brown is a contributing author in the books *Heal Us Emmanuel: A Call For Racial Reconciliation*; *Representation and Unity In the Church*, and *Keep Your Head Up: America's New Black Christian Leaders, Social Consciousness, and the Cosby Conversation*. He serves on the board of trustees for Covenant College. He is also an advisory board member for Gordon-Conwell Theological Seminary-Charlotte and Reformed University Fellowship. A Charleston, South Carolina native who loves Clemson football, Howard fishes every chance he gets. He and his wife, Kellie, are foodies who enjoy listening to music and watching movies and TV together. They are the proud parents of two boys, Harrison and Clark.

Rev. Anthony Carter (MA, Reformed Theological Seminary) is Lead Pastor of East Point Church in East Point, Georgia, an organizing member of the Council of Reforming Churches, and a Council member of The Gospel Coalition. He is the author of two books, including *Black and Reformed: Seeing God's Sovereignty in the African-American Christian Experience*. Anthony and his wife, Adriane, have five children.

Bruce Fields, PhD, was Professor of Faith and Culture at Trinity Evangelical Divinity School in Deerfield, Illinois. Dr. Fields has served on the staff of Campus Crusade for Christ in the Native American Ministry, with Athletes in Action, and on campus staff at the University of Michigan. His areas of expertise include the book of Philippians, liberation theology, and Black theology. He has taught theology and chaired the Biblical and Systematic Theology Department at TEDS and has taught New Testament and theology at Trinity College. During the production of this book, Dr. Fields tragically passed away in April of 2020 after a long battle with cancer. We are indebted to his scholarship and will be forever inspired by his humility, grace, perseverance, and strength.

Natalie Haslem, DNP, RN, PMHNP-BC, is a psychiatric nurse practitioner with Naphcare, Inc. at the Fulton County Jail in Atlanta. Her specialization is psychiatry with a BS from Spelman College, a BN from Kennesaw State University, a MS in Nursing from the University of South Alabama, and a Doctorate of Nursing Practice also from the University of South Alabama.

Rev. Ken Jones is the pastor of Glendale Missionary Baptist Church in Miami, Florida. He has taught seminary extension courses on the book of Galatians and church history. Rev. Jones has contributed articles to *Modern Reformation* and *Tabletalk*.

Rev. Lance Lewis is Senior Pastor of Soaring Oaks Presbyterian Church in Philadelphia, Pennsylvania. Lewis holds an MDiv from Chesapeake Theological Seminary and a BA in English from Temple University. Prior to serving at Soaring Oaks, Pastor Lance was a church planter in the Philadelphia area at Christ Liberation Fellowship and served as Assistant Pastor of New City Fellowship in Fredericksburg, Virginia.

Rev. Eric Mason, DMin, is the founder and lead pastor of Epiphany Fellowship in Philadelphia, Pennsylvania. Dr. Mason, aka "Pastor E" and affectionately called "the Bishop," is married to Yvette and has three sons, Immanuel, Nehemiah, and Ephraim, and one living daughter, Amalyah. After over two decades of gospel ministry, Dr. Mason has become known for his unquenchable passion to see the glory of Jesus Christ robustly and relevantly engaged in broken cities with the comprehensive gospel. Urban ministry is the heartbeat of his ministry and calling. He is the founder and president of Thriving, an urban resource organization committed to developing leaders for ministry in the urban context. Dr. Mason has written four books: *Manhood Restored, Beat God to the Punch, Unleashed,* and *Woke Church.* Dr. Mason received a DMin from Gordon-Conwell Theological Seminary and a ThM from Dallas Theological Seminary.

Rihana Mason, PhD, received her PhD in experimental psychology with an emphasis in cognitive psychology from the University of South Carolina. She served as an associate professor in psychology at Emmanuel College for several years, where she helped to expand the undergraduate curriculum to include courses which emphasized research and writing in psychology. She was awarded the Firebaugh Memorial Faculty Award from Emmanuel College in 2015. She was formerly the project director for the Quality Rated Improvement System Evaluation Project and now leads the Hearst Cox Campus Evaluation and L4 DOE projects the Urban Child Study Center at Georgia State University. She is an adjunct faculty member at Spelman College, her undergraduate alma mater. Her primary research interests include vocabulary acquisition, reading comprehension, and the assessment of language and literacy in diverse populations.

Yvonne RB-Banks, PhD, is a Professor in the School of Urban Education at Metropolitan State University and an adjunct instructor at The University of Northwestern St. Paul. Prior to coming to Northwestern, Dr. RB-Banks worked in the public school system for approximately seventeen years. She started her professional career by using her training as a teacher to work with students placed in special education. Over the course of her career she has been a classroom teacher, team lead, and district coordinator for special programs. In addition to her teaching responsibilities in the core curriculum, she coordinates the Special Education Minor program. Her primary field of research has been on the population of students labeled emotional/ behavioral disordered and specific learning disabilities needs, and the impact of such placements on their academic experiences. In addition to studying the academic outcomes for the special needs populations, Dr. RB-Banks often researches and presents on how cultural norms influence the learning experiences for children from diverse backgrounds, especially African American males. She holds professional memberships in the Association of Black Women in Higher Education (ABWHE-Minnesota Chapter); the Minnesota Association for Continuing Adult Education (MACAE); the Midwest Educators of Color Association (MECA); and the Minnesota Association on Higher Education and Disability (MN-AHEAD).

Ralph Watkins, PhD, is the Peachtree Associate Professor of Evangelism and Church Growth at Columbia Theological Seminary. Dr. Watkins's work and research centers around building twenty-first-century churches. His writing and research is done with congregations as they partner to be faithful to the call of being the body of Christ. He is presently working on ways the church can use multi-media approaches and web 2.0 strategies to be effective at evangelism and discipleship. He is author of *The Gospel Remix: Reaching the Hip Hop Generation*; *I Ain't Afraid to Speak My Mind*; *From Jay-Z to Jesus: Reaching and Teaching Young Adults in the Black Church* (co-authored with Benjamin Stephens); and *Hip-Hop Redemption: Finding God in the Music and the Message.*

Preface

T he Black Lives Matter (BLM) movement grew in response to a number of African Americans who were killed because of the actions of police. These men and women include Trayvon Martin, Renisha McBride, Eric Garner, John Crawford, Michael Brown, Tamir Rice, and others. According to the movement's website,

> Black Lives Matter began as a call to action in response to state-sanctioned violence and anti-Black racism. Our intention from the very beginning was to connect Black people from all over the world who have a shared desire for justice to act together in their communities. The impetus for that commitment was, and still is, the rampant and deliberate violence inflicted on us by the state.

Unlike the civil rights movement of the 1950s and 1960s, BLM has been intentional about keeping black churches on the far periphery of their advocacy for black flourishing. I believe this to be a profound error. Keeping God on the margins, and what God desires for the people he created, will not lead to long-term thriving. In fact, keeping what God desires for the human person on the margins is a predictor of social decline. The authors of this book would not only like to add some perspective on why black lives matter but also explain why the church matters to Black Lives Matter. The central thesis is this: black lives matter because African Americans are made in the image of God, and black thriving is, therefore, derivative of God's desire for human flourishing as we address various issues of this generation.

This book first began as a continuation of a conversation started by Bill Cosby and Dr. Alvin Poussaint in their 2007 book *Come On People: On the Path from Victims to Victors*. The first edition of this book, in conversation with Cosby and Poussaint, was published in 2012 as *Keep Your Head Up: America's New Black Christian Leaders, Social Consciousness, and the Cosby Conversation*. Poussaint did not mince words when speaking about the state of black men, the social tragedies wreaking havoc in low-income black neighborhoods including children not being parented well, children suffering in substandard public education, media that glories in the dehumanization of women and men, unhealthy eating habits, black-on-black violence, and lack of economic empowerment. *Come on People* was an honest challenge for blacks from all walks of life to pay attention to a group of Americans that have been ignored by many, including the black middle-class. The issues raised by the Black Lives Matter movement call for renewed attention to be paid to those principles and practices that have historically produced black thriving. We believe that we will not make progress until we hear from black religious leaders who hold the work and person Christ in high esteem. This is why we are repositioning this discussion with *Why Black Lives Matter.*

Historically, the black church has been a place of spiritual formation and cultural renewal in black communities. Because the church remains relevant today that tradition must continue, since people need help and hope. The election of Barack Obama to the presidency of the United States was a wonderful example of social progress but can only offer limited hope to address the deeply differentiated social and spiritual issues that have many black communities in America in a new kind of oppression. We need to hear from the Lord. We have assembled some of the most dynamic and progressive black pastors and theologians in America to move this conversation forward because we believe the church must lead in initiating the type of renewal needed to rightly answer the deep questions about solutions to the crisis and to provide insight on why black lives matter.

In chapter 1, Vincent Bacote sets the stage for this new movement by addressing the issue of African American identity and the victim mentality that Cosby and Poussaint discuss in their book. Bacote sets the dynamic realities of personhood and dignity in a theological framework that seeks to establish the best framework for understanding the human person in light of God's intention for human life. In chapter 2, Bruce Fields provides a powerful vision for strengthening the black family to cast a vision and offer hope for redeeming the most important social institution in black communities. Without strong black families, there is not much hope for sustainable change. With chapter 3, Yvonne RB-Banks explains the need for the church to pay particular attention to the needs of black girls. Howard Brown, in chapter 4, writes forthrightly about sex and sexuality in the black community. Some of the issues Poussaint addressed reveal the consequences of divorcing sexuality from the covenant of marriage.

Is there anything redeemable about hip hop? Can hip hop encourage black thriving? Can we learn anything from the genre that might help us know how to help people? These questions and more will be addressed in chapter 5 by Ralph Watkins. The celebration of misogyny, violence, and materialism in popular hip hop provides an easy target for criticism. Poussaint and others point out many of the negative aspects of the music. What may not be so clear, however, is that hip hop provides signals of pain and suffering that we certainly do not want to miss if we want to accurately apply the gospel to the sin and brokenness experienced in daily life for many African Americans. Hip hop can show us the issues in black lives that need to be addressed. Additionally, popular hip hop presents an image of what it means to be a black male in America that the gospel needs to address. Eric Mason in chapter 6 "makes it plain" by challenging the distorted vision of black masculinity in our culture and provides a way forward in light of the gospel and role of the church. Black men's lives matter in the church. In chapter 7, Rihanna Mason uses important research to show a scientific approach to the matter and to explore ways that Christians can support black thriving on college campuses, and Historically Black Colleges and Universities (HBCUs) in particular.

Does the church have any role to play in healing the black community? Since the time of American slavery, black churches in America served as the cement that kept communities and families together within the context of oppression. The church has a central mission to provide the spiritual formation necessary to ignite virtuous social mores in communities and has been doing so for centuries. Lance Lewis in chapter 8 discusses the redemptive power local churches can have in helping communities wrestle with complicated issues as we press towards making a Christian case that black lives matter. In chapter 9, using Isaiah 61:1–4, I introduce readers to a vision of redemptive transformation that takes broken people on a journey toward liberation with a life redirected to the kingdom of God. It is a road map for how black lives become victors and agents of mercy, justice, and faithfulness to the priorities of the mission of God. Natalie Haslem continues the mental health discussion in chapter 10 by applying these issues to the criminal justice system.

We conclude the book by focusing on the church, which forms the people who do all of the great work mentioned in the previous chapters. In chapter 11, Anthony Carter, with great clarity and insight, addresses the need for biblical orthodoxy in black churches if the church intends to be what it always has been for black people and the world—the central destination for renewal. One of the greatest impediments to the healthy mission of the black church has been the rise of the prosperity gospel. The prosperity gospel has devastated the lives of many people needing help from God by distorting the core message of the gospel. In chapter 12, Ken Jones discusses the prosperity gospel in historical context and offers important biblical and theological corrections to a movement that has exploded in black communities all over America.

It is my hope that this book will be read critically and will create new questions for a national dialogue about the black church and her connection to the black community as we think about the telos for black lives and why they matter. We are all independent thinkers from multiple traditions and bring different perspectives to the table. The richness of this volume is a type of viewpoint diversity that keeps the resurrection of Jesus Christ at the center. While we do not agree on specific prescriptions for change in all areas we do share a central conviction that there needs to be a resurgence of black religious leadership to properly form the Black Lives Matter movement. Without the church, black lives cannot be truly liberated to be the persons that God created them to be. We hope for this book to serve as a first step in inspiring more black religious leaders to lock arms and provide the moral voice that our communities need as we pursue what it means to say, "Black lives matter."

Anthony B. Bradley
The King's College
New York City

Chapter 1   **More Than Victims: The Benefits of a Theological Vision**

—VINCENT BACOTE

Alvin Poussaint and Bill Cosby's *Come on People: On the Path From Victims to Victors* sounds an alarm about a crisis in the African American[1] community. The subtitle suggests that this emergency can be construed as an identity crisis, at least in part. From the vantage point of Cosby and Poussaint, a victim identity and/or mentality only facilitates and entrenches the crisis at hand. How should we think about African American identity, particularly when we look at it through a theological lens? This chapter will first look with Poussaint at the circumstances that have given rise to a victim mentality, some of the response to Poussaint, and then consider a vision of African American identity rooted in some of the categories we find in the biblical narrative.

Elements of the Crisis

The subtitle of *Come on People* reveals the desire to promote a positive African American identity. In order to properly address the issue of identity, we must accompany the authors as they address the various challenges which have led some (perhaps many) to see themselves as victims. Each chapter addresses a particular set of problems. My first task is to identify the elements from each chapter that can comprise a victim identity. The path to a helpful theological response requires us to face the various aspects of this dilemma with a clear, unadulterated vision.

Cosby and Poussaint begin with the crisis of the African American male. Linked to lamentable community decline and a loss of parental skills, the plight of African American men has emerged unexpectedly. Despite the legal protections from segregation and discrimination won in the civil

---

1. In this chapter I will use both "African American" and "black" as a descriptor.

rights era, a new legacy of success in mainstream America has not emerged, particularly for those inhabiting a lower economic station. However, one startling change has occurred:

> In 1950, five out of every six black children were born into a two-parent home. Today, that number is less than two out of six. In poor communities, that number is lower still. There are whole blocks with scarcely a married couple, whole blocks without responsible males to watch out for wayward boys, whole neighborhoods in which little girls and boys come of age without seeing up close a committed partnership and perhaps never having attended a wedding.[2]

For African American males, this drastic shift in poor communities has set the stage for a number of specific problems—chief among these is the absence of fathers. While there are many virtuous and strong black women in these communities, this fails to adequately compensate for the vacuum of positive male influence within families. The effects of this absence reverberate broadly, from deficient visions of success to education to dating. In spite of Daniel Patrick Moynihan's prediction about the effects of the welfare system, it is unlikely that anyone would have expected the effects to be so devastating.

Poussaint identifies problems beyond criminality, such as the emotional problems that lie beneath a veneer of "coolness," the contrasting tendency to resort to violence upon the slightest hint of "getting dissed," careless sexual promiscuity that leads to unplanned pregnancies—and men with no interest in responsible fatherhood—and mutual disrespect between men and women in romantic relationships—sometimes with the consequence of abused male children in fatherless homes.

The second chapter has a specific focus on community and explicitly draws attention to the detrimental effects of the myth of white supremacy on black identity. One prominent manifestation of this is the tendency to equate education and success with "being white." While acknowledging the role of systemic racism in United States history, Poussaint is more concerned with effects of white supremacy on the self-esteem of many African Americans. The internalization of negative stereotypes and the tendency to live down to the expectations of low education and criminality along with other forms of failure facilitates and catalyzes a form of mental inertia within youth. The authors wonder if this has meant accepting the lie that an entire culture primarily produces bottom-dwellers. The central concern in the entire chapter is the failure of communities to

2. Cosby and Poussaint, *Come on People*, 2.

function as a village that supports its members and encourages even the most downtrodden to move toward success. It is particularly interesting that the church does not escape Poussaint's critical gaze. While he does not universally criticize the church, he makes the point that many churches have failed to encourage their congregants to tend to their communities as an expression of the mandate for humans to care for God's world. Put differently, the church is failing to combat the rampant victim mentality that immobilizes the range of responsibility necessary to have flourishing neighborhoods despite the challenges of the past.

Children are the focus of the third chapter, which begins with an emphasis on the responsibility of childcare, though the specific focus is on parenting. In their efforts to prompt readers to elevate themselves beyond a victim mentality, Cosby and Poussaint address a combination of ignorance, neglect, and pathology that has conspired to keep African Americans from flourishing. They proceed from the womb through the teen years and begin by drawing attention to a range of concerns such as proper prenatal and postpartum care, the role of nurture and positive attention, and the virtue of patience in parenting. The absence of such vital modes of care leads to children who struggle to thrive. These are the children who enter the educational system already at a disadvantage.

Poussaint also criticizes physical punishment as an approach to discipline, particularly because such expressions can escalate to abusive violence and send the message that violence is the way to resolve problems. While not asserting that physical punishment inevitably leads to a broken spirit, the clear argument is that this approach to discipline can play a role in creating certain kinds of victims rather than producing productive citizens: "We're not saying that parents who occasionally spank children will damage them. The adults who feel spankings helped them were more likely to be the ones who were occasionally spanked. Unfortunately, those who were spanked excessively or abused as children are less likely to show up in our audiences as responsible adults."[3]

Physical violence is not the only concern; verbal, sexual, spousal, and sibling abuse is also part of a larger problem. The hope is that less violence of any kind in the home will reduce criminal violence elsewhere. A final notable concern in this chapter is self-concept. What concept of identity do parents convey? Is there shame related to skin color, beauty standards, education, and language? How many parents are unwitting allies in the construction of an identity of black victimhood and inferiority?

---

3. Cosby and Poussaint, *Come on People*, 70.

The fourth chapter, focusing on education, might be understood in part as a lament that learning has somehow become linked to a bad public relations campaign. The authors state that apart from a well-trod path of educational uplift, "most of us would still be struggling at the fringes of society. Given this glorious history, it troubles us that so many black youth are as thrilled about getting an education as they are about getting head lice."[4] Why the lack of interest in getting a good education? Bad schools in poor areas, homes and communities that rouse little interest or inspiration for learning, and low literacy and high dropout rates are not the components of good advertising for education. Yet, this is the context in which many poor blacks live every day. While Poussaint traces a path toward uplift, the lived experience of many in such settings is comprised of an existence where it is "normal" to have little chance to be educated and have successful lives.

Media is the topic of the fifth chapter. After the success of positive programs such as *The Cosby Show* and *Roc*, the return of negative stereotypes through certain Hollywood films and music videos—along with the tendency to connect beauty with lower concentrations of melanin—disheartens. The pervasiveness of violence, careless and promiscuous sexual behavior, and a disturbing proliferation of the N-word from the mouths of some black entertainers washes over the minds of African American children in wave after wave of media. Models of decadence, self-destruction, and self-hatred are marketed, packaged, and sold to youth who often imitate the "reality" presented by their favorite celebrities. The role of advertising is also challenging. One example: some very popular celebrities promote liquor in magazines and television marketed to black communities. The authors point to research that shows a greater likelihood that children exposed to such ads will drink alcohol heavily. While media is not inherently detrimental, many films, video games, television programs, and websites wield great influence, often negatively.

The domain of health care is covered in the sixth chapter. Discrepancies in health care are one legacy of racism that continues to this day, in spite of a notable decrease in discriminatory practices in medicine. While the era of uninformed participation in research protocols is now past, a lingering distrust in the medical profession remains. I can attest to this personally; my mother had a basic distrust of the medical profession because of the many people she knew that had substandard health care, especially the elderly. This suspicion may have been a factor in the late discovery of the disease that killed her. The chapter indicates that deaths from cancer are also linked to the tendency to wait until it is too late for a proper diagnosis; Poussaint

4. Cosby and Poussaint, *Come on People*, 101.

notes that this is quite typical for the black poor who don't have insurance or access to adequate care. For the black population overall, life expectancy is lower for males and females compared to their white counterparts by close to five years.[5] Passivity about health is as much of a problem as suspicion of the medical profession. Ignorance combined with inadequate vigilance about diet and exercise contributes to a range of problems from tooth decay to diabetes to cancer. Mental health is perhaps a greater area of crisis because of a lack of awareness and understanding of depression and the stigma associated with mental illness in black communities. Unsound bodies and minds are certain roadblocks to abundant life.

The specter of violence appears in several chapters but gets direct focus in chapter seven. While in the past many in the South projected their own violent behaviors onto black men, the stereotype of the dangerous, sexually predatory, stupid, and violent male prevails in the minds of many today. Though black crime against whites is relatively rare, there is indeed much crime and violence within black communities that suggests that black men are prone to violence. A glance at the statistics listed above from the first chapter reveals an epidemic. Although there has been a decrease in violence in recent years, this hardly means that the core problems have seriously abated. Deficient parenting, gangs as stand-ins for family units, drug culture, access to and use of guns, and disrespect for authority (particularly the police) mix together in communities in a cocktail that often produces violence.

The final chapter charts a course from poverty to prosperity. The topics from the previous chapters often contribute to poverty. "There are many causes of poverty among African Americans, some direct and some indirect. Here is a partial list: institutional racism, limited job opportunities, low minimum wage, mental illness, physical disabilities, drug and alcohol abuse, lack of a high school diploma, incarceration, and a criminal record."[6] The authors admit that these are challenging conditions for anyone, yet their message is that such conditions need not guarantee a life below the poverty line. Yet, this struggle remains today.

Here is what many African Americans live with every day: black males as an endangered species, unstable communities, children subject to poor parenting, deficient education, seductive and misleading media, poor health, excessive violence, and poverty. The relentless drumbeat of these elements would make anyone perceive themselves as a victim, yet Poussaint believes that these factors do not need to have the last word. While

5. Bond and Herman, "Lagging Life Expectancy for Black Men," 1167.
6. Cosby and Poussaint, *Come on People*, 223.

it is beyond dispute that the legacy of racism and white supremacy has victimized the black community, the central question of identity focuses on whether a legacy of oppression has the definitive voice. Adam Serwer's review of Claude Steele's *Whistling Vivaldi* helps us see some of the difficulty. Here are notable observations quoted at length:

> Racial identity . . . affects people's thinking and action in countless ways but often without any awareness or malice. People pick up on cues—a topic of conversation, the language used in an employment brochure, the number of people of their own race or gender in a classroom or office—and react on the basis of internalized concerns about being stereotyped. While people in every group register these signals, members of racial minorities often experience a threat—what Steele calls "stereotype" or "identity" threat—that impairs their performance.
>
> In *Whistling Vivaldi*, Steele primarily focuses on underperforming college students, particularly blacks and women, who by reaching college might be thought to have conquered negative stereotypes. But the research that Steele and others have done indicates that when facing identity threat—that is, when they are reminded of the shortcomings associated with their group— these students tend to underperform in comparison to their male or white counterparts with similar scores.
>
> Steele's experiments show that identity threat can affect a member of any group given the right context, but minorities and women face more of a problem because the stereotypes that work against them are so deeply rooted in our culture. The stress caused by identity threat then becomes an ever-present burden. Steele points to high rates of diseases such as hypertension among African Americans as an example of the physiological effects of coping with identity threat on a constant basis.
>
> *Whistling Vivaldi* conveys an understanding of why race remains such a powerful factor even in a society where racial discrimination is seen as abhorrent and prohibited by law. And while Steele's research gives some measure of hope, I'm not betting that people would change even if they learned about his findings. Dealing with stereotype threat requires a willingness to admit the power that group identities have over our minds and actions, and most of us don't believe that we're susceptible

to bias, whether we're the guy whistling classical music or the person sighing with relief and deciding not to cross the street.[7]

The legacy of white supremacy has tenacious and lingering effects that explicitly and implicitly penetrate the consciousness of many African Americans. This at least suggests that an identity as a victim of some sort can be present even in those who are not in circumstances as dire as those presented in *Come on People*. The goal of this chapter is to present a theological path toward a more whole, positive, and responsible identity. Before bringing a theological voice to this conversation, however, we briefly turn to some of the response to a former leader of the community, Bill Cosby.

Talking Back to Bill

It is important to remember that the response to Bill Cosby (there is far less criticism of Alvin Poussaint) is not only to *Come on People*, but also related to his famous 2004 speech given at the fiftieth anniversary commemoration of the *Brown vs. Topeka Board of Education* decision (called the "Poundcake" speech by some). In the speech, Cosby criticized irresponsibility in the black community, particularly in poorer areas. The speech attracted much affirmation and criticism. Was this a matter of someone finally telling the truth, or was this yet another example of class warfare where upper- and middle-class blacks look down on and leave behind the underclass they hold in disdain? One of the most notable respondents was Michael Eric Dyson, who wrote the book *Is Bill Cosby Right, or Has the Black Middle Class Lost its Mind?* In various media, Dyson took Cosby to task for blaming the victim and betraying those still subject to an unfair society. *Come on People* was published in 2007, and some regard it as a response to the initial criticisms. The book was also subject to affirmation and critique. In addition to Dyson, other critics primarily focused on Cosby; they felt he used flawed data and preached about responsibility without considering the structural problems that have inhibited the success of many African Americans. For example, Earl Ofari Hutchinson stated the following in the *Huffington Post*:

> [Cosby] did not qualify or provide a complete factual context for his blanket indictment of poor blacks. He made the negative behavior of some blacks a racial rather than an endemic social problem. In doing so, he did more than break the alleged taboo against publicly airing racial dirty laundry; he fanned dangerous and destructive stereotypes.

7. Serwer, "Our Racial Interior."

This is hardly the call to action that can inspire and motivate un-
derachieving blacks to improve their lives. Instead, it further de-
moralizes those poor blacks who are doing the best to keep their
children and themselves out of harm's way, often against towering
odds, while still being hammered for their alleged failures by the
Cosbys within and without their communities. Worse, Cosby's
blame-the-victim slam does nothing to encourage government
officials and business leaders to provide greater resources and opportunities to aid those blacks that need help.

Come on People, intended or not, continues to tar the black
communities and the black poor as dysfunctional, chronic
whiners, and eternally searching for a government hand-out.
Come on, Cosby.[8]

The criticism of Cosby presents an interesting dilemma: how do you
regard those who are living with these difficulties? Is it possible to be a critic
of Cosby while also resisting the temptation to identify blacks as victims
primarily? It seems that even while acknowledging that there is a place for
responsible action—none of the critics deny this—the critical responses
direct our focus to some form of perpetual victim status. What path do we
take to find an identity beyond this label?

Who Tells the Story?

In the late 1980s I once had a dream where Spike Lee came to me and asked,
"What does it mean to be black?" I don't think I gave an answer before I
woke up, but I remember being disturbed by this question that assumed the
existence of an "authentic" black identity. In answering this chapter's question about identity, it is important to briefly draw attention to the effort made
to strengthen the African American community by overcoming the false
identity formation that results from the legacy of racism. While there may
be some broad agreement that the history of slavery and Jim Crow in the
United States devastated and enslaved the minds of many African Americans, there are different approaches to healing, uncovering, or creating a
proper identity. Perhaps one of the most significant strategies has been to
discover the "true" history of African Americans as a remedy. Eddie Glaude
Jr. refers to this as the "archaeological approach" in which "black identity is
concerned with uncovering our true selves and inferring from that discovery
what we must do. Black identity is interpreted here in terms of reality and
appearance. There is a *real* way of being black and a *false* way. Something

8. Hutchinson, "Come on People, No, Come on Cosby."

out there is essentially black, and when we lose our way, as some of us have because of white supremacy, we need only find "it" and all will be well.[9] One might say that the aim of the approach is to replace a false narrative (given by the oppressor) with the true one (uncovered and passed on by those who have learned about, for example, our true African selves). The idea is that an authentic story will yield authentic practices and facilitate liberation. This archaeological approach locates identity in a cultural retrieval project. This strategy may have some relevance, but it relies upon the idea of an authentic ancient history that all African Americans must know in order to be properly self-actualized. It also seems to run the risk of trading one dominant narrative for another, with the notable exception that the storytellers are no longer white oppressors. Correcting the lies of a white supremacist narrative is a genuine moral obligation, but is it enough to replace the lies with some version of another cultural history? How do we affirm our cultural uniqueness and our common humanity and resist the siren song that would exalt essential or ontological blackness as the answer to the norms of whiteness? Our cultural stories alone will not suffice. A theological vision can help us have a deeper sense of identity that incorporates the gifts our culture without requiring us to go on an expedition for a mythical conception of "blackness."

What Does God Say?

The Bible tells the story of our salvation. In this story, God reveals our identity. The term *story* does not mean "myth" or "fable," but reflects the fact that there is an overarching narrative—some use the term "metanarrative"—in Scripture from which doctrines emerge that should inform the way we view ourselves. Creation, fall, redemption, and renewal are vital categories/doctrines for understanding who we are and how we should live. If we desire to understand our plight as humans as well as the promise that catalyzes a hopeful existence, then we should put our specific focus on theological anthropology, which answers the question "what does it mean to be human?" The four categories/doctrines can be seen as four chapters of the story, which each provide vital content perspective as we attempt to solve the riddle of our identity. It is very important to have all four of these chapters. In answering this anthropological question, we discover our ultimate purpose, which in turn helps frame our approach to life, whether our circumstances are favorable or otherwise. A partial answer would be more detrimental than helpful because it fails to truthfully show how God's revelation addresses the plight of those who could easily see themselves as victims.

9. Glaude Jr., *In a Shade of Blue*, 53.

Creation

Genesis 1 and 2 give us two complementary perspectives on God's creation. Regarding the creation of humans, Genesis 1 emphasizes that the one true God has created human beings in the divine image. While some draw a distinction between the words *image* and *likeness* in Genesis 1:26, it is likely that they refer to the same idea; for example, Genesis 1:27 uses "image" alone and later Genesis 5:1 uses "likeness" alone and both texts are expressing the same meaning respectively.[10] Genesis 2 brings a sharper focus to the making of the first person and to the specific responsibilities given to humans as the stewards of God's creation.[11] As created in the image of God, humans are distinct from the rest of the created order and the only ones who are made to be like God in certain ways.

In light of the concerns of this chapter, there are some important implications of humans as divine image bearers. First, it is important to recognize that the biblical text makes no reference to skin color. While this may seem obvious, this is important because the significance of being human has nothing to do with the percentage of melanin in one's skin. While the Bible later acknowledges differences in appearance, it does not link the value of persons with their skin tone. Humans as divine image bearers have in common a shared dignity that is based in God's pronouncement that "it was very good."[12] God calls the entire creation good, and that includes humans. This truth is echoed in Psalm 8:5–6:

> Yet you have made him a little lower than the heavenly beings
>
> and crowned him with glory and honor.
>
> You have given him dominion over the works of your hands;
>
> you have put all things under his feet.[13]

All humans are crowned with a glory and honor bestowed upon them by God, and they also have the tremendous privilege of caring for the entire creation. This great task of creation stewardship is given as a functional expression of humanity created in the divine image. Some call this the "cultural mandate" or "creation mandate." This mandate is an expression of God's

---

10. Hoekema, *Created in God's Image*, 13.

11. An interesting book specifically focused on this is Headley, *Created for Responsibility*.

12. Genesis 1:31; Given our culture of superlatives, "very good" should be understood in its best sense, as excellence, or as many would say today, "awesome."

13. Unless stated otherwise, all biblical quotations come from the English Standard Version.

desire that the entire creation flourish. Genesis 1:26 states this dominion over creation as part of God's creational intent and Genesis 1:28 presents this great responsibility as a command given to our first parents.

Why is this important? There are two points to make here. First, the responsibility for the entire created order implicitly means that humans have the responsibility to seek the flourishing of other human beings, the very crown of creation. This mandate compels us to seek the best for everyone. Second, responsible participation in God's world is central to our purpose as human beings. One constant emphasis in *Come on People* is the need for blacks to act responsibly. What is the most fundamental reason why anyone should act responsibly? Is it because of our parents or our community or our loyalty to some group? I suggest that all of these reasons should be subordinate to the recognition of our creational purpose. God created humans to be responsible people, bestowed with an inherent dignity. How much does the frame of creation influence our concepts of responsibility?

Fall

The story does not end with creation, unfortunately. While we are given dignity and purpose as divine image bearers, the story takes a horrific turn. In Genesis 3 the first sin occurs, and all of us have been victims ever since. Though it is still God's good creation, the fall introduces massive distortions. Four relationships are altered, as humans are fractured internally, have breaches with God, with the created order, and enmity with other humans.

As a result of sin, the divine image is altered in a way analogous to a cracked mirror or the hall of mirrors in carnival funhouse. Humans retain the image of God but fail to consistently or properly express any likeness to the creator. The fall leads to a change in our natures. We are prone to act sinfully; it is difficult for humans to act in ways that seek the flourishing of others and to express love to others in selfless ways. In contrast, the responsibility given to humans becomes twisted. Power is often used in oppressive ways and some apathetically disregard the various kinds of stewardship necessary for a flourishing creation. Some want to control everything, some want to fight, others want to give up, and some are simply apathetic.

Fallenness makes distortion "normal" and leads us to see ourselves and others in incomplete and false ways. It is as if we made our home in the hall of mirrors and base our perception on the ubiquitous warped reflections. We struggle to understand and appreciate the dignity that God has given to all of us and instead it is typical to regard ourselves either too high or too low. Sometimes we make those "like us" into objects of worship and "others" into objects of disdain. In other instances, we loathe ourselves and make others into idols. We humans vary like sheep who do not know who they are or who they should follow. If we take the effects of Genesis 3 seriously, it should not be a surprise that a general glance at human history or a specific focus like that in *Come on People* shows us many ways that things have gone wrong for our race. The carnage and subsequent reverberations of white supremacy are but one example of the cycles of oppression and victimization that go back as far as Cain's murder of Abel. Post-fall reality is often a living hell.

Redemption

If the fall were the final word, then "victim" is the proper label for every human (even the ones that don't know it as they bask in self-worship). Genesis 3:15 promised that the serpent's head will be crushed one day by the Messiah. Even though human history moved forward with consistent expressions of sinful distortion, God promised that one day the world would be set right; God told Abraham "in you all the families of the earth shall be blessed."[14] This blessing begins to come to fruition with Jesus, the divine-human Son of God who at the beginning of his ministry announces the advent of God's kingdom. The good news of the gospel is that through Christ the ruptures of the fall will be healed.

Here is a place where we must be careful, because it is important to convey that the gospel is not merely a spiritual pacifier which comforts us in the face of difficult challenges. In terms of identity specifically, the good news of the gospel is that our full humanity is given back to us in Christ. Christ, who is the fullness of the divine image, not only demonstrates a completely human existence but sends the Spirit to believers to not only make us alive to God but capable of living in accordance with the creational intent. This is not an immediately complete transformation, but a process where we "have put on the new self, which is being renewed in knowledge after the image of its creator."[15] When we talk about being "saved," it is certainly the reconciliation we have with God through justification, but much more. We are participants in a process of sanctification that is not only concerned with our internal holiness but also our private and public practices that spring from obedience to the cultural mandate and the first and second greatest commandments. Matthew 22:37–40 tells us that all the commandments are expressions of our love for God and neighbor. Redemption is the good news

14. Genesis 12:3.
15. Colossians 3:10.

that we are God's children, members of his family who model the realities of God's kingdom wherever we find ourselves.

What does this mean for the challenges that concern Poussaint? First, it means that we can never see ourselves as victims if we see our true humanity through the lens of the gospel. The story of redemption must counter the multiple narratives that emerge from the legacy of racism, corrosive media, and the desperation on display in poor communities. We acknowledge the reality of fallenness but move beyond that to practices empowered by hope. Second, it is important to emphasize the path to improvement as an expression of sanctification. God's transforming work through the Spirit enables Christians to live as kingdom witnesses. This includes attending to the needs of the most downtrodden but also stewarding our personal agency in efforts to improve our own circumstances. Christians are kingdom citizens who celebrate our common humanity and praise God for the richness of our diversity as creatures. We can praise God for our ethnic/racial particularity without the need to deify our culture.

Renewal

Eschatology is the end of the story, when God will bring all things under the reign of Christ. While there is often a focus on the debates related to the final sequence of events (tribulation, rapture, millennium, etc.), it is also important to consider how eschatology can inform our identity. If we think of eschatology as the final culmination of redemption, we can also think of it as the full restoration and fulfillment of our humanity. Humans rightly related to God through Christ will become the realization of God's original intent in creation. For the present time, this becomes a source of hope that is based on Christ's resurrection and anticipated return. We live in an "already, but not yet" kingdom that Christ inaugurated when he conquered death: "And he is the head of the body, the church. He is the beginning, the firstborn from the dead, that in everything he might be preeminent."[16] Our hope in the future directs our gaze to a day when we are free from our personal, relational, and societal dysfunction. An eschatological vision tells us where we are going. In the words of the band King's X, "we are finding who we are," an echo of 1 John 3: "Beloved, we are God's children now, and what we will be has not yet appeared; but we know that when he appears we shall be like him, because we shall see him as he is."[17] We continue to discover the profound truth of our God-given identity until the final day.

16. Colossians 1:18.

17. 1 John 3:2.

This perspective helps us to resist any sense that current circumstances are final and reminds us that God is in control of history. God will change us and transform the world into the kingdom. The promise of our future humanity gives us hope while we practice sanctification, expressed as faithful responsibility to ourselves and for our communities. As dire as some of the crises above appear, we press forward in light of an assured victory. Eschatology at its best is far from "pie in the sky" theology that leads us to escape. Instead, our vision is set on what we will become and where we are going. At the end, we will be made perfect in God's image.

A Plea for Catechesis

God's story of salvation should be prominent and foundational in the identity formation of Christians. The great problems identified by Poussaint will not be sufficiently addressed if we seek our identity and best practices in our cultural uniqueness or if we are so terrorized by the magnitude of the crises that we can only lament our status as victims. We should also remember that while these great problems present themselves intensely in the black community, these problems are not only ours; these challenges are present throughout the human race in ways similar and distinct. The path forward must include the church as a context for identity formation.

How do we do this? There are many strategies that we can take, such as the recently proposed Male Investment Plan (MIP) that emerged from "The Gathering" in March 2010. Over 6,000 people from the three African American Methodist denominations (A.M.E., C.M.E., and A.M.E. Zion) met in Columbia, South Carolina to address the crisis among African American males. Bishop John R. Bryant states that the MIP will "focus on spiritual enrichment, mentoring, education, economics, health and wellness, prevention of imprisonment and job preparation. We will also seek advice from our churches and community partners across the country, which have been actively engaged in male mentorship and male strengthening programs. And we are still listening to God, who will shepherd us through a process we are confident will change lives."[18] This is an encouraging multifaceted effort that offers a lot of promise.

I would like to offer another suggestion based on the educational function of the church. One of the best things churches can do is develop a range of ways to teach their people biblical and theological truth. Preaching, Bible study, Sunday school, and special seminars or classes are opportunities for practicing what the ancient church called catechesis (teaching). The

18. Kwon, "Churches Unveil Plan."

purpose of catechesis is to educate those who enter the church so that they understand what it means to be part of God's people. How many people who occupy pews on Sunday understand what God says about their identity? The church is the place that plays a role in identity formation, but to what degree? What message is conveyed?

It is vital to examine the curriculum that we are using and consider how we can make sure that identity formation occurs when people become church members. Admittedly, we are in an attention-challenged society where the idea of teaching church doctrine in a classroom format can be very daunting. This does not mean abandoning the direct oral communication of biblical and doctrinal content, but it is important to recognize that learning happens in a number of ways. Catechesis does not need to be limited to the verbal transmission of information; churches can brainstorm and devise ways to convey the content of the faith linked to concrete expression of our responsibility as humans.

For example, if church members participate in planting gardens in their neighborhoods, commit to cleaning up an entire street blocks, or initiate tutoring programs in educationally challenged areas, they are exhibiting a central aspect of their identity as those created in God's image. Another idea could be encouraging those with an interest in media to write and stage one-act plays or short video clips that present different images than those that marketed in Hollywood films and music videos. One great aspect of these activities is that they can also engage the community not only as an evangelistic witness but also as a message that tells those outside the church that God cares for them. If these kinds of activities are not simply fun church programs but part of the process of bringing people into the church, they can begin to see their identity as image bearers who are being renewed in their minds and deeds. Conveying doctrine does not need to be an arid experience but can be practically linked to everyday life. Creative catechesis can immerse church members in the biblical narrative that informs and empowers them to live a victorious life that contributes to the flourishing of God's creation.

Chapter 2 The Black Family: The Hope of "True Religion"

—BRUCE FIELDS

The way of the good and blessed life is to be found entirely in the true religion wherein one God is worshipped and acknowledged with purest piety to be the beginning of all existing things, originating, perfecting, and containing the universe. Thus it becomes easy to detect the error of the peoples who have preferred to worship many gods rather than the true God and Lord of all things, because their wise men whom they call philosophers used to have schools in disagreement one with another, while all made common use of the temples.

—AUGUSTINE, *ON TRUE RELIGION*[1]

Keep your child in the schools, even if you have to eat less, drink less and wear coarser raiments; though you eat but two meals a day, purchase but one change of garment during the year, and relinquish all the luxuries of which we are so fond, but which are as injurious to health and long life as they are pleasing to the taste.

—BISHOP DANIEL ALEXANDER PAYNE, "WELCOME TO
  THE RANSOMED"[2]

Nothing hinders the perception of truth more than a life devoted to lusts, and the false images of sensible things, derived from the sensible world and impressed on us by the agency of the body, which beget various opinions and errors.

—AUGUSTINE, *ON TRUE RELIGION*[3]

---

1. Burleigh, ed., *Augustine*, 225.
2. Payne, "Welcomed to the Ransomed," 235.
3. Burleigh, ed., *Augustine*, 226.

Alvin Poussaint lauds the opportunities for success that exist in the United States despite the legacy of racism that still influences the present. On the other hand, there are still many harmful behaviors that many black youth take up for various reasons. Poussaint does identify, however, "an important element" that contributes to this troublesome situation:

> We feel that an important element in this crisis is the breakdown in good parenting. We're not telling you something you don't know. In too many black neighborhoods, adults are giving up their main responsibility to look after their children. In all corners of America, too many children are getting the short end of the stick as extended family networks collapse and community support programs fail to replace them in any significant way.[4]

My purpose in this piece is to reflect briefly on matters that will strengthen the black family and facilitate the emergence of a greater number of black youth that will help lead this nation to even greater days ahead.

A legitimate inquiry can be made: "Why would anyone concerned about the contemporary black family begin with quotes from Augustine?" The relevance of the second quote above can be more immediately appreciated, but nevertheless, I will respond to the former question with three propositions that I hope will motivate a fresh consideration of their relevance for any doubters. I want to demonstrate that the wisdom of the ancient, corporate church is still applicable today, even for the black family.

First, my reflection is aimed primarily at the church of Jesus Christ, comprised of those who have put their faith in him alone as their atoning sacrifice for the forgiveness of sin and reconciliation with God. Augustine has been an influential theologian and philosopher in the church, with elements of his thought being embraced by much of Christendom since his death in 430 AD. This North African bishop was, however, simply a churchman who attempted to minister to his flock through the multiple aspects of his ministry. In short, he was a pastor—concerned about the life and thought of that segment of the church entrusted to his care. The church has selectively embraced its past in the search for instruction and wisdom, and Augustine is an authoritative contributor to this search.

Second, Augustine taught not only from Scripture and church tradition, but also from his own life's lessons. An immediate connection between his life and the issues of this piece is his family life.[5] Things were not very smooth in his household or in his life in general. He struggled with his father and had a periodically strained relationship with his mother. He had

---

4. Cosby and Poussaint, *Come on People*, 57.

5. Augustine, *The Confessions*, 1, 11, 17.

a son born out of wedlock, Adeodatus, a gifted young man who died at an early age. At one point he put aside his son's mother to position himself for a marriage that would advance him socially while holding the position of chief rhetorician in Milan. At a pivotal time, God got a hold of him and enabled him to be a grace-empowered minister who could speak biblically to many important matters. The foundational truth that Augustine embraced more and more in the course of his life was that the only stable thing in life is the Lord himself. Life can have much in terms of uncontrolled variability, but God remains who he is and what he is about.

This leads to my third proposition. Augustine contributes to the wisdom of the church and to the wisdom needed for the benefit of the black family with his emphasis on the pursuit of true religion as the proper orientation for all aspects of life. This orientation is good for the church in general, but it is also the hope, specifically, for the black family. To flesh out this concept for the sake of greater applicability, I will need to explain it in a manner sufficiently nuanced for it to speak to the hope of the black family.

True religion is the pursuit of the one true God. This pursuit tests the nature of all things in life and shapes all visions and goals in life. The church is to be a sign and model of this pursuit. The black family, understood through the lenses of the Scripture and the church, should be also a sign and model of this pursuit. Despite the horrors of slavery, Jim Crow segregation laws, and the present, pervasive effects of racism and poverty, the family has survived and will survive. The foundations for the perpetuation of the family and the enhancement of its effectiveness in the African American community must incorporate some historical reflections, beginning with an analysis of the devastating effects slavery had on the black family in America.

Slavery created a situation of profound dehumanization demonstrated in numerous ways, but concretely shown in the lack of integrity present in slave marriages and child rearing.[6] Families could be easily broken up with family members being sold simply at the master's whim or because of economic necessities. Jim Crow allowed some advancement for the African American community, but its humiliating effects had economic ramifications as there were fewer opportunities for jobs. Recently, racism has taken the form of disparate advantages for members of the dominant white culture when compared to those given to blacks.

During the 1960s Great Society initiative, Daniel Patrick Moynihan advanced the controversial case that there were other factors besides

---

6. Frazier and Lincoln, *The Negro Church in America*, 37–40.

racism that were harming the African American community.[7] The problem was essentially the embrace of a culture that denigrated marriage, creating environments where many children were being raised in single-parent families—a potentially harmful situation—where children were often growing up without the regular presence of fathers. This enhanced not only the number of out-of-wedlock births, but also raised the percentage of people living in poverty. Moynihan and his cohorts were accused of racism and insensitivity to other key factors affecting the black community, but his findings have been affirmed in recent times.

Despite its good intentions, the Great Society's war on poverty hurt the black family in the long run. The original intent of the program was admirable. President Lyndon Baines Johnson described it as, "A place where men are more concerned with the quality of their lives than the quantity of their goods."[8] As an extension of the program and in response to a number of riots taking place in Harlem (1964), Newark, and Detroit (1967), culminating in the assassination of Dr. Martin Luther King, Jr. (1968), Johnson appointed the Kerner Commission to investigate the causes of such unrest. The commission concluded, "Chronic poverty is a breeder of chronic chaos."[9] Eliminating poverty, it was believed, would eventually bring about the elimination of the frustration and rage that bred chaos. Giving blacks, particularly black males, jobs would enhance the stability of the black family.

The Great Society had noble goals. However, harmful developments in the black family began to emerge, despite good intentions and government "equalization" programs. Kay S. Hymowitz observed that the Johnson administration initially embraced the findings of the Moynihan report. The administration, however, also distanced itself from it based upon charges of racism in the report as well as pressure from feminist critics who viewed the two-parent family as the "oppressive ideal of the nuclear family . . . Convinced that marriage was the main arena of male privilege, feminists projected onto the struggling single mother an image of the 'strong black woman' who had always had to work and who was 'superior in terms of [her] ability to function healthily in the world' . . ."[10] Hymowitz concludes with a statistic also found in Poussaint's book: "70 percent of black children are still born to unmarried mothers."[11] Poverty and the perpetuation of

---

7. Moynihan, "The Negro Family."

8. Johnson, "The Great Society."

9. National Criminal Justice Reference Service, "Report," 265.

10. Hymowitz, "The Black Family."

11. Cosby and Poussaint, *Come on People*, 14.

poverty in subsequent generations is often due to joblessness, but in many situations, fatherless families also cause it.

A sociocultural analysis of this breakdown in familial relationships can often lead to discussions about the effects of poverty, joblessness, and the lack of the sacrifices needed to build and maintain a family. These sacrifices, for example, take the forms of commitment to one's spouse even in tough times, learning to control one's emotions for the family's well-being, and postponing the fulfillment of desires for the good of the family. From a biblical/theological perspective, I believe that the Great Society invited a radical departure from a focus and dependence upon God and his ways for solutions to the problems facing blacks in America. The embrace of the Great Society was essentially the movement from dependence on the one true God to dependence on the human institution of government. This is a theological assessment of a historical, economic, sociocultural phenomenon. Such programs may indeed take on concrete sociocultural, political, and economic forms, while still being oriented in ways that reflect the acknowledgment of, and respect for, God. The church is the community that should primarily reflect this perspective, the orientation that I see as the continuation of true religion.

Because of God and his ways, any solutions that only involve governmental programming and do not intentionally protect and preserve the black family are doomed to failure. I will attempt a survey of biblical and theological considerations to advance the case for such protection and preservation. The first part will examine some biblical passages that reflect the importance of honoring marriage. Admittedly, I will not be able to address all relevant biblical material, but some foundational passages will be identified. The second part will engage some theological categories and propose what implications they have for the black family. Through such reflections, I will attempt to explicate the meaning of "true religion," particularly as it relates to pursuing a life before God that provides an orientation and evaluation of all areas of life, including the life of the family.

Biblical and Theological Reflections

Biblical Passages

The instructive contributions of specific passages are a function of how they fit into a biblical story line. The story line is made up of many people, substories, and teachings, but many would agree that the overarching story line is the story of God's redemptive plan for humanity and creation (Romans

8:22–25). The pivotal figure for the accomplishment of this redemption is Jesus Christ. The view of marriage, its meaning, and its significance is an essential part of this story line. My purpose is to show that the biblical view of marriage is portrayed against the backdrop of God's redemptive plan. When appropriately oriented in God's plan, a person, a couple, or a people are about the business of practicing true religion.

I will be looking at a few texts from Genesis, Deuteronomy, Proverbs, and the Gospels. Many others could be cited, but my intention is simply to demonstrate the type of biblical narrative where marriage is portrayed.

Genesis

Genesis 1:26–27 speaks of God creating humanity in his image. The passage entails many possible meanings of "image" that cannot be fully discussed here. It will suffice to incorporate a couple of observations. Millard Erickson summates the meaning of the image as "the elements in the human makeup that enable the fulfillment of human destiny. The image is the powers of personality that make humans, like God, beings capable of interacting with other persons, of thinking and reflecting, and of willing freely."[12] Charles Sherlock correctly observes that the text does not tell us specifically what the image is; rather, we are told what it "*involves*: living in a series of relationships."[13] The capacity to form relationships creates the elements for the institution of marriage.[14] God brings it about and facilitates a bond of a deep, profound nature. The relationship between Adam and Eve produces children of both a troublesome—Cain—and a more positive nature—Abel.[15]

God's concern for the integrity of marriage is shown early to his special servant, Abram. It is through his servant that God reveals his concern to others. In Genesis 12:15–16, Pharaoh takes Sarai into his household because Abram had previously lied and said that Sarai was his sister, leading Pharaoh to believe that she was "available." Genesis 12:17 speaks of the Lord afflicting Pharaoh and his household with diseases because he had taken Sarai, Abram's wife, as his own, albeit unknowingly. Pharaoh confronts Abram with his earlier lie where Abram said that Sarai was his sister. Elements of God's overarching plan had to be fulfilled, and part of that fulfillment was the protection of Abram and Sarai's marriage.[16]

12. Erickson, *Christian Theology*, 532.
13. Sherlock, *The Doctrine of Humanity*, 37.
14. Genesis 2:24–25.
15. Genesis 4:1–8.
16. Genesis 12:1–3; 15:4.

Much of the rest of Genesis records relationships where a number of the patriarchs had multiple wives or relationships that produced a child. Concurrently, however, is the presence of multiple references to a singular "wife" in the narratives, suggesting a foundational relationship. I will identify a few examples. Genesis 12:5 reads: "And Abram took Sarai *his wife*," (emphasis mine).[17] Abraham, formerly known as Abram until God changed his name, forbids the eldest of his servants to find a wife for Isaac among the Canaanites, but in Genesis 24:4, he commands him to "go to my country and to my kindred, and take *a wife* for my son Isaac" (emphasis mine).[18] Jacob had sons by his wives, Leah and Rachel, and by their maidservants, Zilpah and Bilhah, respectively. Nevertheless, after Isaac blesses Jacob, he commands him: "Arise, go to Paddan-aram to the house of Bethuel your mother's father, and take as *your wife* from there *one* of the daughters of Laban your mother's brother" (emphasis mine).[19]

There are other such references in Genesis. These are mentioned to show that even though many men took more than one wife, it seems that "one" was elevated to a status above the other wives. In the example of Abram, this is undoubtedly a demonstration of the sanctity of this marriage relationship. The sanctity of marriage between a man and a woman is more clearly demonstrated in Deuteronomy.

Deuteronomy

Deuteronomy gives a great deal of attention to the covenant that God established with the people of Israel. Within the context of the reaffirmation of the covenant, Moses re-establishes the authority of the Ten Commandments. Two of the commandments have specific application to the protection of marriage, while a third assumes a one-to-one correspondence in a marriage relationship. The fifth commandment, "Honor your father and your mother, as the Lord your God commanded you, that your days may be long, and that it may go well with you in the land that the Lord your God is giving you," suggests marriage is a relationship between *two* individuals.[20] J. G. McConville observes:

> The Fifth Commandment moves into the realm of the social order. Respect for parents includes the obedience of children, the

17. Genesis 12:5.
18. Genesis 24:4.
19. Genesis 28:2.
20. Deuteronomy 5:16.

most obvious modern inference from this command. In Israel, however, the requirement of obedience lasted beyond childhood, to the point where young people had to answer for their failings in this regard before the representatives of the whole community.[21]

This concept's application to the contemporary scene can be illustrated through a lament from Poussaint. He reminds the reader of earlier days when if one was tempted to do something foolish, like stealing, one always considered how that action would reflect on one's parents. "If you get caught stealing it, you're going to embarrass your mother . . . You're going to embarrass your family."[22] He laments that such a perspective is not as pervasive in the African American community as it once was.

The seventh and tenth commandments show a more immediate burden to protect the marriage relationship: "you shall not commit adultery," along with, "you shall not covet your neighbor's wife. And you shall not desire your neighbor's house, his field, or his male servant, or his female servant, his ox, or his donkey, or anything that is your neighbor's."[23] Adultery is understood typically as parties engaging in actions or levels of relationship only appropriate within a marriage relationship, with people outside of their current marriage. It can be more easily understood as unfaithfulness to one's marriage vows.

Much could be said about Deuteronomy 24:1–4 if I was discussing the matter of divorce,[24] but 24:5 contributes to understanding a healthy marriage. The Jews allowed young couples to have some time free from normal responsibilities, with hope that a foundation would be built that would help avoid potential negative developments down the road. McConville observes that there was also an economic incentive to allow this stretch of freedom from normal responsibilities: "Behind the hope of a happy marriage, there were also economic tensions that might arise on the death of a young man who was childless."[25] This was a social, cultural, and political environment that encouraged the protection of marriage in a unique way. The word of the Lord commanded it. It was recognized that marriage was a foundational part of society. It still is.

Many more implications addressing the ideal nature of marriage could be drawn from Deuteronomy and other sections of the Old Testament. Nevertheless, I will have to limit the rest of my observations to a primary

21. McConville, *Deuteronomy*, 128.

22. Cosby and Poussaint, *Come on People*, 2.

23. Genesis 5:18, 21.

24. See, for example, McConville's treatment, *Deuteronomy*, 357–60.

25. McConville, *Deuteronomy*, 360.

representative of the wisdom literature, Proverbs. As in the previous sections, I am not attempting an exhaustive study of all relevant material. I will
be content to continue a demonstration of how the story line of Scripture,
though its overarching theme is God's redemptive plan, nevertheless reveals
insight about God's perspective on marriage. These insights give more con-
creteness to the possibility of living in the realm of true religion.

Proverbs

Proverbs speaks often of the "fear of the Lord." This "fear" is a profound
reverence for God and is supposed to be the organizing principle for all
aspects of life. This organizing principle is summarized in Proverbs 3:5–6:
"Trust in the LORD with all your heart, and do not lean on your own understanding. In all your ways acknowledge him, and he will make straight your
paths."[26] This is the proverbial equivalent to Augustine's concept of "true
religion." One of the areas that Proverbs addresses throughout the book,
and that is fundamental to a proper life before God, is marriage and family.
If applied specifically to the black family, the family is strengthened and
prospers when it models and sustains life "in the fear of the LORD," or in
the realm of "true religion." Proverbs reveals the wisdom and necessity of
protecting the husband/wife relationship, while also providing guidelines
for a healthy life for the members of a family.

First, much in terms of this protection focuses on staying away from
the adulterous person. The frequency of such concern is a demonstration
of God's desire to protect life in general, but certainly to protect marriage.[27]
Second, there is a great deal of blessing to be had when the covenant-mar-
riage relationship is respected. The teacher encourages a husband to "rejoice
in the wife of your youth."[28] Many other exhortations could be identified,
but one that has particular meaning to me is 19:14: "House and wealth are
inherited from fathers, but a prudent wife is from the Lord."[29] The epitome
of a wise woman is also described in Proverbs 31:10–31.

Finally, I will mention a few examples of family life as portrayed in the
book of Proverbs. Parents are admonished to raise up a child according to
his way.[30] Though there must be consistent principles that parents should

---

26. Proverbs 3:5–6.

27. Another helpful section in this regard is Proverbs 6:27–35. There can be legitimate, harsh consequences when a man becomes involved with another man's wife.

28. Proverbs 5:18.

29. Proverbs 19:14.

30. The ESV reads (Proverbs 22:6): "Train up a child in the way he should go; even

enforce consistently with all their children, there must be an accompanying awareness of the dispositions of each child. It sometimes takes a bit more prayerful effort to train a child with a respect for how they process and respond to the parents's consistently held principles. Discipline of a non-abusive sort helps to instill such principles in the deep recesses of the child's soul. Coupled with this are the commands that the child should listen to his/her parents. For example, Proverbs 6:20–21 encourages such commitment: "My son, keep your father's commandment, and forsake not your mother's teaching. Bind them on your heart always; tie them around your neck."[31] The commandments, of course, are assumed to be reflective of God's revealed directives. If a child wishes to honor his/her parents and give them joy in life, the child should pursue a pathway of wisdom. Shame and reproach come to one who does "violence to his father and chases away his mother."[32]

At no time have all of God's commandments been obeyed, but the Scriptures do provide ideals to pursue. History, as well as the contemporary environment, shows that abuse can run rampant in families, and the Scriptures recognize this by guarding against it. My point is that living in "the fear of the Lord" still requires an advocacy and protection of marriage and the family. I will explore only one passage from the Gospel of Matthew to show the Lord Jesus' concern for marriage. Again, others could be discussed, but Matthew 19:3–9 is pivotal for a number of reasons.

Matthew 19:3–9

> "And I say to you: whoever divorces his wife, except for sexual immorality, and marries another, commits adultery."[33]

My point in reflecting on this passage is to counter any interpretation of this text that entertains a clear, sure-fire case for divorce. There are simply more factors to consider. The Lord Jesus himself was an advocate for the protection of marriage. He was also one who insisted on the practice of children honoring their parents.[34] Marriage was to be intensely protected

---

when he is old he will not depart from it." I am following the lead here of Miller, *Proverbs*, 159–60.

31. Proverbs 6:20–21.

32. Proverbs 19:26.

33. Matthew 19:9.

34. Jesus accused the Pharisees and scribes of "breaking the command of God" (Matthew 15:3) for the sake of their tradition. They could withhold aid to their parents by declaring something as a "gift" to God. Jesus held them accountable because "tradition" presented them the opportunity to disobey the Lord.

because of the command of God, in part because so much could be determined about the orientation of a people before God by what they thought and practiced about marriage.

This section follows a passage in chapter 18 dealing with the magnitude of God's forgiveness and the call for others to forgive similarly. The Pharisees try to draw Jesus into a debate on the proper interpretation of Deuteronomy 24, which was the basis for the different opinions on divorce represented by the schools of Hillel and Shammai.[35] Jesus bypassed the whole discussion by appealing to what God intended for marriage from the beginning. He combines in Matthew 19:4–5 references to Genesis 1:27 and 2:24, and then emphasizes two fundamental understandings regarding marriage in 19:6. First, he says, "they are no longer two but one flesh." Keener suggests that the force of "one flesh" is "the language of family ties and alliances (as in 2 Samuel 5:1)."[36] Second, in the same verse, there are the accompanying words: "What therefore God has joined together, let not man separate." Marriage is something with which God is intimately involved. Thus, from a biblical, narrative perspective, marriage is far more than a mere sociocultural institution.

Of course, if one denies the authority of Scripture, this will affect one's view of marriage. Another consideration for the rejecters, however, is to reflect on the question: Why is it that in societies where marriage and family relationships are in widespread disarray, the society does not last much longer in maintaining its identity and power? "Much longer" refers to a comparison with the length of time that it may have been in existence.

The meaning of 19:9 must also be understood in relation to the question Jesus is asked regarding why Moses allowed for a certificate of divorce. He confronted the Pharisees with the fact, "Because of your hardness of heart Moses allowed you to divorce your wives."[37] It is very important for readers to read the rest of the verse: "but from the beginning it was not so." Jesus would again bring them back to God's original intent reflected in Genesis. The exception, then, for divorce in 19:9, is for *porneia*—"sexual immorality." This is a word that can have a broad range of meanings: fornication, adultery, something indecent.[38] Towards a proper conclusion on the significance of this passage, we must consider a bottom line—marriages without some practice of forgiveness will not last. The force of the passage is more geared towards one who has a long, unrepentant engagement with sexual

---

35. Keener, *Matthew*, 295.

36. Keener, *Matthew*, 295.

37. Matthew 19:8.

38. Carson, *Matthew*, 413–18.

immortality. This then in a very real way can be considered a fundamental violation of the covenant/marriage relationship.

The biblical-redemptive story line demonstrates that God intends to guard the perpetuation of marriage. Admittedly, many more passages could have been studied, but I believe that this is sufficient to establish this perspective as the biblical one. What happens in the family greatly influences other familial and societal developments.

Much could be said about such developments through sociocultural and economic lenses. For example, young people can learn about the importance of education from their life in a family. This would enable them to engage and assist society, where there is an inherent interdependence among members. They could learn about the importance of courtesy and respect for people in general, especially for the elderly and for those who have achieved great things through hard work and sacrifice. An ideal would be learning the importance of having honest, skill-building work. I hope that through various forms of modeling, a young person can learn that there is much to be gained by maintaining faithfulness in all aspects of work. I am old enough to insist that young people in the African American community learn that it is a privilege and a responsibility to vote.

Nevertheless, I also want to offer some needed reflection about the theological teaching that could take place within a context of solid marital relationships where there is a strong desire for the wellbeing of children.

Some Theological Categories

These will not be extensive treatments, but I wanted to entertain some possibly valuable lessons that could be learned through the family, particularly believing families, reflecting on doctrines related to God, Christ, and the church/community.

Children process various impressions and understandings about God that they encounter early in their family life. Is God near? Does God comfort and protect? Is God reliable? What does it mean that God is love? What does it mean to refer to God as our Father, as in Matthew 6:9? These questions only illustrate the types of developments that can take place in the mind of a child. These developments can have great effect upon subsequent learning and understanding. Having said this, I would admit that I have personally struggled with my own understanding of God because my father was not as present in my childhood as he should have been.

The long and short of it is that through the grace of God, I determined that my children were going to know who their father was, whether they liked it or not. I had begun to understand that the development of their personal faith would be greatly affected by what they saw in me, as well as what they saw in their mother and in my relationship with her. I have sometimes communicated to our children that they are the "fruit" of our love. Their mother and I are one couple, though we are each a distinct person. We are one family, yet each of the members is a distinct and precious person. This is not an attempt to draw an exact correspondence with the doctrine of the Trinity, but such a balance of relationships can build a unique understanding of individuality, leading to an enhanced ability to understand the Trinity. The appropriate conception is to view oneself not as an autonomous self, but as both an individual and a member of a family. This can contribute greatly to building identity and establishing a sense of belonging.

The doctrine of Christ traditionally consists of a study of both the person and the work of Christ (the meaning and significance of the atonement). Though numerous observations and applications can be made in this area, I will offer only one observation on his atonement that can provide a helpful lesson that can be effectively internalized in a family setting.

The Apostle Paul writes that "Christ died for our sins in accordance with the Scripture."[39] In Philippians 2:5, he begins a pivotal passage on the person and work of Christ: "Have this mind among yourselves, which is yours in Christ Jesus."[40] Paul then speaks of Christ's radical obedience, submitting to death to accomplish the Father's will. The principle seen here is that meaning in life often involves some elements of self-sacrifice. This means focusing on others and their needs rather than your own. Teaching children to consider how their actions affect others, and to always consider the consequences of an action, will be very beneficial to their development into responsible adults. Much can be accomplished when Jesus is set forth as the example for our life, and the Holy Spirit is acknowledged as the power behind our life. With concrete examples and the empowerment that God makes available through the Holy Spirit, a young person can consistently practice the type of sacrifice that Christ displayed on Calvary.

Critical Teaching and Application for the Church

The church must continually focus on a multifaceted response to the challenges facing the black family. In terms of an overarching theme, the church should actualize a teaching-preaching-modeling strategy that places the divine institution of marriage within the context of God's

39. 1 Corinthians 15:3.
40. Philippians 2:5.

redemptive plan. Pastors and church leaders must teach the biblical story, keeping the climactic figure of Jesus Christ in the forefront. An essential and fundamental part of the biblical story is God's view of marriage and what it takes to build a family. In terms of true religion—seeking the Lord and living appropriately before him—the family, along with the church, must model and perpetuate this perspective. I will offer some generalized suggestions on how the church can be a more effective servant in bringing greater health to the black family.[41]

Witnessing to the Gospel

All that I have said thus far about what is needed for the health of the black family and the black community in general is futile apart from the transformative power of the gospel of Jesus Christ. The church must continually witness to humanity's need for the forgiveness of sin and reconciliation to God that is only available through faith in Jesus Christ. The Apostle Paul writes in Romans 5:10–11: "For if while we were enemies we were reconciled to God by the death of his Son, much more, now that we are reconciled, shall we be saved by his life. More than that, we also rejoice in God through our Lord Jesus Christ, through whom we have now received reconciliation."[42]

Humanity's greatest need is to be reconciled to God. This insistence, admittedly, may lack sociocultural, economic, political, and historical sophistication, but it is the foundation for all hope. Elsewhere, the apostle speaks of the reality of empowerment. In 1 Corinthians 2:3–4, Paul talks about his "weakness," "fear," and "much trembling" in the fulfillment of his ministerial responsibilities, but his hope is the power of the Spirit. So, it is possible to speak of principles and strategies that would be beneficial for the life of the black family, but it is another matter of the power needed to fulfill said principles. True religion begins with a living, vital relationship with God through faith in the Lord Jesus Christ.

Centers for Study, Sharing, and Prayer

The formal aspects of the church, in terms of Sunday school and the various worship services held at the church, are indeed important. There is another level of aid that can be applied effectively at the lay level. I refer to "centers,"

---

41. For greater attention to a specific training program, see Richardson, *Reclaiming the Urban Family*.

42. Romans 5:10–11.

but this simply means small groups giving attention to Bible studies and mutual counseling. This level of interaction and accountability is crucial. Pastors and pastoral staff teams cannot cover all the needs of a congregation. There is a level of vulnerability and encouragement that can take place only in small groups. The church should identify lay leaders who are able and willing to open up their homes for these types of engagements. Prayer practiced in these kinds of settings facilitates comfort and accomplishes much.

Reconciliatory Liturgy

Pain, misunderstandings, and divisions happen in families. The church can do much to strengthen families through teaching on the blessings of good communication and forgiveness. People must communicate with one another to have to hope of maintaining healthy relationships. The church should aid the development of such conversations. Reconciliation is best achieved when there is acknowledgment of wrongs (confession) and the asking of forgiveness for whatever one has done to contribute to pain and division. There may even be a need for some sort of ceremony to seal the meaning and significance of what has transpired to the people involved. Though I am sure that some churches already practice such reconciliatory liturgy, perhaps there could be a libation, or some symbolic passing of an object, that recalls the meaning of the forgiveness and reconciliation that has occurred. It may be ideal to have witnesses to hold the parties accountable through prayer and to observe the responsible parties' future behavior. They promise to each other that they will move beyond the painful events that transpired in the past in order to experience the healing and peace of reconciliation. With these proposed guidelines, I am assuming that the family members involved are believers in the Lord Jesus Christ. Reconciliation with God and the power of the Holy Spirit are required for the effectiveness of such liturgy.

Outreach to the Surrounding Community

The church prepares itself for outreach by following through on the suggestions above. Modeling is so important for service to the community. A concrete way of engaging the community regarding marriage and family is to provide lay "listeners." This does not require formal training, though that would be helpful. This involves having lay people who are able and willing to listen and pray with people in the neighborhood who need someone to talk to. So much in terms of witness and modeling can take place at this level.

Because of the dangers of abuse in the family, some people advocate offering alternative structures for relationships, projecting more "open" understandings and greater toleration for less than the biblical "ideal." For the black family, however, our more recent history has demonstrated that such a view has been devastating to the community. Evidences have pointed to this fact, but there are those who benefit politically and economically from such devastation. Because of this, poor family habits and practices will still occur, and the "listeners" will still be needed. They will occupy the place of "spokesperson." They will be needed to take care of the masses from the storehouse of their compassion.

Marriage and family life must be conducted in the context of Augustine's understanding of true religion, pursuit of the true knowledge of God and his ways. Many elements of life are changeable and beyond personal control. Yet in the flow of true religion, there will emerge not only instruction, but also encouragement, comfort, and power. This is the blessing of the family. This is the hope of true religion.

Chapter 3 Black Girls Rise: Yes, It's Time! A Call to the Church of the Black Community

—Yvonne RB-Banks

S chool-age black girls are mangled in a crisis of double jeopardy. This jeopardy only exists because they are black and female in America. Who is responsible for attending to this crisis? Who is responsible for sending them off to school to succeed? Addressing how such matters affect their academic success requires a look into the many layers that force them to face educational dilemmas. Questions about how to address this matter and who should be involved make one point clear. That is the immediacy of need. Due to the far-reaching nature of what is happening to black girls, the matter may be best confronted in the context of the black community's role in eliminating this crisis.

The social context of needed change requires the influence of what the black community has used in the past to bring about any major social force for change—the black church. According to the Pew Institute, 89 percent of blacks in America are Christians.[1] Therefore, in addressing the severity of the disenfranchisement of black girls by the school system, this writing seeks to stimulate the 89 percent's role in championing and securing educational equity for black girls. Without immediate interventions on their behalf, black girls will continue to face a harsh road. Their school experiences are laden with barriers that leave very little hope for change as they mature and move into adulthood.[2] Extensive research lays a foundation for what needs to change in America's schools for black students to progress.[3] Areas related to culturally responsive pedagogy, advocacy, assessments, teachers's dispositions, discipline policies, self-determination skills, and a curriculum

---

1. Masci, "5 Facts."
2. Center for Law and Social Policy, "Young Women of Color."
3. White, "The Invisible Victims."

designed to benefit black girls are in the most need of attention. The merits of their needs warrant the influence of the black church.[4]

Questions of Change

What can 89 percent of a population do to bring about educational change? What can that population do to defend black girls in America's classrooms? What actions of responsibility should the black community, known as The Village, take to rid black girls of the crisis they face daily? Critical to answering these questions is to turn to black Christians for actions on their behalf. There is guidance about the role of all Christians, according to James 2:6, regarding how we should use a collective impact in ways that harvest social inclusion. James 2:6 in this context is for the educational equity of black girls. As well, we have Micah 6:8, which outlines what we have been called to do and how to walk in justice.[5]

A stream of narratives about academic outcomes for black girls and the overarching history of demonizing and dehumanizing images about blacks, especially females, starts early. This is harmful most notably because black girls are "styled by their perceptions."[6] Therefore, blacks identifying as Christians must be asked about their collective leverage of advocacy to stimulate policies that change education for black girls. How will systemic attacks on black girls be halted? What help will the black church bring for black girls to rise?

In fairness, individual communities and churches are putting forth efforts to change what black children face in schools every day.[7] However, the alarm is that with the tremendous amount of power coming with 89 percent of blacks in America identifying as Christians, a more systematic movement towards improving outcomes for black girls would be expected. Data provided by Grissom and Redding and others supports experiences told about how this population can't access educational resources due to long-standing bias by school authorities.[8] Black students disproportionately are barricaded out of gifted/talented programs. This includes the lack of academically advanced programs for black girls (e.g., STEM). Such actions from schools leave this group vulnerable later in life.

4. Bradley, "Inner-city Education."
5. James 2:6; Micah 6:8.
6. Muhammad and McArthur, "Styled by Their Perceptions."
7. Bhargaw, "Community Meeting."
8. Grissom and Redding, "Discretion and Disproportionality."

The apparent failure of the black church in protecting black girls from being targeted and disenfranchised from life-changing educational options needs immediate attention. This can be changed with forces of influence bearing down on a system of discrimination. Steps are needed to change a system blocking them from receiving anchors that underline living a productive adult life.

The ongoing recitation on the academic failure of black students offers no good news due to systemic racism, and the matter is exacerbated when black girls move from elementary schools to middle school to high school.[9] The role of the church in the black community—The Village—carries influence and leverage. Therefore, looking forward to addressing issues of race and gender should be done without apology.

Black girls in American schools need the 89 percent from their community to be a powerhouse in sending a message that speaks loudly that their educational outcomes matter! The same power that brought attention to the prison pipeline methods attacking school-age black males is needed now on behalf of black school-age females. We know the importance of early interventions in black children's educational success.[10]

Complacency and Complexity

Research confirms that issues of academic outcomes are complex, especially when it appears that one standardized measure is used for all students. In the book *Why Race and Culture Matter in Schools*, Tyrone C. Howard details the many social factors that created the saturated talk about the achievement gap in American schools, including the problem with assessment measures.[11] Society holds a continuous role in being complacent in sending messages of inferiority about black students. Traditional school assessments, designed and normed on the white middle class, repeatedly affirm their views of being superior and black students as lagging.[12] Christian establishments produce similar reports peppered with statements about how black students don't measure up with white peers. Multiple authors cite that there is no equity found even in Christian schools's hallways for black girls, in spite of messages touting inclusion and diversity.[13] Barriers in and out of

9. Race Forward, "What is Systemic Racism?"

10. Hopson and Hopson, *Different and Wonderful*, 77–91.

11. Howard, *Why Race and Culture Matter*, 25–31.

12. Gaines, "Unity within Diversity."

13. Ohikuare, "When Minority Students Attend Elite Private Schools"; Iloabugi-chukwu, "Not Every Black Girl."

school land on the self-esteem of blacks constantly. The question to pursue is, "Why is such information allowed to be ignored in the educational preparation of black students?"

Institutionalized racism throughout hundreds of years has not changed. Therefore, black children must be informed about what they will face not only in society, but in schools. Cultural knowledge must be used by families, community, schools, and the church to help black students know that they can, will, and are expected to succeed. The platform of educational disparity, when reviewed, indicates no quick remedies, but change is possible with intentional efforts as cited in *Why Race and Culture Matter in Schools*.[14] The Village's stance on addressing the complex issues that bar black girls' academic journey will not be simple, but they should know they are not alone.

This is where hope is found in the advocacy for black girls through the black church based on what noted solidarity can do. According to Professor Jonathan Walton, "For more than 300 years, the Black church in America has provided a significant anchor for black Christians in a nation shadowed by the legacy of slavery and a society that remains defined by race, gender, and class."[15]

Ensuring Black Girls' Academic Success

In the classroom, the conversation around what works best for black girls should be foundational. Seeking their success and teaching them to settle for nothing less is paramount. We want teachers to know about the lives of all students and to use that information to cultivate successful learning environments.[16]

When we look through the lens of the black community, we see the scars of generational trauma from historical oppression and the misrepresentation of the African American culture. How does this influence the positioning of black students regarding the misappropriation of their identity and educational outcomes?[17] This is a valid question if we are to do the work that will ensure educational equity for black girls.

Cultivating successful learning environments can benefit from data on brain research and learner's success. Meyer, a licensed clinical school social worker, and Certified Sand Play Therapist-teacher highlights the importance

14. Howard, *Why Race and Culture Matter in Schools*, 58–59.
15. Episcopal Diocese of Chicago, "Harvard Professor Jonathan Walton."
16. Kozol, *The Shame of the Nation*.
17. Brown and Kopano, eds., *Soul Thieves*, 61–75; 77–90.

of teacher-student relationships and the need for in-depth connections that are required for academic success, especially when working with urban students facing trauma.[18] Reaching and teaching children exposed to trauma requires teachers to bring into the learning environment behaviors that display a willing and welcoming attitude that contribute to the removal of trauma in school experiences.[19] Conversely, teachers who do not take such steps contribute to the demise of black girls' academic pursuits.

Where are the intentional efforts of the black community and church in ensuring needed actions? Important are such questions for The Village to pursue in ensuring black girls have access to teachers who makes connections because "all students can succeed . . . it is educators' responsibility to see that they do."[20]

A Message of Intent

A multitude of shared voices under the heading "Believing Change is Possible" offered authentic and practical examples for effective ways to dig deep into social justice actions on behalf of black students.[21] Such actions address how to counter the negative impact on black students and change the racial barriers black students face. This is a crucial starting point to eradicating the dysfunctional and unfair and separate environments that impede the academic success for black children.[22] Too many games are played in favor of the "race card" on behalf of those labeled white in America. All types of bias deteriorate blacks' education and have a significant impact on them as wage-earning adults.[23] The key is to remove the various layers of bias and deflate actions that derail black girls, thereby denying them being authors of their own stories.

The radical need for action early on in the school experience undergirds the call here to the black community's 89 percent to hold accountable those guarding the gates of educational and economic access for black girls. On behalf of these dynamic students, a message must be sent that carries the intent of Jonathan Kozol's work, which implies that black students—girls—know that they are not waiting for whatever good

18. RB-Banks and Meyer, "Childhood Trauma in Today's Urban Classroom."

19. Sorrels, "Reaching and Teaching Children Exposed to Trauma."

20. Corbett et al., *Effort and Excellence*, 12–13.

21. Dillard, "Black Minds Matter," 11; Al-Shabazz, "Believing Change is Possible," 11.

22. Nelson, "Still Separate, Still Unequal."

23. National Partnership for Women and Families, "America's Women and the Wage Gap."

things may happen for them while politicians and other elitist groups debate their fate. Why? Because it is of little solace to those who are children now and will not get a second chance to live their childhood in the next century because of biased politics and other default measures used by the privilege of this country to keep black children out of reach of the best that is offered to their children.[24]

Gail Thompson's work *Through Ebony Eyes* speaks to the challenging circumstances of childhood that are unfortunately not unique, as classrooms around America are filled with evidence of disproportionate barriers to academic success for black children.[25] When it comes to America's schools it will take serious and intentional advocacy, if the messaging and actions are to prove that Black Girls Too Matter!

Advocacy

The current educational system is a perilous journey to navigate without advocates who care, support, and guide black students. To some, it may appear that this academic crisis for black girls is going unnoticed by the black community. However, actions are taken on behalf of educational equity; it is clear that there are advocates seeking change on behalf of all black students. There are advocates for black students' right to learn in environments that are ripe for their success. The benefits of advocacy targeted towards addressing rooted barriers tied to race, class, and gender, unlock what holds black girls back.[26] The *Journal of Insight and Diversity* highlights how advocacy is paramount in efforts to "Bridge the Gap" in the academic experience of black students.[27] Accessing the determination of advocates and channeling their influence along with 89 percent of black Christians offers a hopeful and formidable resource for improving black girls' education.

Order of Business, Self-Determination and Identity Politics

Ensuring that black girls know they matter starts with teaching them self-determination skills. Such skills build resiliency and foster success. Collaboration between home, community, school, and church offers influence

24. Kozol, *Amazing Grace*, 193.
25. Thompson, *Through Ebony Eyes*, 130–31.
26. Council of the Greater City Schools, "Annual Report."
27. Vollman, "Health Professions Schools."

for protecting black students. In a range of reports calling for change, the National Education Association provides steps for effective change on behalf of black students.[28]

A key point for black girls's advocacy is found in the fact that many have access to the black church early in life. The role of the black church in making it a part of their order of business is key when it comes to informing black girls' skills in the areas of self-advocacy and self-determination. The church holds an essential role in improving outcomes. As part of the African diaspora, blacks in America have traversed, survived, and succeeded in a culture of steady hostility, sabotage, oppression, and brutal infringement because of their leaning into self-determination. Therefore, the role of self-determination in the intersection of preparing for overcoming barriers can't be overlooked in the strategy to arm black girls to succeed. In The Village, the black church is a strong focal point in navigating social, educational, and economic justice.

Tom Burrell, inducted into the advertising hall of fame, published *Brainwashed: Challenging the Myth of Black Inferiority*, which highlights the importance of building resiliency through the removal of systematic strategies that impact educational outcomes for urban black youth. He tells in interviews how through his forty years in advertising that, "Images and words are very powerful . . . and carry out the whole idea of African Americans being less-than . . . not good as . . ."[29] Such work should be a lightning rod to inform the urgency in removing barriers black girls face on their academic path. Building resiliency leads to self-determination skills and should be an expected norm in changing the educational trajectory for all black students. Self-determination skills are not skills in isolation, rather they are the principle that holds valuable insight, motivation, learnings, and self-efficacy that lead to change.

The black community has a collective responsibility for teaching self-determination skills. The endeavor here is to make it an order of business for the black church to be involved in that partnership and engage in actions that enrich the development of black girls' identities, thereby counting the daily images that attempt to defeat their purpose.

Actions: Teaching Who I Am

The American Psychology Association detailed how "numerous studies found that students who are more involved in setting educational goals are

28. National Education Association, "Race Against Time."
29. Burrell, "Negative Images."

more likely to reach their goals . . . [I]ncreasing student success through instruction in self-determination appears to be the bedrock of academic success."[30] When assumptions about black girls are examined, when their education is designed in ways that are culturally centered, and when preventative measures are in place then we will see success because they will be stopped from falling through the cracks.[31] Our children need to see what they are capable of, expected to do, and set goals to achieve such outcomes. They should accept no less than the best from themselves and those around them, including their schools. Resources such as *Black Firsts: 4,000 Ground-Breaking and Pioneering Historical Events* support such success and lay a foundation for black girls on a theme of "Who I Am."[32] Such engagement screams, "You are relevant!"

Families, communities, and the black church have a responsibility to ensure that the curriculum reflects the strengths of who we are from the day our children enter. Black girls must be prepared to speak with a voice of self-advocacy that says "I have a Village and my Village cares!" Such actions prepare black girls to face inevitable injustices and rise!

No longer can what it means to be black in the American educational system be ignored. Intentional interventions targeting the double barrels of racism and sexism are needed for black girls' success. For change to occur, only the black community can effectively start the process with a keen focus on educating each black girl about her greatness. The problem to correct at the start is believing that looking out for black boys will carry over and produce similar results in favor of black girls. However, we can learn from works that appear effective.

The Problem Before Us

> Black people are not dark-skinned white people . . . they are much more. They are survivors of the Middle Passage and centuries of humiliation and deprivation, who have excelled against the odds, constantly making a way out of "No way!" At this pivotal point in history, the idea of black inferiority should have had a Going-Out-of-Business Sale.[33]
>
> —TOM BURRELL

30. American Psychology Association, "Increasing Student Success."
31. Ricks, "Black Girls in Education."
32. Smith, *Black Firsts*.
33. Burrell, "Negative Images."

School data indicates that black girls do not receive supportive or restorative efforts that help them excel as they go through what all children go through while growing up. Focus groups and interview reports tell how black girls are treated as problems by school officials. Historically, white school officials bring biases against black adults and that bias is extended to black children. Extensive collaborative research between Kimberlee Williams Crenshaw, Columbia Law School, the Center for Intersectionality and Social Policy Studies, and the African American Policy Forum tell of the reality that black girls are suspended at a rate of 12 percent compared to white girls who are suspended at a rate of 2 percent.[34] Such unfair discipline practices are problems that lay the groundwork for systemic obstructions to their success. School officials engaged in dangerous actions towards black girls carry long-term and devastating outcomes.

The school experience for black girls continues to be an experience of foreboding. The deep impact of race and gender in the disciplinary actions towards black school-age girls is clear through the work started over thirty years ago by Diane Scott-Jones and Maxine Clark.[35] Unfair school discipline creates an atmosphere that promotes vulnerability, poor attendance, targeted bullying, stereotype threats, sexual exploitation, and early involvement in the juvenile system. Startling recent documents show the youngest black girl suspended from school was of preschool age.[36]

Such experiences are not minor and offer a clear view of how black girls stop mattering almost immediately in the American school system. This harmful historical truth shows itself in what happens as they mature in a society committed to engaging in trauma and violence against African American girls, damaging their educational experiences. Well documented is the legal system's failure to stop the historical violence bestowed upon black girls.[37] This dual impasse between race and gender has historically justified sexual assault and preserved racially biased social power structures that discount sexual violence against black girls and women, allowing such assaults to persist and go disproportionately unpunished.[38] The trauma against black girls is as real today as it was in the past. Trauma, sexual harassment, assault, community violence, and the daily stressors of racism and sexism have negative effects on academic performance. Also, "When addressing sexual violence faced by black women, it is important

---

34. Crenshaw et al., "Black Girls Matter."
35. Scott-Jones and Clark, "The School Experiences of Black Girls."
36. National Women's Law Center, "Unlocking Opportunities for Black Girls."
37. Equal Justice Initiative, "Sexual Exploitation of Black Women."
38. West and Johnson, "Sexual Violence."

to understand the unfair stereotypes and destructive misrepresentations of black women that perpetrate crimes against women of color," and how this adds to the vulnerability black girls' experience in schools today.[39] This negative school climate is dangerous to black girls and brings forth questions: 1) What happens to young girls removed from what should be the protective boundaries of the school day? 2) What happens when parents are forced to choose between multiple caregivers, and work to provide for the family because the school day is made unavailable due to lenses that are not culturally sensitive? Such questions should move the black community into collaboration with the black church.

Practices Matters

An effective academic system reflects practices that understand students' culture is essential to their success.[40] Far too long there has been a missing link between schools and students of color's culture. The respected works of Gloria Ladson-Billington hit hard how intentional relationships are needed for schools to matter to all students. The curriculum is foundational to good teaching, and specific pedagogy is needed for working effectively, as it allows students to see themselves in it.[41] Natalie King's work indicates that when teachers connect with black girls the impact is significant, even in the most challenging academic fields.[42] Cultural applications in schools are being left out when it comes to understanding black girls. The funneling of black girls into special education has taken on a serious pattern very similar to the one black male students faced from mostly white, female, and middle-class Americans.

If there is any doubt that educational strategies matter in confronting educational inequities, Fatima Gross-Graves stated; "[A]nd many African American women and girls are simply stuck on a school to poverty pathway, in which poor educational opportunities result in limited job prospects, concentrations in low-wage work and disproportionately representation among those in poverty. [Therefore] it's time to address the educational crisis facing African-American girls."[43] When effective practices are ignored,

39. National Organization for Women, "Black Women and Sexual Violence."

40. Hernandez-Sheets, *Diversity Pedagogy*, 38.

41. Science Education Resource Center, "How to Engage and Support Urban Students."

42. King, "When Teachers Get It Right."

43. Goss Graves, "How We Can Help."

institutionalized racism gives those unwilling to educate black students the privilege to neglect and over-discipline.

Emphatic are groups such as The Center for Intersectionality and Social Policies Studies when they discuss how "We can no longer afford to leave young women and girls of color at the margins of our concerns with respect to the achievement gap, drop-out rate, and school to prison pipeline."[44] This type of information should alarm us as an assessment of what is intentionally happening through the use of biased disciplinary policies. The black church should be on fire and in motion against this injustice toward black girls!

Assessment Matters

Programs made available to black students/black females for true educational access are done best in learning environments that do not tolerate institutionalized racism. Practitioners who respect diverse use of language and communication styles use such knowledge to inform educational practices.[45] Such practices include assessments that are relevant to students' diversity. Without corrective actions in the assessment of black girls, there will continue to be an echo that there is no serious interest by any to remove barriers.[46]

The work of Lesaux and Marietta gives a resounding message for assessments to be designed in ways that work for diverse students.[47] Their research stressed that schools need to create a new relationship with data that is tied to strategies that produce outcomes for students from diverse backgrounds. Structured interventions, tied to culturally normed assessments, offer accountability measures that impact academic outcomes, leading to educational equity. The fact that students learn differently is not new information and should not be a surprise to schools.[48]

The combined investments of culturally relevant pedagogy, teaching self-advocacy, partnering with families and communities, a curriculum for empowerment, and master teachers who want black students to successfully produce outcomes can't be denied. In "The Pedagogy of Poverty vs. Good Teaching," an essential question is asked about reform and accountability for working with urban learners: "Why is a minor issue like improving the

44. Crenshaw et al., "Black Girls Matter."
45. Hernandez-Sheets, "Diversity Pedagogy," 108.
46. Hing, "New Report Details Barriers."
47. Lesaux and Marietta, *Making Assessment Matter*.
48. Willingham, "Do Visual, Auditory, and Kinesthetic Learners," 31–35, 44.

quality of urban teaching generally overlooked by popular reform and re-structuring strategies?"[49]

We know that black students are and can be successful. Black children succeed in dire circumstances, yet more often what is reported and portrayed are messages of collective failure vs. historical fortitude to succeed. Re-envisioning success starts with re-examining and understanding how success is defined in a specific cultural/social construct. The work done by the North-side Achievement Zone is an excellent summary of such works.[50]

School officials hold power over curriculum, testing materials, and how seriously teachers take personal responsibility for the learning process.[51] Until teachers care and there is a no-excuse policy for the lack of teachers accountable in matters of assessments, unfortunately, nothing will change. We can't police the heart, but we can police results and demand what is needed to do just that on behalf of black girls.

Teachers Who Care Matter

The book *Reflective Teaching* takes us deep into the importance of a teacher's ability to self-assess and take personal responsibility to teach all children.[52] This level of reflection allows a teacher to learn and use cultural practices that matter to black students. As well, when responsible teachers under-stand the impact of a child's exposure to poverty, low employment rates, inadequate health services, malnutrition, and more, they can take steps to support change in the school experience in ways that matter.[53] Needless to say, having teachers who care about such a foundation is essential in the work ahead for improving black girls's outcomes.

Pioneers in the work to help black children thrive and overcome their underachievement in American schools have a long history.[54] Work by Lois Weiner titled "Preparing Teachers for Urban Schools" outlined thirty years of reform.[55] Amos Wilson's work outlined the importance of having master teachers in the classroom. His work went on to talk about the actions of a master teacher who is an essential anchor in the movement to change black girls' school experiences. Wilson says, "Master teachers are someone who

49. Haberman, "The Pedagogy of Poverty vs. Good Teaching."
50. Northside Achievement Zone, "A Game Changing Approach That Is Working."
51. Douglas et al., "The Impact of White Teachers."
52. Zeichner and Liston, *Reflective Teaching*.
53. African American Policy Forum, "Did You Know?"
54. Elias, "Social-Emotional Skills."
55. Weiner, "Preparing Teachers for Urban Schools."

has the gift to teach, inspire, uplift, spread knowledge and promote mental growth. Master Teachers are as precious as Rubies and Gold. They are the vehicle which many of us use to travel the journey of increasing our knowledge. We are empowered by their words, enlightened by their philosophies. We read their books, listen to their audio, study their teachings long after many of them have passed on to be with the Ancestors."[56] This trail of documentation is rich and tells why we must remove the stubborn root of racist education in galvanizing the black community in a quest raise up black girls! The call here is not only for qualified and fully prepared teachers, but for master teachers to address the stubborn roots of racism.

> Today our very survival depends on our ability to stay awake, to adjust to new ideas, to remain vigilant and to face the challenges of change.[57]

—REV. DR. MARTIN LUTHER KING JR.

Conclusion

Schools are the battleground! Once again, the black community is faced with a quality of life crisis, and this time the spotlight is on our black girls. We know these battles are about educational suppression to control the stratified economic divide that continues to be reconstructed in America as a form of oppression against black and brown populations. Change for black girls will require intentional nurturing and educational strategies that foster their success. Without this work, the crisis of a long history of destructive intersections related to gender and race will continue. What black girls face in schools is not the fault of any one event, one entity, social program, or person, but the outcome of historical scars from institutionalized racism in America. Therefore, to move forward, the black church must set a beacon on the path for black girls to flourish.

For the required level of respect to be experienced, it will take not only deep listening but deep actions. Such action can be found in the voice of the young, as they have proven themselves to be strong, resilient, and carrying forth wisdom. Such wisdom is found in the statement below given to us by Angie Thomas, a young black female scholar who guides us and captures what is needed to bring forth ideas about why new soil is needed in the schools around this country. "Yeah, a li'l damaged, but alive.

56. Wilson, *The Developmental Psychology of the Black Child*.
57. King Jr., *Where Do We Go from Here*, 171.

I am going to try something different with them. Putting them in new soil can be like hitting a reset button."[58]

The reset button for black girls' education rests in the hands of the 89 percent of black Americans who are Christians and their allies as advocates. The crisis faced will not go away easily because we see evidence daily that America is in crisis. What is happening in society will only amplify what black girls face because schools don't exist in a vacuum. Blacks as a collective community have always seen the strongest systemic changes when they rallied to advance a cause. Historically, the black church has been the center of such change and most effective when out front, focused, and determined on a specific social issue. The cultural disconnect being faced in today's schools is a social crisis and warrants the black church stepping in to eradicate the problem. The black church has an essential and extraordinary opportunity now to hit the reset button. We know the importance of the black church's role in resetting black girls' path because:

> Family and religious social capital are the most potent predictors for positive student college aspirations—students who attend church and believe religion is important may be more likely to interact with more adults who can help them with their school work and even provide guidance about their future goals and plans.[59]

Black Christians are essential players in the work needed to ensure that black girls received the capital to access their ambitions; it is like the "moral vision at the center of all things."[60] Therefore, black girls' fate is at the center of the black community. So yes, black girls need the unwavering commitment of all blacks, especially the church of the black community, to send them off to succeed in school, flourish in college, lead in ways that the world has never seen, lift others, demonstrate self-determination, and make their climb in society; rising without limitations. Yes, it's time!

---

58. Thomas, "The Hate U Give," 435.

59. Bradley, *Something Seems Strange*, 198.

60. Williamson, *Healing the Soul of America*, 132–33.

Chapter 4 **Sexuality in the Black Community**

—Howard Brown

The Place Our Sexuality Began

T he Bible begins with a creation story in which God created man and woman and made them naked, but in that nakedness, they were unashamed. In other words, they were known, could know each other, and know God in their nakedness. They were not afraid to be touched and seen by each other. No dangerous or deceitful motives or covert agendas existed. Adam and Eve's full frontal, physical, uncovered presentation said with sensual candor, "This is who I am." What you saw in the beauty and the acts done in the body perfectly reflected the souls wonderfully encased within. That raw, uncensored, benevolent ability and exercise to know, be known, and explore one another is called intimacy. Human sexuality, in terms of sexual intercourse and interactions between men and women, is only one God-given way to express physical intimacy.

The story of Adam and Eve goes on to tell us that humankind broke away from God and, in doing so, became a broken creation. Having lost the *full* ability and desire to reflect the image of God and relate intimately with God, humanity literally sought to "cover its losses." This "cover-up" dimmed the light of their knowledge about themselves and each other. Intimacy—naked freedom and benevolence toward one another—suffered. Shame, fear, hatred, and destructive behavior remained, now hindering and harming the intimacy necessary to be sexually whole. At the same time, we continue to harbor a God-given, yet broken, desire and drive to be intimate sexual creations. Our intimate longings hobble along, leaving a jagged, damaged path of broken relationships in their wake.

Although damaged, our sexuality continues to make us "naked." It lays bare much of what is right and wrong on the inside. It expresses who we really are and what we really feel. At the same time, it opens us up to experience and exposes all sorts of internal, invisible damage. Our sexuality and its behavior mirror the condition of our souls and the souls of our community.

This is no different for black people. Our sexuality reveals our humanity. The expressed result of that sexuality confirms that black people, along with other human beings, are beautiful but broken. The cultural peculiarities of black sexuality, seen in ethnic statistical data and exploited on the stage of popular culture, provide an important picture of the souls of black people. What does it tell us?

The Place of Sexual Brokenness

In *Come on People*, Alvin Poussaint highlights many concerns about broken black sexuality. Among them are the number of single mothers, absent and apathetic fathers, the lack of two-parent homes, teenage pregnancy, and the spread of STDs. The statistics accompanying Poussaint's account are somewhat alarming:

> Sixty-two percent of black families are single parent families with children under eighteen years old. Of that 62 percent, 90 percent of those are maintained by a single mother.[1]

> The STD rates among African Americans can be 6 percent to 18 percent higher than whites depending on the disease. Among black teenagers fourteen to nineteen, 48 percent have an STD compared to 20 percent of young white women.[2]

> Minority women constitute only about 13 percent of the female population (aged fifteen to forty-four) in the United States, but they underwent approximately 36 percent of the abortions.[3]

That means that, on average, about 1,800 black babies are aborted daily. In the timely words of Poussaint—come on people! It is time to examine seriously the results of our sexual behavior, what it reveals about us. Obviously, we are a passionate people, hungry to be known and to know each other. We have the potential to achieve a high degree of fulfilling relationships. Unfortunately, it seems that we are only having a lot of sex. These statistics show us that many of us are behaving like a shell of a person and have disconnected our sexuality from our God-given sense of worth and intimacy.

1. Strauss, "Abortion Surveillance."
2. Strauss, "Abortion Surveillance."
3. Black Genocide, "Abortion and the Black Community."

God created black people, along with all human beings, to fulfill their humanness. Any failure of intimacy in our sexuality short-circuits our emotional and relational processes. Judging by its product, our sexual behavior (the manifestation of our sexuality) declares that we are broken. Clearly, this failure is an internal malfunction of the soul and heart. But how did this happen?

The Place of Family in Our Sexuality

As Cosby states, the family is central to understanding and moving toward sexual dignity as a people, because the family shapes our sense of sexuality and our understanding of its proper expression. God created human beings to influence each other. This means we are responsible for shaping each other. Genesis says that God brought Eve to Adam. Adam blessed her, declaring to her, the world, and to himself, that she was a dignified bearer of God's image. By declaring "This at last is bone of my bones and flesh of my flesh; she shall be called Woman, because she was taken out of Man," Adam announced that Eve shared in the same essence of humanity that God had created in Adam.[4] What was "this" became "woman" through the infusion of God's created image. God later ratifies this blessing by calling Adam and Eve to be fruitful and multiply. They were to pass on who they were, based on who God had made them—examples of healthy relationships between men and women. God made it so we would learn how to properly approach and express sexuality, dignity, and intimacy from our elders, parents, and community; and he made it so we would learn by word and by deed.

The Place of Marriage in Our Sexuality

If men and women are not present, active, and engaging in committed, rightly intimate relationships with each other, sexual mess occurs. As Adam proclaims, the marriage between our original parents refers to a psychosomatic unity. "Therefore a man shall leave his father and his mother and hold fast to his wife, and they shall become one flesh."[5]

This one flesh refers to a spiritual unity between the man and the woman. Adam declares just as much about the soul of Eve as her body. Their sexuality functions properly only if they are socially, emotionally, and spiritually one. If the latter fails, so will the former. Marriage makes

4. Genesis 2:23.
5. Genesis 2:24.

one beast out of two distinct creatures, man and woman. Their sexuality is the physical expression of that "beast." No wonder sex malfunctions outside of marriage! No wonder a lack of committed relationships brings so much pain and struggle! We cannot live the lie of having sexual wholeness outside the sanctity of marriage. Our sexuality problems are also our marriage problems, and we have passed them on to the next generation. Below is an excerpt from a writer who in 2006 visited a sixth-grade class in Washington, DC for a career exploration:

> "Marriage is for white people."
>
> That is what one of my students told me some years back when I taught a career exploration class for sixth graders at an elementary school in Southeast Washington. I was pleasantly surprised when the boys in the class stated that being a good father was a very important goal to them, more meaningful than making money or having a fancy title.
>
> "That's wonderful!" I told my class. "I think I'll invite some couples in to talk about being married and rearing children."
>
> "Oh, no," objected one student. "We're not interested in the part about marriage. Only about how to be good fathers."
>
> And that is when the other boy chimed in, speaking as if the words left a nasty taste in his mouth: "Marriage is for white people."
>
> He is right, at least statistically. The marriage rate for African Americans has been dropping since the 1960s, and today, we have the lowest marriage rate of any racial group in the United States. In 2001, according to the U.S. Census, 43.3 percent of black men and 41.9 percent of black women in America had never been married, in contrast to 27.4 percent and 20.7 percent respectively for whites. African American women are the least likely in our society to marry. In the period between 1970 and 2001, the overall marriage rate in the United States declined by 17 percent; but for blacks, it fell by 34 percent.[6]

A number of really difficult and heartbreaking reasons exist for the decline of marriage in our community. It can feel more freeing to leave behind, or let go of, what for many has become the disappointing institution of marriage. Our people resort to what I would describe as a "neo-nihilism" that masquerades as freedom but is really a loss of hope. In a world that remains

6. Jones, "Marriage Is for White People."

disappointing and hard, God calls us to live and be healthy. We must dig for and ask the Lord for ways to redeem what he has created as good for us but has been destroyed and demeaned by so many.

All said I must take a step back and confess: I do not believe marriage, in and of itself, is the answer to our sexual brokenness. Marriage itself can be only as healthy as the people it unites. I agree with bell hooks, in part, as she discusses what she describes as an "idealized fantasy" presented by shows like *The Cosby Show*:

> If there was a man in the house, a father, everything would be perfect; they would be happy . . . When black pundits, whether political figures or intellectuals, talk about the black family, they too seem to buy into the romantic myth that if only there was a black man in the house, life would be perfect. Like children, who know better, they refuse to accept the evidence that there are plenty of homes where fathers are present, fathers who are so busy acting out, being controlling, being abusive, that home is hell and children in those homes spend lots of time wishing the father would go away . . . Dysfunctional homes where there is no love, where mother and father are present but abusive are just as damaging as dysfunctional single-parent homes.[7]

Hooks rightfully asserts that even in a context of marriage, damage occurs. Marriage alone cannot shoulder the entire burden of our sexual dysfunction. At the same time, we must resist the temptation to dismiss it as merely beneficial to our sexuality. It is where our sexuality begins and departs. If intimacy between a man and a woman forms the core of the sexual act, a departure from the God-given context of psychosomatic unity will only compound the damage of our sexual brokenness. If marriage becomes the exception instead of the norm, we are doomed to sexual weariness. Marriage defines the sexual act and sets its stage and scope. Marriage frees intimacy to convey dignity and worth. Marriage says, "You are my destination, not just what you've got." Without the commitment and sanctity of marriage, intimacy can never fully manifest itself, and we will be disconnected and disoriented in our intimacy and sexuality. We will then pass this distance and disconnection on to our children.

---

7. hooks, *We Real Cool*, 102.

The Place of Broken Relationships in Our Sexuality

So, we must ask ourselves, what does the sexual act become outside of a context of intimacy and commitment? Before Adam and Eve ate from the tree of the knowledge of good and evil, they were "naked and unashamed." They did not fear exploring and being explored by each other. Adam and Eve were not afraid that they would use that unguarded existence to hurt, take advantage of, or abuse each other. Their differences did not make them insecure; their differences connected them to each other. However, when Adam and Eve sinned against their Creator, they lost their sense of worth, respect, and trust for God. This meant they also lost their sense of worth, respect, and trust for themselves and each other.

> So when the woman saw that the tree was good for food, and that it was a delight to the eyes, and that the tree was to be desired to make one wise, she took of its fruit and ate, and she also gave some to her husband who was with her, and he ate. Then the eyes of both were opened, and they knew that they were naked. And they sewed fig leaves together and made themselves loincloths.[8]

For out of the desire of something different from God's provision, Adam and Eve not only sold out on God, they failed to protect and cover each other. Eve fed it to Adam, and Adam, who was with her, failed to stop her from being seduced by the serpent's lies. They both traded their nakedness for security in their own wisdom. From that point on, humanity could no longer trust that they would not be used, overlooked, and unprotected in their nakedness. According to the Scriptures, we should fear intimacy with others—as we are open to all sorts of abuses. The fall caused humanity to break their proper relationship to everything and everyone around them. Shame entered each one of us. We covered our nakedness and our newfound guilt and fear with fig leaves that did not work. Adam and Eve covered themselves from each other and their God. They now viewed their sense of intimacy and their freedom to know each other with fear and distrust. They were ashamed of their dispensability, frailty, and culpability. Intimacy was dangerous, and when intimacy is dangerous, we want to be divorced from it. Without true intimacy, sex is nothing more than a cheap counterfeit. On one hand, because sex is intimate by its very nature, we use it as a cover-up and healing agent to provide some of the intimacy that we once had. On the other hand, because we are divorced from the true intimacy Adam and Eve knew before the fall, and because we share their fear of nakedness, we also

8. Genesis 3:6–7.

use sex as a tool of violence, rage, and control. In his chapter on "What's Going on with Black Men," Poussaint says:

> The fact is though, that many of the black females who used to get married when they became pregnant are no longer doing so, there is less shame and less embarrassment . . . Not long ago a television show featured a thirteen-year-old mother who had somehow managed to have two of her suitors appear on the show for a paternity test. One of the boys was black, the other Puerto Rican. They were fifteen- and sixteen-year-old best friends, who both had had sex with this young girl during the general time she conceived. The word shameless comes to mind. Why these people would wash linen this dirty not just in public but on national TV is still another sign that all is not well in the world.[9]

I agree with Poussaint that these examples are a sign that all is not well in the world, but I do not agree that shamelessness or a lack of shame is the problem. I believe it is shame exactly that has driven these people to seek an antidote for their brokenness. Sometimes the antidote looks and feels like justice and being known and respected (opposites of shame) when it is actually another way of responding to the shame of their insecurity, abandonment, and disgrace. *Shameless* behavior is an outward cry of the inner rage and sorrow of a person whose humanness is unmet, untouched, and unknown. They rightly feel sold out, used, and desperate enough to display humiliation in order to reclaim the sexual dignity that has escaped them.

The Place of Men in Our Sexuality

Our people, especially our men, are hiding something and hiding from something based on the issues of our sexuality. Poussaint says:

> The more socially impotent the black man is feeling, the more he will rely on sexual conquests to prove his manliness. There is much bragging among black men when sex and paternity are the main claims to fame. Some will see getting a girl pregnant and having a child as proof of their virility. But what it really proves is their insecurity . . . Real men act responsibly, and they sure as hell don't walk away from the mothers of their babies. Real men make a commitment to these young mothers. If they do not marry them, at least they should take care of their children.[10]

9. Cosby and Poussaint, *Come on People*, 14–15.
10. Cosby and Poussaint, *Come on People*, 13–14.

Black men are having a hard time being "real men" as Poussaint describes because many are running and hiding from what responsible manhood will be sure to reveal—their lack of "manliness." Black men suffer from being boys who cannot handle the internal rigors and demands of committed relationships and adult responsibilities. They refuse to grow up because they fear being weighed, measured, and found wanting. Our men wrongly believe sexual acts will cover and remove the pain of not feeling man enough in a fallen world. They are tempted to try to outrun the overbearing weight of their sexual and relational responsibilities. "Hit it and quit it," becomes the modus operandi of the black man who is afraid to be found emotionally and financially incapable of being a "real man." Poussaint writes:

> Some black women simply don't want to marry the fathers of their babies because these men appear to have little to offer beyond sperm. Many of these men are unemployed and unemployable . . . Because so many black men are unemployed, underemployed, and incarcerated, they are not proposing marriage and if they did, their proposals might not be taken seriously. A father takes care of his children. These men have trouble taking care of themselves. The relationship between them and the mothers of their babies is often strained or worse.[11]

If a black man's worth hinges upon his ability to provide financially, he will run away from his responsibilities in shame. Though provision is not, and should not be, excluded as a dignifying attribute of manhood, provision is not, and should not be, exclusive or premier among those attributes. If it is made an issue between him, his woman, and his child, a black man, or any man for that matter, provision will malfunction. Those who should be the object of his affection and attract his sacrificial attention simply become reminders and aggravations of his failure. Bell hooks writes:

> Most black males have consistently received contradictory messages from society about what it means to be responsible. Patriarchal socialization says you are responsible if you get a job, bring your wages home, and provide for your family's material well-being. Yet poverty and a lack of job opportunities have prevented many black males from being responsible in the patriarchal sense of the term. Many black males accept this definition of responsible manhood and spend their lives feeling like a failure, feeling as though their self-esteem is

11. Cosby and Poussaint, *Come on People*, 14–15.

assaulted and assailed on all sides, because they cannot acquire
the means to fulfill this role.[12]

Out of sheer rage and anger toward the women who appear to rob his
sense of worth, some men become vigilantes of lost manhood by conquering
women sexually. They will wrongly seek justice for what they deem unjust
and unfair measurements of their manhood by being "sexual Robin Hoods."
Most men, in their bragging, boasting, and violent objectifying behavior, are
seeking to conquer and defend in what seems to be a war against their manhood. Tragically, this means men will demean, depress, and destroy their
familial responsibilities in an attempt to remove their condemning presence
over them. This can lead a man to enter the same type of irresponsible relationships and father more children, continuing in a lifestyle that will only
increase his sense of shame.

If he will not wage war against what serves as a mirror to his weaknesses, he will simply run away and hide from his shame. He will turn away
from his woman and children all together, disowning them as not just irrelevant to his manhood but malevolent. Therefore, children and mothers
may not see the father for days, months, or years, and in extreme cases, the
father may disappear from their lives forever.

Some men have abandoned being in sexual relationships with women
at all, turning to homosexuality as a safe haven from the constant reminders of their lack of true manliness. It can be more comforting and safer to
take on an effeminate persona, especially if they think being a man in the
wake of failure is too difficult and too disgracing. Men are hiding from and
warring against the condemnation and exposure of their broken and fallen
manhood. Let us look back at the account in Genesis.

> And he said, "I heard the sound of you in the garden, and I was
> afraid, because I was naked, and I hid myself." He said, "Who
> told you that you were naked? Have you eaten of the tree of
> which I commanded you not to eat?" The man said, "The wom-
> an whom you gave to be with me, she gave me fruit of the tree,
> and I ate." Then the LORD God said to the woman, "What is this
> that you have done?" The woman said, "The serpent deceived
> me, and I ate."[13]

All men shield and cover their nakedness and their exposure to guilt
and condemnation from their women and children. Man seeks to escape
facing himself, God, and his responsibilities, because he does not have an

12. hooks, *We Real Cool*, 85–86.

13. Genesis 3:10–13.

answer for his internal or external corruption. Women have responded to this neglect with equal anger and apathy.

The Place of Women in Our Sexuality

Women, rightly offended by the often-abusing sexuality of black men, turn to protective mechanisms too. A black man who walks out on her and her children is a constant reminder that she is not worth the effort or the attention. Black men have succeeded in their passive and active sexualized aggression. The black woman is theirs to be sexually conquered and impregnated and that is it. Our women, wanting to be touched and known, even if falsely, will fold to this pressure. Some women actually believe having sex with uncommitted men means that they are loved. This creates a "sexualized intimacy" between a man and a woman. They both seek to answer their deep longings with superficial sexuality. They fool themselves into thinking that this will satisfy their longings to be known, cherished, and encouraged. In the end, both people feel the letdown of sex that is handled like a drug—it only temporarily masks the symptoms of an unmet, deeper desire for intimacy. Women, as with men, easily turn to sexually addictive and foolish behaviors in a failed attempt at wholeness.

In a sexualized intimate relationship, it is easy for a woman to see the child created in the process as the emblem of worth and value after the man has abandoned the relationship. Motherhood becomes a way of keeping her dignity and grace intact. She was not good enough to be someone's wife or, if married, emotionally cared-for wife, but she does have a consolation prize—her children. Thus, the cycle continues for her and her children. Black community leaders have rightly focused on drug addiction and abuse as a source of many problems with the black community, while having failed to focus on the consequences of sexual addiction and abuse on our people and their sense of dignity.

This can happen to the married or the unmarried. There are a number of marriages where sex is divorced from intimacy. The husband and wife stay married out of convenience, shame, or to sustain their fantasy of being good people. Nevertheless, both men and women participate in the dance. Like a man who runs away out of shame, a woman may refuse to invite her man to anything higher or better as far as intimacy is concerned. If she has already felt like a sexual object, conquest, or prescription, she will protect what is left of her on the inside. She will not be vulnerable with the man, or demand that he become a better man, because his potential failure is too great a risk. She will seek to protect herself by being strong, living life on her own, and raising children by herself. She will take control of her sexual life, by enjoying her sexuality as objectively as the men around her enjoy it, or she may turn to the comfort and safety of a same-sex relationship; she will not allow her heartfelt desire for deeper respect from men to surface. To do so would open her up to more pain, stigmatize her as being "over-demanding." In that way, she allows the man to maintain his behavior as they both behave as wary, jaded consumers of each other.

Only after the high of having sex, being in a fake relationship, or having a child wears off will a woman's own sense of rage surface. However, that often perpetuates the problem. She will rage against the father of the child or blame the child as the remnant of a disgracing experience with a man. She may be tempted to use the child to cover her shame and exact justice against the cavalier and disappointing father. She can do this by not allowing the father to see the child or to be in the child's life. An emotionally abandoned mother, single or married, may use the man as a scapegoat for all that has gone wrong, indoctrinating her children and other young women along the way. She may even transfer her unmet longings to the child, forcing a young boy to become mama's protector, or the new man of the house, or her counselor, or sounding board for her grown-up issues. Sometimes these children witness their mother's lonely and empty sexual pursuits with man after man. The mother is trying to stay alive emotionally but like a drowning victim grabbing for life, she may drown her children with her in her sexual brokenness. No wonder young girls can grow up believing that a man is good for babies and sex, but bad for long-term emotional relationships.

The Place of Children in Our Sexuality

In his book *Silently Seduced: When Parents Make Their Children Partners,* Dr. Kenneth Adams describes what he coins as "covert incest" in contrast to the physically abusive overt incest:

> Covert incest occurs when a child becomes the object of a parent's affection, love, passion, and preoccupation. The parent, motivated by the loneliness and emptiness created by a chronically troubled marriage or relationship, makes the child a surrogate partner. The boundary between caring and incestuous love is crossed when the relationship with the child exists to meet the needs of the parents rather than those of the child.[14]

---

14. Adams, *Silently Seduced,* 9.

Adams goes on to describe covert incest in many ways: as mama's "prince," mama's "confidant and advisor," or mama's "little man." However, no matter the profiles, the violation and abuse complicate their sexual lives. This abusive pattern, so common in the black community between mothers and sons, ironically often makes the boys into womanizers. Their womanizing covers the shame and anger of unhealthy relationships with their mothers. They seek justice and freedom from the abuse—either by never entering into a meaningful relationship with a woman outside of the sexual act or by becoming Casanovas who, like little boys with an adult sexual drive, seek to "comfort" all the emotionally distressed women in their lives. Worse, some become straight objectifying misogynists who are sexually addicted and driven to have sex with as many women as they can demean. These men are ashamed, angry, and empty. They do not allow themselves to condemn the only person who seemed to love them; they do not acknowledge their emotionally stunting, shaming abuse. Thus, the downward spiral continues.

However, this "covert incest" is not exclusive to mothers. Father-to-son sexual abuse and overt incest occurs often in the black community. It occurs when black men brag about their sexual conquests to pubescent and pre-pubescent boys incapable of committed emotional relationships with women. These boys observe crass, even pornographic, descriptions of male exploits. The mere discussion of such things with adolescent, teenage, or younger boys is a form of sexual abuse causing much of the same damage as physical sexual abuse. The images, deposited by men they trust, rip their way into the tender psyche of our boys leaving deep scars that surface in their later sexuality. Compounding the problem is the belief that these misogynistic exploits and portrayal of women affirm their entry into manhood. In other words, boys face rejection and shame from men, whose respect and love they want to gain, unless they participate in this emotionally disconnected and sexually broken lifestyle. If they do not, they are derided and demeaned. No wonder so many brothers are on the "down low." They are running away from abuse, seeking unconditional love from men who will not belittle and shame them. Boys grow into men who want relief from the traumatic teaching that sexual exploits are a rite of passage. This leads to the same downward spiral as these men are confused and frightened by anything that is more than just sex. As bell hooks writes:

> Many womanizing black males have experienced traumatic sexual abuse in childhood. It scars them for life. And when they receive the message from the culture that real men should be able to endure abuse as a rite of passage and emerge with their sexual agency intact, there is no cultural space for them to

articulate that they were sexually abused, that they are damaged and in need of sexual healing.[15]

As black men and women, we bear the scars of this abuse and neglect. Unless we are touched, known, healed, and forgiven, we will live according to the longings, emptiness, and offense of that neglect and abuse.

As we discussed earlier, God created humans with an ability to pass on our sense of worth. This is not completely "good news" according to what we have discovered thus far. This means that married or not, if our parents are not healthy sexually, we probably will not be either. If our parents do not have nurturing relationships, we will not. If our parents treat each other with derision, we will do the same. Married or not, parents play a central role in developing and contributing to the ethos of our children's sexuality. Malfunctioning sexuality stems from a shared lack of worth passed on to us by our parents, particularly our fathers.

If parents are emotionally and sexually anemic, their children will grow up to be emotionally adolescent adults who struggle with a profound and deep appetite for unmet intimacy. Unfortunately, for many, sexualized intimacy becomes the "food" of choice. Confused and heart-hungry men and women feast on each other sexually in a futile attempt to fill the void. This hungry emptiness is an epidemic among our black men and women who have become, and are creating yet another generation of, sexual addicts and deviants. But is there hope? Is there help? Is there a place of healing and sexual wholeness? Indeed, there is.

The Place of Redeemed Sexuality

Extreme pain and death mark the road to this place. Facing and realizing the abandonment, abuse, and neglect caused by our sexual brokenness, while necessary for rehabilitation, overwhelms the sinner. Who can or wants to hear and face all of that condemning truth? Some of these issues will take more than one lifetime to change as we continue to walk and live in present ruins.

Poussaint wisely looks and points us to education, advances in civil rights, and better health care as being helpful in dealing with the symptoms of our sexual brokenness. As a pastor, I propose that we have one more place to explore. Poussaint characterized many of our churches as clouded and represented by leaders and institutions more committed to being economically successful than spiritually relevant. Nevertheless, in the message of the Bible, the gospel, there is still a place.

15. hooks, *We Real Cool,* 80.

After Adam and Eve sought to control their sense of worth, which separated them from God's dignity and shackled them with sin-laden shame, God called them out and back to Him. "And they heard the sound of the LORD God walking in the garden in the cool of the day, and the man and his wife hid themselves from the presence of the LORD God among the trees of the garden. But the LORD God called to the man and said to him, 'Where are you?'"[16]

Like Adam and Eve that day, living and crouching in fear and disgrace, the best words for our black men, women, and children to hear from God are "Where are you?" In this profound question, God invades our world of hiding and covering and calls us together before him to face what we would not and could not face on our own—our sin. God calls us to examine and confront the mishandling and abuse of others and ourselves. He calls us to a place where we can look squarely at ourselves and see our failure. In addition, as God turns us around to face our self-destruction, he also turns us to face him, a position that allows him to heal our hurt. In all the ways intimacy has escaped us, God does not let his broken people escape him. God promises to recognize black people; he does not ignore or reject his own.

Moreover, God delivers on his promise. Though like Adam and Eve, we bear the just effects of our sexual sin, God does not seek to shame or condemn us. He lovingly calls broken people to approach him for healing and redemption. "And the LORD God made for Adam and for his wife garments of skins and clothed them."[17]

God brings his people to a place where we can be redeemed from our sexual sins. Though often skewed by malpractice, the church remains the place where broken people can find refuge. Where we, both sexually offensive and offended, can be unashamedly known and invested in without fear of condemnation. The church, the people God has called to himself, remains the place where we practice the message of God's transforming grace in healing our sexual sin. In this place, people provide each other with counseling, confrontation, and reconciliation. In this place, we call men to see and be seen by their Creator in ways powerfully intimate enough to call them out of a fallen image of sexuality into God-ordained manhood. In this place, women can hear the words of God that pronounce they are God's beautiful creation. This place is a clinic—a spiritually therapeutic place that redeems the emotional, social, and mental souls of people. But this community is a place of healing because a person of healing is central to it.

16. Genesis 3:8–9.
17. Genesis 3:21.

We know how great an impact (albeit in this discussion, damaging) a mother, father, boyfriend, or girlfriend can have on our progeny and us. Just imagine if there were a new Adam. Imagine if there were a new source of our humanity that could have just as great an impact as Adam and Eve's on our sexual lives. Without a new Adam, redemption could not occur, and the world would continue to bear the brokenness caused by Adam's sin. But God has provided a new Adam to heal our sexual brokenness. God sent someone to be intimate with us and to meet us in our shameful condition. God sent someone who feels all that we feel in our sexual pain, and yet does not let it make him hate, despise, use, or condemn us. He works and speaks transforming life to us. When God speaks judgment to the serpent that misled our first parents, he says the following: "I will put enmity between you and the woman, and between your offspring and her offspring; he shall bruise your head, and you shall bruise his heel."[18]

He is the second Adam, the intimate knower of our condition, the Lord Jesus Christ. What this Scripture tells us is that he will be born into our sin, into the broken sexual experience and heritage of black people, and will not let it remove him from us. He will not let it keep us from true and lasting dignity, if we only choose to follow him. He is promising to restore and redeem us. He will do this by becoming the power and hope that guides our pursuit of sexual wholeness through education, health reform, and civil rights. He has come to create a place of forgiveness, confession, and courageous disclosure of our sexual dysfunction, a place without shame and with real hope that we will be made right through him. Come on people! For I know a place where redemption and healthy sexuality can be found.

18. Genesis 3:15.

Chapter 5 Gangsta Rap Made Me Do It: What's Really Goin' On?

—*RALPH C. WATKINS*

If I act like a pimp ain't notin' to it
gangsta rap made me do it.

If I call you a nappy headed ho ain't nothin' to it
gangsta rap made me do it.

If I shoot up your college ain't nothin' to it
gangsta rap made me do it.

If I rob you of knowledge ain't nothing to it
gangsta rap made me do it.[1]

—ICE CUBE

He has showed you, O man, what is good.

And what does the LORD require of you?

To act justly and to love mercy and to walk humbly with your God.

—MICAH 6:8

I t is hard to listen to rap music. I can only speak for myself, but for me, it is sometimes difficult to have an appreciation for hip-hop culture. There is a lot about hip hop that makes me cringe and at times scream. Although this is the case, I am still compelled to listen. I am called to lean in and hear what's going on in the lives of the hip-hop generation. Those things that repel me are worthy of criticism. The American values of lust, misogyny, sexism, greed, materialism, hyper-sexuality, and violence that I hear in rap music and commercialized hip-hop culture must be addressed. They make me sick to my stomach. There is room for criticism of rap music and commercialized hip-hop culture. In this chapter, I try to bring balance to the conversation. While the critics of hip hop are many, and with a valid argu-

1. Ice Cube, "Gangsta Rap Made Me Do It."

ment, those who have leaned in to listen with an empathetic ear tend to be in the minority, especially when it comes to the church. I am not defending hip hop, but I am asking that we listen a little closer. I am appealing to the church to be that loving community that hears pain and heals the wounds. I am arguing that the problems our young adult and youth are facing is bigger than hip hop and we can't place all the blame on hip hop, although hip hop has to bear some degree of the blame. A deeper socio-demographic-theological analysis is needed if the church is to respond effectively to the hip-hop generation and heal the wounds of despair and alienation that exist between the hip-hop generation and the elders.

On Ice Cube's *Raw Footage* CD on his song "Gangsta Rap Made Me Do It" he rings out in each chorus, "Gangsta rap made me do it."[2] The chorus above is the second of the three different choruses on the song that identifies the things gangsta rap is blamed for, in each chorus what gangsta rap is blamed for is changed and becomes ever more outrageous. In the third chorus Ice Cube says, "If I f*** up the planet ain't nothin' to it gangsta rap made me do it." What Ice Cube is exposing is how gansta rap is blamed for the ills of society. Don't worry about what you do, be you a rapper, a kid from the hood, a preacher, or even a white radio talk show host, "If I call you a nappy headed ho ain't nothing to it gangsta rap made me do it." Ice Cube is pointing out that human behavior is much more complex than being the result of a single variable. The struggles African American youth and young adults are facing can't be blamed on hip hop. This is the point Ice Cube is trying to make. When you put Ice Cube in dialogue with Alvin Poussaint it should at least make us think. Ice Cube is chosen as a dialogical partner because he is one of the founders of what Poussaint points to in hip-hop culture as the culprit—gansta rap. So, what is the historical foundation of "gangsta rap"?

In 1988, NWA dropped the classic album *Straight Out of Compton*, and it is really at this point in hip-hop history that the West Coast got national attention from the hip-hop community. Jerry Heller and Eric Eazy E were the masterminds behind the exposure that the group received. But more than savvy marketing and a shocking name was the story that *Straight Out of Compton* told. It told a story of what the group called "street knowledge." These then-young brothers were coming as they said on the opening track "Straight Out of Compton!" The story opens with them announcing who they were and where they were coming from, "Straight outta Compton mother f**** named Ice Cube from the gang called N***** With Attitudes."[3] They were boys from the hood who had something to say and they were

2. Ice Cube, "Gangsta Rap Made Me Do It."
3. NWA, "Straight Outta Compton."

going to say it with an attitude. The next logical question is, "Why did they have an attitude?" The reason they had an attitude was because they had been abused by the police. Not only them, but they make it clear in the story that the police are a part of the larger systemic problem of racism and classism. If the listener missed this in the opening song/story, it came through loud and clear in the next cut, "F*** tha Police." NWA saw themselves as a different kind of a gang, but they were a gang.

NWA, the fathers of gangsta rap, were a gang that was designated to be the storytellers of the pain that their brothas and sistas in the hood on the West Coast were going through. Eithne Quinn's book *Nuthin' but a "G" Thang: The Culture and Commerce of Gangsta Rap* tells how this revolutionary story of exposing pain became a product for sale to the highest bidder.[4] While Quinn's assessment and link with gangsta rap and commercialization singles out what happens with West Coast hip-hop culture, the story isn't unpredictable. Hip-hop culture was being bottled and sold in the early 1990s. Jerry Heller and others like him were now on board and the days of the mid-1970s (the birth of hip-hop culture, that would later be exploited by the hip-hop industry) would never be again. The story of the West Coast is chronicled not only in Eithne Quinn's book but also in William Shaw's *Westside: The Coast-to-Coast Explosion of Hip Hop*. This can also be read as a complementary commentary to the work of Eithne Quinn in Ronin Ro's book *Gangsta: Merchandising the Rhymes of Violence*. Finally, there is Joel McIver's book *Ice Cube Attitude*. Much of the West Coast history is in the work of Too Short, Ice T, NWA, Dr. Dre, Snoop Dogg, The Dogg Pound, Daz and Kurupt, and of course, Ice Cube, especially after he left NWA. The work of the artist in hip-hop culture tells more about the culture than the books that are published on the topic. Those of us who write about culture are usually trying to interpret for our readers, but I want to encourage readers to become listeners, watchers, and participants of hip-hop culture. It is important to go back to the original sources. If one wants to learn the story of West Coast hip-hop culture, one is encouraged to listen to that story straight from those who tell the story in time and rhyme.

When you go back and listen to the dialogical partner in this chapter, Ice Cube or O'Shea Jackson—the son of a two-parent home—you hear a young man who was more about reporting what he saw in the hood and not promoting violence. In many ways Ice Cube is a participant observer in the traditional sociological sense when it comes to his reporting on the violence, poverty, and struggle of inner-city poor in Los Angeles. The concern I have with some critics of hip hop is that in most cases their critique, which

4. Quinn, *Nuthin' but a "G" Thang*.

tends to be shallow and surface, proves that they haven't looked intently at hip-hop culture or engaged the complex stories in rap lyrics. It was in high school that the son of parents who worked at UCLA and a mother who was an active member at Bethel African Methodist Episcopal Church in Los Angeles that Ice Cube began to write his rhymes that told the story of his times. Ice Cube was the first member of NWA. When NWA hit the rap scene on the West Coast they were compared to Public Enemy on the East Coast. These were conscious rap groups who were raising issues and fighting against the system. Ice Cube's eventually leaving of NWA and striking out on his own was his personal stand against what he saw as the hip-hop industry's pimping and abuse of hip-hop culture.

Ice Cube is the father of gangsta rap, and he has a right to that legacy. On his *Laugh Now Cry Later* CD on the cut "Child Support," Ice Cube critiques the direction of some rap artists who claim to be heirs to the gangsta rap sub-genre.[5] As the father of gangsta rap, Ice Cube stands as a senior critic who at forty years old is saying some of the music is not reflective of a true West Coast gangsta. A true West Coast gangsta, like Ice Cube, is one who is the hood's CNN. They aren't promoting violence; they are critiquing the social conditions that create, sustain, and maintain conditions for the violence they see in the hood. In Ice Cube's body of work from 1988 to the present, as the father of gangsta rap he has been both socially conscious and critical of the oppressive forces that have produced what we see in the inner cities of America. Once again on his *Laugh Now Cry Later* CD he has a cut, "Why We Thugs," where he is clear that the conditions of poverty in inner cities are not the result of gangsta rap. Ice Cube asserts that forces outside of the hood send in guns and drugs, two keys as to why what happens, happens in the hood. Ice Cube talks about the deplorable working conditions and the lack of jobs that create a crime frenzy in the hood, the decaying social networks, and the dilapidated civic organizations—and you want to blame gangsta rap? Ice Cube recognizes the limitations of the self-help theory. Noted sociologist William J. Wilson put it this way:

> For the first time in the twentieth century most adults in many inner city ghetto neighborhoods are not working in a typical week. The disappearance of work has adversely affected not only individuals, families, and neighborhoods, but the social life of the city at large as well . . . A neighborhood in which people are poor but employed is different from a neighborhood in which people are poor and jobless. Many of today's problems in the inner-city ghetto neighborhoods—crime, family dissolution,

5. Ice Cube, "Child Support."

welfare, low levels of social organization, and so on—are fundamentally a consequence of the disappearance of work.[6]

What Wilson and Ice Cube are saying is that if you want to understand what is happening in the hood, one has to point the finger at an infrastructure that has been destroyed over the last forty years. What Wilson and Ice Cube are alluding to in their work is that the issue isn't gangsta rap or the decay of values in the communities of poor African Americans. It's larger systemic issues that in fairness to Poussaint he points to but fails to take into account just how powerful these forces are in the lives of those who are trying to make it in the hood. Poussaint says, "Gangster rap . . . promotes the moral breakdown of the family. It deliberately influences women to become pregnant before they have finished their education and influences men to shuck their responsibility when this happens."[7] Poussaint goes on to use a scene from a fictional movie, 8 Mile, as an example to amplify his point. "In the climactic scene in the film 8 Mile, Eminem disses Papa Doc, his black opponent in a freestyle rap showdown, for being named 'Clarence' and having 'two parents.' The wound is lethal. Eminem prevails. In the world of hip hop, to be educated as Papa Doc was, and to live in the suburb with both parents, is to be less 'black' than even a white guy."[8] Poussaint misses the point of the scene. Eminem isn't dissing Clarence because of social status and family lifestyle. The diss is based on Clarence trying to pretend he isn't those things. The name Papa Doc and pretending to be hard and from the hood is what exposes Clarence; Clarence was rapping a lie; hip hop calls for authenticity. If you are going to talk about the hood and represent the hood, then you have to really be from the hood. 50 Cent really did get shot. Jay-Z, Biggie, and Tupac did have struggles growing up. DMX really did do time. Eminem was poor. Gangsta rap isn't about promoting, but rather, real gangsta rap is about reporting.

William J. Wilson says,

> Our research that the beliefs of inner-city residents bear little resemblance to the blanket media reports asserting that values have plummeted in impoverished neighborhoods or that people in the inner city have an entirely different value system. What is so striking that despite the overwhelming joblessness and poverty, black residents in inner-city ghetto neighborhoods actually

6. Wilson, When Work Disappears, xiiii.

7. Cosby and Poussaint, Come on People, 143.

8. Cosby and Poussaint, Come on People, 143.

verbally endorse, rather than undermine, the basic American
values concerning individual initiative.[9]

Values have not plummeted; inner city African Americans embrace
mainstream values. They want the good job, house, white picket fence, dog,
mini-van, and two and a half kids. The reality is that the structural forces are
so strong that it impedes their ability to fulfill the American Dream. Gangsta rap isn't stopping them or even encouraging them not to dream. When
you listen to hip hop, it is thoroughly American. Hip hop is capitalism at its
best. Hip hop's story is a broke kid from the ghetto works hard, makes beats,
write rhymes, gets signed by a major label, and makes it good. Hip hop is the
Horatio Alger myth on steroids. Hip hop doesn't dis American values. Just
like poor inner-city African Americans, gangsta rappers are trying to live
the American dream while living in an American nightmare.

The reality is that when young African Americans go looking for jobs,
they find that the jobs simply aren't there. The key argument in William J.
Wilson's *When Work Disappears: The World of the New Urban Poor*, that
is supported with hard research, is simply what the title says, "work has
disappeared." The employment base for the inner-city poor isn't there. There
aren't enough jobs to support them. When inner-city African Americans
compete for the few jobs that do exist, they face overwhelming odds as they
confront what is gently referred to by Wilson as "selective recruitment."

> Selective recruitment practices do represent what economists
> call statistical discrimination: employers make assumptions
> about inner-city black workers in general and reach decisions
> based on those assumptions before they have had a chance to re-
> view systematically the qualifications of an individual applicant.
> The net effect is that many black inner-city applicants are never
> given the chance to prove their qualifications on an individual
> level because they are systematically screened out by the selec-
> tive recruitment process.[10]

In the end we have two key variables at work: lack of jobs and the ra-
cial/class discrimination when inner-city African Americans apply for jobs.
These two variables have nothing to do with gangsta rap. At the foundation
of the problems in the hood are the systemic forces that have worked against
African American working-class progress. The conversation of Poussaint put
in a book is evidence for a socially constructed reality that is not based on
research. As one reads the unbalanced critique of hip hop and the blame game

9. Wilson, *When Work Disappears*, 179.

10. Wilson, *When Work Disappears*, 137.

that Poussaint and his "call outs" suggest, one has to stop, reflect, and ask the questions: Can their assertions be supported by empirical data? What the empirical data tells us in the final analysis is that gangsta rap and hip-hop culture have little to do with creating the world of the inner-city poor.

This generation of inner-city poor African Americans are trying to make it in an economy that has transitioned from an industrial economy to a service economy. They are going to public schools that are overcrowded, underfunded, and understaffed. As Joan Morgan says of the hip-hop generation, "We are the first generation to grow up with all the benefits of Civil Rights (i.e., Affirmative Action, government-subsidized educational and social programs) and the first to lose them. The first to have the devastation of AIDS, crack, and black-on-black violence makes it feel like a blessing to reach twenty-five."[11] The odds are stacked against them; gangsta rap didn't create these conditions. The world inner-city African Americans live in isn't that enclave of class diversity that my generation was raised in, but these residents are socially isolated and socially dislocated. They live in communities that are filled with poor, unemployed neighbors who can't help them get a job. As a result, they are not connected to the workforce, as Wacquant and Wilson suggest:

> The poor are presented as a mere aggregation of personal cases, each with its own logic and self-contained causes. Severed from the struggles and structural changes in the society, economy, and polity that in fact determine them, inner-city dislocations are then portrayed as a self-imposed, self-sustaining phenomenon . . . the urban black poor today differ both from their counterparts of earlier years and from the white poor in that they are becoming increasingly concentrated in dilapidated territorial enclaves that epitomize acute social and economic marginalization . . . The economic and social buffer provided by a stable black working class and a visible, if small, black middle class that cushioned the impact of downsizing in the economy and tied ghetto residents to the world of work has all but disappeared. Moreover, the social networks of parents, friends, and associates, as well as the nexus of local institutions, have seen their resources for economic stability progressively depleted. In sum, today's ghetto residents face a closed opportunity structure.[12]

A closed opportunity structure—this is the reality. It isn't gangsta rap that has closed the door on opportunity for inner-city African Americans.

11. Morgan, *When Chickenheads Come Home to Roost,* 61.

12. Wacquant, "The Cost of Racial and Class Exclusion in the Inner City," 25–26.

In the words of Biggie, "Things done changed."[13] If the church is going to respond prophetically to this crisis, they have to realize that *things done changed* and the church has to engage the powers that be to kick open the doors of opportunity.

Things Done Changed: A Call for a Prophetic Encounter

> He has told you, O man, what is good;
> and what does the LORD require of you
> but to do justice, and to love kindness,
> and to walk humbly with your God?
>
> —MICAH 6:8

> Gangster rap makes our young people tough, but not so tough that they can walk through prison walls. It can jazz them about sex, but it can't begin to make them good fathers. No matter how often or how publicly they grab their crotches, crotch-grabbing isn't even going to get them a bus ride downtown.[14]
>
> —ALVIN POUSSAINT

> The ghetto is a n**** trap, take the cheese
> Soon as you do it here come the police
> Invented and designed fo' us to fail
> Where you gon' end up, dead or in jail
> Concrete slave ships, never move
> Where n***** like us get used like a mule
> Don't let 'em catch you, arrest you
> Strip and undress you, throw you in a cesspool
> You wanna know the crime of the century
> A ghetto elementary, a mental penitentiary
> Black man, you never been friend of me
> Boy you kin to me, why we enemies?
> The ghetto is a trap.[15]
>
> —ICE CUBE

13. The Notorious B.I.G., "Things Done Changed."
14. Cosby and Poussaint, *Come on People*, 13.
15. Ice Cube, "The N**** Trap."

When you actually listen to the father of gangsta rap—Ice Cube—and engage him, what you see is not the monolith that some critics want to present. Rather, you hear a social critic engaging the social conditions of the hood and speaking prophetically. In the quote above, you hear Ice Cube interrogating "being tough." He isn't promoting black-on-black violence; he isn't promoting toughness. Ice Cube says, "Boy you kin to me, why we enemies?" Cube is saying we are not to be shooting each other. Cube is asking young brothers and sisters to sit back and reflect. We are not meant to be enemies. He is pointing out how the "ghetto" is a trap. It is a trap that has been socially constructed by an economic system this is designed to profit from the pain index of the poor. The trap is set to lead young African Americans to a life of crime and violence. This "cheese" of crime and violence is set in the trap— the trap door is that prison door that slams shut. Ice Cube isn't promoting that kids walk through that door; he is trying to help them see how they are being set up as lifelong slaves in a prison industry. Kids who aren't equipped to succeed in ill-prepared school systems ensures that prison and the inner city become no more than concrete slave ships. Ice Cube is prophetically critiquing what he calls a new form of slavery. The socio-critical-prophetic voice of hip hop needs to be heard here. If we were listening to Ice Cube, we would hear him, but this is part of the problem. As Dyson puts it, "The arguments of many of hip-hop's critics demand little engagement with hip-hop. Their views don't require much beyond attending to the surface symptoms of a culture that offers far more depth and color when it is taken seriously and criticized thoughtfully . . . Such critics seem afraid of the intellectual credibility of complex truths they might find where they to surrender their sideline seat and take an analytical plunge into the culture which they comment [on]."[16] While I will admit there are problems with hip hop and some manifestations of gangsta rap, if the church doesn't take the art form seriously by embracing it in a conversation, the church may miss the complexities, cries, and truths that are coming out of hip hop. As Dyson suggests, there is room for critique but there is also room for affirmation and an ear for the prophetic that comes out of hip hop.

Marvin McMickle in his book *Where Have all the Prophets Gone?* calls us to task. McMickle calls the church to the task of being prophetic. In order for the church to return to the sacred practice of being prophetic, what we hear from the pulpit has to change. This is a call for prophetic preaching. McMickle says, "Prophetic preaching points out the false gods of comfort. Further, it points out a lack of concern and acquiescence in the face of evil that can so easily replace the true God of scripture who calls

---

16. Dyson, *Know What I Mean?*, xxi.

true believers to the active pursuit of justice and righteousness for every member of society. Prophetic preaching also never allows the community of faith to believe that participation in the rituals of religious life can ever be an adequate substitute for that form of ministry that is designed to up-lift the 'least of these' in our world."[17] To act prophetically means that the church must engage the world. The church must hear the cry of hip hop and speak back prophetically. The church must be a theological partner in dialogue with artists like Ice Cube. While Ice Cube has the social critique down, and he even calls the church to task, the church has to offer a theological analysis of what is going on in the hood.

The church's critique and prophetic voice has to be rooted in the tradition of Amos, Jeremiah, and Micah. The theological and biblical engagement of the church must be rooted in the witness of that Jesus who shouts in Luke 4:18, "He has sent me to proclaim liberty to the captives" and then in Matthew 25:40, "Truly, I say to you, as you did it to one of the least of these my brothers, you did it to me." Part of the theological response is a call to action to understand how the social structures of a stratified society which keeps the poor, poor, and makes the rich wealthier needs to be critiqued based on the witness of a Jesus who came to set the captives free. As McMickle says, "The prophets preached truth to power, attacking the monarchs and the ruling elite."[18] While Ice Cube calls the powers that be out and says you are creating stationary slave ships, the church has been silent. Cube is pointing to the fact that the absence of prophetic preaching implicates the church in the creation of the current conditions that inner-city African Americans are struggling to survive. Ice Cube says on the cut "Thank God" on his *Raw Footage* CD:

> I do gangsta rap
>
> They wanna blame world problems on gangsta rap
>
> It's our fault, cause mother f****** is dying in Iraq
>
> It's our fault, cause mother f****** is starving in Africa
>
> It's gangsta rap fault, that people are poor can't get
>
> enough to f***** eat or live their life
>
> That's rap music fault
>
> It's rap music fault, that we got all this god damn laws
>
> and restriction and s*** we can't do
>
> They blame it all on us

17. McMickle, *Where Have All the Prophets Gone?*, 2.
18. McMickle, *Where Have All the Prophets Gone?*, 3.

I'm blamin' them for gangsta rap,

because if they didn't create this kind of condition

I wouldn't have s*** to rap about

You know what I mean?[19]

Do we know what he means? He is pointing the finger back at the church. Ice Cube is saying you are blaming gangsta rap for creating the conditions that he raps about. No! Ice Cube is saying that the prophetic call reverses the blame game and realizes that what Jesus said in Matthew 7:1–5 about pointing fingers and judging others is true. The church has to deal with its plank. What can't the church see? Can the church see what has caused and continues to cause the conditions that poor inner-city African Americans are laboring under? If the church listened to hip hop as a weeping prophet, how would that change their take on gangsta rap?

Part of the active socio-theological response of the church has to be the practice of sacred listening. I am convinced that hip hop has not been heard by the church. The cry, the pain, the sense of abandonment by the elders, a lack of appreciation for the art of hip hop has not been heard. The hip-hop generation is in pain. Joan Morgan, the hip-hop feminist, tells us why she listens and why we should listen. Morgan says,

> My decision to expose myself to the sexism of Dr. Dre, Ice Cube, Snoop Dogg, or the Notorious B.I.G. is really my plea to my brothers to tell me who they are . . . As a black woman and a feminist I listen to the music with a willingness to see past the machismo in order to be clear about what I am really dealing with . . . I believe hip hop can help us win. Let's start by recognizing that its illuminating, informative narration and its incredible ability to articulate our collective pain is an invaluable tool when examining gender relations. The information we amass can help create a redemptive, healing space for brothers and sistas.[20]

When we listen with ears of love, we hear the hurt. We hear the pain. While hip hop shouts louder and angrier, we have to ask: Is this because they feel like they haven't been heard? Why does Ice Cube at forty years old run around defending his art form that he has been developing for over twenty years? Ice Cube, a businessman, father, husband, movie star, and gangsta rapper/prophet, still has to scream because the elders refuse to listen. The interesting thing about Jesus is he always had time to listen. Jesus heard the cries for help. Jesus had time to stop and heal, resurrect, and give hope.

19. Ice Cube, "Thank God."

20. Morgan, *When Chickenheads Come Home to Roost*, 80.

A prophetic response via preaching and social action from the church is not simply to condemn the abuses of capitalism but as McMickle says, "The great need that faces preaching today and that is badly needed by the people who hear that preaching is the reclaiming of this tension between action and accountability, between distributive and redistributive justice, between obeying God's command to do the work of justice and facing God's judgment and wrath when we fail or refuse to do so."[21] The church must embrace this tension of action and accountability as they do the work of justice. What does this mean? It means the church doesn't have to excuse hip hop but it must lovingly engage hip hop as an informed engagement that is contextualized in present social realities of oppression. The church must look inwardly and critique itself or at least listen to the critique the hip-hop generation has by and large lodged at the church. The silence of the church's prophetic voice and engagement with youth and young adult culture has made the church irrelevant in the lives of most young, inner-city African Americans. It was in the 1990s that C. Eric Lincoln cried about the pending irrelevance of the African American church. Did the church hear him? C. Eric Lincoln and Lawrence Mamiya said, "A major challenge to the black church concerns a growing sector of unchurched black youth, largely teenage and young adult black males from the underclass."[22] This growing sector of unchurched black youth and young adults still remain unchurched and untouched. Where do they lodge their cry? Who comes to their aid? Who walks with them? Who talks with them? Who develops them? Do they feel heard in hip hop? Do they feel loved by hip hop? Has hip hop become their pastor?

Praying for Our Children and Young Adults

What I suggest in the end is that churches start by listening to hip hop. There are the radio cuts, or what we call club bangers, that will repel most church folk right away, because in most cases they represent the worst of hip-hop culture that has been abused by the hip-hop industry. Therefore, let me suggest a first stage listening playlist to begin to engage the conversation and practice of sacred listening. I would suggest the following cuts:

- Mack 10—"The Testimony" on *Hustla's Handbook*
- Ice Cube—"Why We Thugs" on *Laugh Now, Cry Later*
- Ice Cube—"Gangsta Rap Made Me Do It" on *Raw Footage*

21. McMickle, *Where Have All the Prophets Gone?*, 46
22. Lincoln and Mamiya, *The Black Church*, 322.

- The Game—"My Life" on *LAX Files*
- T.I.—"Prayin' for Help" on *Urban Legend*
- Lil Wayne—"Tie My Hands" on *Tha Carter III*
- Fabolous—"Stay" on *Loso's Way*
- Pharrel—"Our Father" on *In My Mind*
- Kanye West—"Pinocchio Story" on *808s & Heartbreak*
- Jay-Z—"Lost One" on *Kingdom Come*
- Talib Kweli—"Black Girl Pain" on *The Beautiful Struggle*

These songs will give the church an initial window into the pain coursing through hip hop. If this is a church's first engagement with hip hop, I would suggest they listen to the clean version of the music.

Are we prepared to listen and respect each other? If not, how do we get to this point? I want to suggest that the elders provide the leadership God has called them to provide. We are the ones who need to step forward and call our people in the kitchen as we prepare a meal and begin the discussion. We start by setting the table and asking our younger sisters and brothers to begin the dialogue. We ask them to start us off. We should have begun the listening process prior to dinner. We should watch their culture as it is portrayed in accessible formats. This means we may watch some videos, listen to the radio, or better yet make our way to the local book and record store and carefully select the voices we choose to hear. We may want to select those more conscious voices who don't get the radio airtime. My only caution would be that we don't ignore the more commercial aspects of hip hop because it has a greater hold on our youth and young adults. We may want to simply begin by having mini conversations in many places with those who look like us but are much younger than us. We may call up a nephew or niece and listen while they talk. We have to make room for them to be honest about us, the church, and our faith tradition. This is a conversation that must be rooted in love. We have to suspend our desire to defend our ways and be willing to engage in conversation of give and take that moves us closer together in spite of our generational divides.

It is the power of language that we tell the story in our own words. Ngugi Wa Thiong'o tells us that language carries culture.[23] We must speak in our language. We must use the rhythm, style, tone, and lyricism to tell it. This means we must make room for a time to tell our stories. We must recreate the kitchen and the sitting rooms of our culture. The village cannot

---

23. Thiong'o, *Decolonising the Mind*.

be sustained without intentional times of sharing. We must listen to some of hip hop's most outspoken leaders. When we listen and talk back to them, we will hear the ancestors leading us back while pointing us forward. We have to take the walks in the park that Jill Scott has called us to. We have to look for Zion with Lauryn Hill. We have to come and hear the political rhetoric of Mos Def and Dead Prez as they critique the very system or industry that produces the worst and best of hip hop. We have to answer the call to discipleship as ushered by Nas. We even have to go to Chicago and testify with Common and Kanye West as they raise the right questions in their complex works. There is a world in hip hop, there is a world on the streets, in the academy, and in the church. These worlds that are built on the Word must be brought into a concerted family conversation about who we've been, who we are, and who we shall become.

We have to go back to the basics. The church has to reach out and reach up. God is love, and God is calling the church to love the hip-hop generation. As elders we have the responsibility to call the children in the house for a conversation. I remember growing up in the South and my mother calling me in the house when the streetlights came on. I hated that call, and I loved that call. I never wanted to stop playing, but there was no more secure place than home at my mother's dinner table. The love and support I found in our home are what propelled me to get up the next day and do it all again. It is time for us to call hip hop to church and say we love you and we are glad you are at the table—now, let's talk. In the end this is about discipleship and spiritual maturity. How can the church help our young people see where hip hop is good and where it has gone wrong as it has emulated the larger popular culture? In discipleship we don't excuse our young people, but we lovingly develop them. I am reminded of Proverbs 22:6 that says: "Train up a child in the way he should go; even when he is old he will not depart from it."[24]

I ask the question: Have we trained the children? If the promise implied in the text is true then we have to ask why the departing? Some may say, I am just proof texting. Ok, but the question still remains, have we trained them? When I visit churches with empty Sunday school rooms, micro-Bible studies and part-time youth ministries, I wonder when did this happen? This is not the church I was raised in with full Sunday schools and capacity Bible studies. On the one hand, we have to hold hip hop accountable as wrong, and on the other hand, we have to assume our responsibility as the church to reach the young and teach them the word of God and what it means to live according to the word of God. I was taught and was raised by my nuclear family and a little church, St. James African Methodist Episcopal

24. Proverbs 22:6.

Church in Eatonville, Florida, that taught me to love God, respect women, and not be trapped by the ways of the world. As I have gotten old, I haven't departed from what they taught me. Let us be about our Father's business and train our children in the gospel.

Chapter 6 **Black Men and Masculinity**

—Eric M. Mason

Yo, Bruthas, Where You At?

Recently, much discussion has occurred attempting to assess the issues blacks face in America and the problems that are faced in the uniqueness of our journey. As of late, there have been many who have highlighted important issues, but we must have multifaceted, comprehensive, and systemic innovations to create long-lasting solutions. Moreover, all of these must flow from the transforming power of the gospel of Jesus Christ.

To be honest, things didn't seem too bad for white men during the era of second and third wave feminism from the fifties through the nineties. It is impossible to talk about manhood in the experience of black men without a basic overview of the history. It has been said that history is the road map for what to do and what not to do. I have heard much about manhood in my life as a Christian man, but most of it has come from white Christendom. Sometimes I will hear great information, but I still feel a bit unclear about the idea's historical background.

On one occasion, I was going through some manhood material contextualized for suburban, white, middle- or upper-class men. The information and curriculum were excellent, but one section of the material disturbed me. The section was entitled, "The Historical Roots to Our Present Crisis in Masculinity."[1] The author spoke of the sociological place of manhood during the Industrial Revolution, World War II, and the current time.

This same time period, viewed from an African American perspective, would consist of drastically different key events and figures such as slavery, Jim Crow, the civil rights movement, the Black Power/Black Bourgeoisie era, the Soul Baby Era, the Hip-hop generation, and the Eclectic era. What has driven black history in America is the fight for freedom. For many it is the fight to experience what has almost always been available to whites. Blacks and whites are on two completely different sociological and economic planes. The fight

1. Lewis, *The Quest for Authentic Manhood.*

for blacks has been off balance because our expectations have been shaped by the experiences of white Americans. Because of this, we have settled for both an American experience viewed through the eyes of whites, and a Christian experience that reflects that of our white brethren. Because of this, we must show that the social issues each race must deal with are extremely different, although all are a result of the fall. We must remember that Jesus, not another man, is the one who gives us our image of the ideal man as he embodied true humanity. With this in mind, we must be willing to transport our vision of Christology across the bounds of various social, cultural, and ethnic barriers. We will discuss this in more detail later.

During slavery, black men were emasculated primarily by not being allowed to marry, either at all, or only to women on the same plantation and by watching black women become the unwed playthings of white slave owners.[2] We could continue with examples until the break of dawn.

In the post-slavery Jim Crow South, blacks were free from slavery, but racism and repression were as strong as ever. The doctrine of "separate but equal" was intended to maintain equality between the races while preventing the civil strife that would supposedly result from mixing the two races. However, in reality, this principle became another means of repressing blacks. Blacks and whites were certainly kept separate, but the opportunities afforded each race were hardly equal.

The civil rights era is known to many blacks as the golden years. Black leaders developed a vision for practical equality that inspired many. But, this vision was still void of an image of masculinity. Masculinity to the African American was still viewed in terms of the social displays of freedom that were portrayed in (white) majority culture. Even the images and comprehensive character of Jesus were portrayed without a proper view of biblical masculinity.

The Black Power side of the post-civil rights generation sought to create a new path and image, forged by blacks of blacks in America. "The Movement" was committed to a rigorous affirmation of blackness, racial pride, and an insistence on the economic and political liberation of black people, independent of whites.[3] During this period, masculinity was expressed through art, fashion, black intellectualism, and historical identification with African roots. Blacks became extremely proud of our heritage, but something was still missing, as comparisons to white America were still the measuring stick for black progress.

2. Franklin and Moss Jr., *From Slavery to Freedom*, 127–28.

3. Obgar, *Black Power*, 37.

The black bourgeoisie was a different breed of blacks who were social-ized during and after the civil rights movement. They were the first to reap the rewards of the civil rights movement. Many black nationalists viewed them as sellouts. E. Franklin Frazier states that,

> In attempting to escape identification with the black masses, they have developed a self-hatred that reveals itself in their de-preciation of the physical and social characteristics of Negroes. Likewise, their feelings of inferiority and insecurity are revealed in their pathological struggle for status within the isolated Ne-gro world and craving recognition in the white world.[4]

As harsh as this analysis is, it serves as an apt summary for the previous points. Masculinity during this era was still being defined according to the definition proposed by white America. Art attempted to paint a multifaceted image of black manhood during the 1970s, even with "blaxploitation" movies. "Masculinity" was all over the place. Shaft, the Jeffersons, and *Good Times* were some of the most prevalent models of that period. Our current society still bears the effects of these images. In addition, the black preacher and the church were seen as the worst images of manhood in America. These points are not intended to place blame on white America for black issues, but rather to partially explain why things are the way they are today.

The Hip-Hop/Soul Era

The Hip-Hop/Soul Era is becoming more of an eclectic movement in our contemporary culture. However, hip hop has been one of the most profound global influences on multiple cultures since the rise of rock. Its influence has spread to every continent except Antarctica, and it continues to expand and diversify its subgenres. As it relates to masculinity, hip-hop culture has been critiqued and criticized on many occasions. Whether it is gangster rap, pimpology, extravagance unleashed, womanizing, Islamic underpinnings, or even the conscious aspects, hip hop has had its share of troubles when it comes to scrutiny of its influence on both men and women. Along with all of its components that people would have trouble with, hip hop presents a skewed image of black men. Whether we admit it or not, art has had an undeniable influence on culture's perception of manhood. As much as many are able to identify with the indigenous connectivity of hip-hop culture, many of its components are irredeemable. Hip hop has made both positive and negative contributions to the masculinity of black men. One negative

4. Frazier, *Black Bourgeoisie,* 213.

effect is the insatiable need to amass wealth, glorified in much of hip hop. As spoken by the west coast poet Warren G:

> I want it all; money, fast cars
>
> Diamond rings, gold chains and champagne
>
> S***, every damn thing
>
> I want it all; houses, expenses
>
> My own business, a truck, hmm, and a couple o' Benz's
>
> I want it all; brand new socks and drawls
>
> And I'm ballin everytime I stop and talk to y'all
>
> I want it all, all, all, all
>
> I want it all, all, all, all, all.[5]

The Eclectic Era

The Eclectic Era has had a great effect on culture's view of masculinity. In what many consider an era in which white racial and ethnic issues are less discernible or understood by those under age forty, a fusion of the arts and gender specificity has become normal. This era is filled with positives but also has many negative repercussions in relation to masculinity. What manhood looks like is determined by the roles one accepts in society, attitudes towards other people, and even the clothing one wears.

Jay-Z released an album on September 11, 2009 called *The Blueprint 3*. He has proven to not only be a trendsetter artistically, but also in people's understanding of manhood and maturity. On the day of the album release, he had a live concert on Fuse. In an interview before the concert, he stated his desire to transform the art of hip hop, especially the content that artists are coming out with.[6] One of the most profound statements that he made was on race. Jay stated that, because of the global-local connection of the arts and technology, black and white issues have taken a back seat to issues affecting the global multi-ethnic community. His point was that people are gathering around what connects, rather than divides, them.

His track "Death of Auto-Tunes" is a call to musical authenticity and the execution of true talent, but the call is masculine in tone. Jay speaks to rappers not only about the heart and soul of hip hop, but also the elements missing from its culture of masculinity.

5. Warren G, "I Want It All."

6. Jay-Z, "Jay-Z."

For black men who had not had any cultural identity, hip hop provided a vision. When we saw the Motown artists—as much as we enjoyed their music—before the 1970s we weren't dreaming the way they were. During the crack era and the creation of turbulent inner cities, we were caught between a rock and a hard place. In light of this, hip hop was indigenous, and it gave vision through the creation of music videos, BET, and later MTV, of what an external manhood could look like. Out of all the other parts of history, hip hop gave us the most vivid images of manhood: images of violence and rage providing (illegitimately and without redemptive value) lust, love, and most importantly, freedom.

Contemporary Significance

Today, images of masculinity appear to be a casualty of history. Many have attempted to defuse this claim, but everything unredeemed is a casualty of the fall, whether it be human nature or the world in which we live. Because of this, we hear about statistics that reflect some type of connection.

Poussaint, in his book, *Come on People*, reveals some startling statistics.[7]

- In the past several decades, the suicide rate among young black men has increased more than 100 percent.

- In some cities, black males have high school drop-out rates of more than 50 percent.

- Young black men are twice as likely to be unemployed as white, Hispanic, and Asian men.

- Although black people make up just 12 percent of the general population, they make up nearly 44 percent of the prison population.

These are just some of the figures indicating that something is severely wrong with many young black men's understanding of masculinity. The solution to this problem can only be achieved through a biblical understanding of masculinity.

Yo brutha, where you at? This is the most riveting question in the Bible. As a matter of fact, this was the first recorded question of God in the scriptures. According to Genesis 3:9, "But the LORD God called to the man and said to him, 'Where are you?'" Yahweh asking this question is one of the most powerful scenes in the Bible. The omnipotent, omniscient, and omnipresent God calls out to the man. After Adam and Eve have disobeyed God, the Missionary God goes after them and calls out to him.

7. Cosby and Poussaint, *Come on People*, 9.

God uniquely holds the man as spokesperson for both himself and Eve. Infinite principles can be gleaned from just this question, but we will limit our discussion to only three.

1. God Was Not Lost, the Man Was

God went looking for the man. He is still doing so, but he is also forging biblical men after the image of Christ.[8] God is not only looking for men but recreating them as well.[9] Through Jesus Christ, God is reconciling all things to himself.[10] Everything redeemable that lost its place because of the fall, God is bringing back to himself, according to the eternal vision he has for this redeemed creation.

2. God Wanted to Show the Man Where God Was and Where the Man Wasn't

Since God knows everything, he wasn't actually unaware of where Adam was. He just wanted the man to know that something in their relationship had changed. The man reveals his position by his answer to God: "I heard," "I was afraid," "I was naked," and "I hid myself." How ironic? The one who prophesied the connectivity of husband and wife is now separating himself from his wife. He makes the first statement of masculinity, but also makes the first statement of emasculation—selfishness. God's question to the first man is the same one he asks us. His purpose is to draw us out of our hiding places and bring us to him. Just as the leaf that Adam used to cover himself died as soon as he removed it from the vine, so man began to die as soon as he separated himself from God.

THUGGISM

Thuggism is an exaggerated form of manhood that uses the smokescreen of anger and intimidation to keep people at a distance. The attitudes and behaviors associated with thuggism are all present in "thug life." A word coined by the late Tupac Shakur, thug is often mistakenly thought to mean "criminal." Thug life is the opposite of someone having all he needs to succeed. Thug life is when you have nothing, yet still succeed, when you have overcome all

8. Colossians 1:15.

9. John 3:5.

10. Colossians 1:20.

obstacles to reach your aim. As pretty as many have tried to paint it, and as many excuses as have been made for its existence, thuggism was one of the most influential forms of manhood training for many men. Having the "cred" of the block, the resources of a CEO, the eyes of the ladies, and the envy of the haters is the mark of the thug. It is not just about survival, but a commitment to not seeing beyond where you are now. Even though many have denigrated the thug life, it is a sign of its influence that it still lingers today as an image of manhood. At its core is survival without direction.

GRAND MAMA

Whether you call her Big Mama, Madea, Nana, Sugar Mama, or Granny, she has been the default leader in many black families all over the country. This transcends the urban context and finds its reality in rural areas as well.

In the days of slavery, and then of sharecropping, when black men generally were unable to achieve economic independence, the black grandmother was often a heroic figure whose role required great sacrifice. The black man was frequently, but not always, emasculated, weakened, or simply neutralized by the social control efforts of the wider white society, and was thus reduced as a competitive force in a male-dominated society. But the black woman was not usually perceived to be as much of a threat to the dominance of the white man as the black man was. According to folklore, such women were then allowed to develop into strong, independent, willful, and wise matriarchs who were not afraid to compete with men when necessary.

As in the past, the heroic grandmother would come to the aid of the family, taking responsibility for children abandoned by their own parents, asserting her considerable moral authority for the good of the family, and often rearing the children herself under conditions of great hardship.

The grandmother's central role has become institutionalized in the black community and carries with it a great deal of prestige, but also a great deal of stress. However, because this role is imbued with such prestige, moral authority, and is so firmly entrenched in the culture, many of those who assume it see it as highly important, if not essential, for the survival of the black inner-city family.

A review of the literature on grandparenthood reveals that the existence of the institutionalized grandmother role is a major feature of black family life, particularly among the poor. Among inner-city blacks, because of this strong tradition, it is often seen as a mandatory role with established rights, obligations, and duties, and those who refuse it may be judged by many in the local black community as having abdicated a vital responsibility. Hence, when called upon, black grandmothers appear constrained to play out their role.[11]

This role became both a blessing and a curse. Despite its many benefits, the cycle of grandmothers becoming midwives, elders, and chiefs of families and neighborhoods has crippled masculinity. Black grandmothers became icons for inner city leadership in the family. With her status as platinum, it was a challenge for black men to realistically understand and accomplish their rightful role. Also, black grandmothers became scapegoats for willful negligence of youth and adults alike, receiving blame for acts and choices they were not involved in. There needs to be a ceremony held in which the grandmothers of the world transfer their authority back to men who are willing to use the mantle wisely and will take responsibility to conduct themselves in a biblical and comprehensive manner.[12]

3. God Is Willing to Go After the Man

When God looks for Adam in the garden, we see first-hand the missionary flair of the Living God. He seeks out man while man hides from him. While we are hiding, he calls to us. Amidst our insecurities, challenges, and failures, he bids us to come.

Towards a Basic Biblical Theology of Manhood

Before we define manhood, we must give a basic biblical portrait of manhood. For the most part, the Bible does not define what a man is, but it does give vivid portraits of manhood and characteristics of masculinity. We will not explore all of them, but we will go through a brief overview of these portraits. These portraits are more powerful than any mere Western, linear definition of manhood. It is impossible to talk about masculinity without speaking of Genesis 1:26–27. These verses are highly controversial, but everything is clear in one respect—masculinity and femininity are distinct:

> Then God said, "Let us make man in our image, after our likeness. And let them have dominion over the fish of the sea and over the birds of the heavens and over the livestock and over all the earth and over every creeping thing that creeps on the

11. Anderson, *Code of the Street*.

12. Matthew 28:18–20; 2 Timothy 2:2.

earth." So God created man in his own image, in the image of
God he created him; male and female he created them.[13]

Manhood and womanhood are distinct and different but should be
unified in their goal, the reflection of the one who created them. Being created in the likeness and image of God is a unified reality for both genders,
but created men and women have distinct, yet complementary, ways in
which to reveal it. We see God putting man in the garden to work, we see
God giving man great freedom and clear boundaries, we see God bringing
all the animals of the earth to man to name and legislating and affirming
his name choice, and we see God giving man a mate.[14] This mate is given
in the context of man naming God's sentient creation. Adam noticed from
a physiological standpoint that he and the other parts of God's creation
were different. However, the difference did not repel him; it drew him to
preach and prophesy. The woman is a co-equal reflector of the glory of
God, who is called to use her femininity to complete God's goal for relative
self-replication of his image through mankind. It is man, however, that is
called to lead this effort.

Man must lead God's creation in reflecting and replicating God's image. In light of the fall, man began to replicate his own image among God's
creation. However, God promised after the fall that he would appoint the seed
of the woman as a redeemer.[15] This redeemer is Jesus, who is the image of
God untainted by sin.[16] Jesus became incarnate to show us who the father is
and what he looks like. The Lord Jesus therefore is the seed of Eve, yet he is
different.[17] He is perfectly able to reflect the image of God and also replicate it.
The cross is the center of God's replication strategy. Jesus gives his life to put
man back in right relationship with God. As an application of that rightness,
manhood is restored to its proper function through the cross.[18]

Romans 5:17 points to Jesus as the embodiment of what it means to
be the new man. The first man (Adam) flunked, but the second man (Jesus)
graduated with honors. Jesus as the new man is the prototype for all that he
died to redeem, and manhood is being restored by being conformed to the
image of God, following the example set by Christ.[19] To be conformed to
Jesus' image automatically reconstructs man into God's image.

13. Genesis 1:26–27.

14. Genesis 2:15; 2:16–17; and 2:19 respectively.

15. Genesis 3:15.

16. Colossians 1:15.

17. John 1:18.

18. Colossians 1:20.

19. Romans 8:29.

Affirmations of a Father or Father Figure

God the Father affirms Jesus as his man and the man that men should follow. God had not audibly spoken from heaven in public since Exodus 20:18–21. However, this was a special occasion, to put it mildly. God said, "This is my beloved Son, with whom I am well pleased."[20] At Jesus' introduction as messianic king, God as a faithful Father shows up to affirm his son, as well as to reveal his presence. Later on God does the same thing, affirming Jesus as his man to the disciples, as "a bright cloud overshadowed them, and a voice from the cloud said, 'This is my beloved Son, with whom I am well pleased; listen to him.'"[21] God lets man know his pleasure with his son.

Key Characteristics of Biblical Manhood

An Initiator

Robert Lewis in his Manhood Curriculum states, "Manhood is the willingness to take the initiative for the benefits of other."[22] Taking the initiative is at the center of our Lord Jesus' philosophy of life. Although he saw himself as sent, he is an initiator of what God has commanded him. One of the challenges of manhood in today's society is passivity. Many view passivity as a characteristic of the soft man. Think of the nerdy dude that wears glasses, high water pants, and is timid around females. However, timidity in the Bible is defined a little differently. It is an unwillingness to execute God-centered mandates. Second Timothy 1:7 states, "for God gave us a spirit not of fear but of power and love and self-control." In context, Paul wants Timothy to walk in God's affirmed gifting and receive the consequences—positive or negative—of reflecting who God has uniquely bred him to be as a man. In addition, he calls him to be courageous in the gospel.

First Timothy 2:8 speaks of men being spiritual initiators. Men are supposed to initiate prayer and worship. Paul makes it a universal axiom. Nothing makes me angrier than to ask for someone to pray and have only women respond first. Husky, raspy, and passionate voices of men should answer that call. Worship in the African American context has become an extremely feminine phenomenon. Expressions of worship often are feminine in nature. Men are repelled by it and do not feel the freedom to worship. The cultural feminization of worship has come from the absence

20. Matthew 3:17.

21. Matthew 17:5.

22. Lewis, *The Quest for Authentic Manhood*.

of men as the initiators of worship. Therefore, we must return to our theological roots. Men must be present and ready to give Jesus his due in public and private gatherings.

Moreover, a famine also exists in the home where men are absent and where men who are present still seem absent. Men are supposed to initiate spirituality in the home. Ephesians 5:26 and 29 point to this. Men are to initiate biblical and theological vitality in the home. Jesus confronts the church about her spiritual needs.[23] Jesus does not merely wait for the church to come and tell him what she needs. Jesus' masculinity patrols the church to inspect and challenge her progress. However, he does it in a way that is nourishing and cherishing. He does not abuse the church in his leading but keeps her safe and protected from evil.

Gospel Courage

Gospel courage is the willingness to be faithful to the gospel in life, despite the negative reactions that may come from men, looking instead to God and his blessing.[24] Men must be willing to fill all their lives with the truth of the gospel. Dying to evil is the gateway into gospel-centered living for the Christian. Jesus' death is the gateway into all that God has for creation. We must have the courage to die, just as Christ did.

Paul speaks of his positional and practical death experience(s). He speaks of the courage necessary to identify with Jesus at the expense of himself. This is manhood at its best. The picture of dying to gain Christ is prevalent in the text. Pressing, suffering, and loss are words of pain and struggle, but the result is a blessing, the gaining of Jesus and true manhood.

Speaking into the Future of Men

One of the greatest manhood chapters in the Bible is Genesis 49. Jacob nearing death called his sons to himself. It is a practice that he received from his dad Isaac.[25] In this section, Jacob shows his vast knowledge of his sons' wiring, actions, and spiritual capacity. He warns them, challenges them, encourages them, speaks prophetically to them, and prays over them. His display is God-initiated; yet God uses his raising of them and his interaction with them as a pipeline for his words.

23. Revelation 1–3.

24. Romans 1:16.

25. Genesis 27.

Jacob, with all of his issues, was a dad who was around. His presence is reflected in his intimate understanding of the lives of his sons. Some of what he said was very blunt, but it was needed for such a rambunctious crew. He calls Reuben "unstable," and calls Simeon and Levi "hot headed." He calls Judah "a King," Zebulun "a beach boy," Issachar "a jackass," Dan "judge and a snake," and Joseph "fruitful."[26] Men having an intimate knowledge of their sons are a rarity. In order to develop men, we must be with them, understand them, and have the courage to challenge them.

Every man knows that even though we all have massive egos that are easily bruised, the wounds inflicted by well-meaning, key men in our lives is deeply valued. Men who, like Jesus, regularly rebuke and encourage are needed. Jesus struck an amazing balance between these two. He challenged Peter's youthful zeal in making emotional commitments, knowing that Peter would not follow through on his promise.[27] But Jesus still encouraged him after his fall.

Setting Men Up to Win

In 1 Chronicles 22:2–19, we see a dad displaying an intimate understanding of his son and the role he must play to set up his son for success. David was told by God that he would not build the temple. As passionate as David was about this, he submitted to the Lord in this matter. The Lord told him that his son would have the honor instead. Although David may have been disappointed, he was man enough to make sure that his son was prepared to succeed in the plans that the Lord had for him.

Since the Lord stated that it was Solomon who would build the temple, David wanted to make sure that his son had everything set in place for this work to occur in a way that would glorify God. Therefore, David used his knowledge of his son and his sphere of influence to aid in the process. He states in verse 5, "Solomon my son is young and inexperienced."[28] This statement is not spoken out of envy of the role Solomon would play in his stead, but a real understanding of where his son was lacking. Solomon himself will later acknowledge his lack of wisdom to the Lord. In light of Solomon's youth and inexperience, David states, "'I will therefore make preparation for it.' So David provided materials in great quantity before his death."[29] The King views his role as helping his son win, all for the glory of God.

26. Genesis 49.

27. John 13:38.

28. 1 Chronicles 22:5.

29. 1 Chronicles 22:5.

It is a powerful statement that David has such a passion for God's glory that he prepares his son to fulfill his role in glorifying God. David stated, "The house that is to be built for the Lord must be exceedingly magnificent, of fame and glory throughout all lands."[30] His concern for how God is viewed motivated him to alley-oop the legacy to his son through preparing him with the resources he would need.

Men prepare men and give them the resources to glorify God. One of the greatest faults among black men is that lack of passion to see younger men win. Many will state a passion for it, but rarely do you see the level of effort taken by black men to establish an environment for winning. Developing a winning environment is of great importance for every man. I am a church planter and 98 percent of the support that we received has been from non-African Americans. One pastor stated, "You have more than I had at the point in which you are currently, so I figured you need to struggle like I did. A part of your learning is earning." I was like, "YOOOOOO!" It blew my mind that he believed that he was setting me up to win by giving me as little as possible. In addition, if resources were given to me, it would make me inadequate, as if the giver thought I wasn't strong enough to do it on my own. We should want the men that come after us to give Jesus more glory than we did. We should want them to be more gifted, more talented, more intellectually astute, more emotionally connected to their wives, more influential, more effective providers, better dads, etc. As time goes on, we should see the abundant lives of those who have gone before fill the next generation with more abundance. Jesus' passion is that his disciples would reach more people with their ministry than he did.[31] He sets them up to win, even in his ascension to heaven.

So many young men in the hip-hop/eclectic generation feel extremely frustrated and un-fathered. Most of the men I shepherd deal with deep daddy deprivation. This deprivation has created spiritual blindspots that set up booby traps along their road to sanctification. The worst of them all is the façade. This façade is a mask the young men use to deceive people who they encounter into thinking that they are all right. Whether it is theological knowledge void of spiritual formation, or comedic relief that aids them in not being taken seriously, these are examples of this façade. Older black Christian men must be able to see beyond that fog, like David, and speak into the life of the young man in light of his chronic weaknesses. Solomon's weaknesses did not de-motivate David but drove him to be a loving resource to his son, so he could bring maximum glory to God.

30. 1 Chronicles 22:5.
31. John 14:12.

Keys to Developing Masculine Men

Able to Use Resources Wisely

Stewardship means to oversee what has been placed within your sphere or under your charge, thereby maximizing its use for the owner's benefit while it is in your possession. The Bible speaks often of this idea. In Luke 16:1–8, Jesus speaks of the shrewd manager. Ultimately, Jesus wanted God's people to understand how to use God's resources to the advantage of the kingdom. In black culture, we speak with one another about what we assume whites teach their children. We assume that whites keep this info for "their own kind" on subjects like money, property, and education. We feel like there is this secret system that white people have to ensure they are better than anyone else. There is this sense of inferiority among blacks, as if our ability to maximize what Jesus has placed under our charge will always be limited.

Able to Emotionally Connect

"We don't love dem hoes," is a colloquialism developed by Snoop Dogg and affirmed by men of the need to maintain emotional distance from women.[32] Continuing the trend, Jay-Z on *The Blueprint 1* had the hit "Girls, Girls, Girls." He speaks throughout the video in a nonchalant way about how connected and into him the girls were, but how disconnected he was from them. We could go on to gangster rhymes that speak of emotional disconnect from authority, or 50 Cent speaking of killing another man and being emotionally disconnected from any sort of remorse.

These and many other examples of emotional disconnect have become staples of unredeemed manhood. To be a distant man has become accepted—and even encouraged! Being emotionally invested in anything but your favorite sports teams, the neighborhood you grew up in, white AF1's, and new Timberland boots is unacceptable. It is okay to be emotionally vested in the woman all the dudes want but only you have. This is because the attachment is self-centered. Some of these issues are generalizations; yet they are embedded on some level in the psyche of almost every black dude who is not a social outcast.

The Bible teaches that God wants worship from every fabric of our being, from both men and women.[33] God wants every part of humanity to worship him. Man was made to love God with his whole being. Although this has

32. Snoop Dogg, "Gin & Juice."

33. Mark 12:29–31.

been defaced by the fall, Jesus died to make it possible for us to holistically love God again. God made the first move through Jesus, demonstrating his love for us before we would for him. God created us with intellect, emotions, and volition. Since that is a part of who we are, we must use everything within our being as an instrument of worship. Men must be taught the skill of emotional connection through the example Jesus Christ.

Men must first be connected with God again in order to apply this reality for a redemptive standpoint. Second, men must acknowledge and resolve the pains of their past. Although Paul states in Philippians 3:13 that we should be "forgetting what lies behind," we must first acknowledge the existence of that past in order to give it to Jesus.

Peter Scazzaro profoundly lists several problems contributing to emotional unhealth:

- Ignoring the emotions of anger, sadness, and fear
- Dying to the wrong things
- Denying the past's impact on the present
- Covering over brokenness, weaknesses, and failure
- Living without limits[34]

For most men, our lack of emotional connectivity can be dated back to some event that we would like to forget. It also does not help that black folks, especially dudes, do not affirm the role of counseling in our lives. The pattern of pretending to be okay when you really are not needs to stop. Time does not fix brokenness; skillful application of the gospel does. If we reconnect broken men with the gospel's healing power, there will be a greater level of health in marriage, friendships, parenting, church community, missional engagement of one's context, and spiritual formation. All of these benefits are on hold until we men are able to face God and our past.

Able to Reproduce Properly and Purposefully Spiritual Reproduction

Black Christian men must understand that you cannot live the Christian life and not strive to reproduce solid disciples of Jesus Christ. Matthew 28:18–20 is a call to everyone in the church, not just the pastor. It is a shame that many of us as black pastors are so insecure and timid that we view men engaging other men and creating disciples of Christ within the

34. Scazzero, *Emotionally Healthy Spirituality*, 24.

local church as competition with our spiritual authority. Pastors must see this as an extension of their spiritual work and a great win for Christ, who is the chief shepherd.[35]

Any pastor who wants to see God work in the lives of men must have a healthy view of spiritual reproduction. Making disciples, leading a small group, communicating with and rallying people, or being called to plant a church is a death wish for many young men who are in the church today. They know too well that the pastor will be saddened, not because he will miss being around you if you leave, or because you will not be as connected to him relationally. It will be because he believes that enabling them to lead will breed competition. Yes, there will be those who will not allow the community to assist them in watching over their charge. That is a part of leading—you get hurt, even by those who you have poured your life into. This is biblical and normal. That is why Paul urges us to maximize our time with the faithful.[36] The only other option is "Controlled Empowerment." CE is when a pastor releases someone, but only with a leash still attached.

Our course of action must be for men to reproduce godly men through discipleship. Spending his life on the faithful was Jesus' passion. This must be a shared passion of ours. In fact, it is a command. You do not need a key program to practice discipleship—just start it. We must make disciples beyond the men's ministry. It must be an organic culture of the church. The leadership should have fewer speaking engagements and spend more time with small groups of the faithful. Go through character studies on manhood in the Bible, books written on gospel-centered manhood, and/or bring them along with you during a natural part of your week and show them biblical manhood.

Physical Reproduction

In Philadelphia, the former mayor stated that 90 percent of the children born in Philly were born to single parent homes. This is a pandemic! Philly is 45 percent black and this is true of our populace. Men need to be engaged with the gospel. We must target men. One of the many problems facing the black community today is that we do not have a problem reproducing, but much of it is done illegitimately. Jesus wants legitimate reproduction. In order to engage men, we must inspire manliness in the culture of the church. Flowers all around the pulpit, first ladies choosing the colors for where the saints gather, and feminine men are the dominant visual. We can

35. 1 Peter 5:4.
36. 2 Timothy 2:2.

have all the social justice programs we want—cool cats will come to that stuff during the week for a handout, and even a hand up—but they will still remain wary of Christianity and the gospel. Once men are engaged, they must see the raising up of godly disciples of Christ as an indigenous Christian trait for men. The raising of godly men will end the cycle. Raising solid Christian children will give people in the next generations a new past. Hopefully they won't have to get over our view of Christianity in order to become children of the father.

Chapter 7   Mentoring as Discipleship at Historically Black Colleges and Universities

—Rihana S. Mason

" What do you want to be when you grow up?" is a common question asked of children and teenagers. When I reflect on my own childhood, the answer to that question changed from becoming a cosmetologist to a traveling dancer to a defense attorney to a psychologist. I dropped the idea of becoming a cosmetologist when I accidentally turned the head of my Barbie mannequin green after mixing several hair products together and applying them with a roller set. The switch to become a traveling dancer came as a result of my middle and high school summer jobs where I worked as a counselor for a performing arts school. I learned how to teach younger children different forms of dance as well as leading them through other activities. I also spent countless hours training to become better at dance. Performing on several stages in the northeastern and southeastern regions of the United States, including Six Flags over Georgia and Universal Studios in Orlando, made me want to share my art form with the world. This dream faded when I was not picked to audition for dance conservatory.

I chased after a more traditional career that was more aligned with the television shows *Matlock* and *JAG*. I had fallen head over heels for the idea of serving as an attorney and being able to win hard-to-solve cases. In preparation for my new career pathway, I attended a summer preview program at the United States Naval Academy. I had the chance to talk to sailors who were attorneys, see the campus of the Naval Academy, and spend time in a trial run of classes on campus. After participating in this program, the idea of proving innocence or guilt through the use of virtual reality and crime simulation sealed the notion of pursuing a career in law.

Sadly, my dream of practicing law ended on the day that I attended a pre-law society meeting during my freshman year in college. Given the lengthy discussions about the Constitution and the absence of the conversations about the science of the mind, I sorted out that I was more interested in studying the minds of clients than defending them. I defaulted to pursuing a career in psychology since at the time it was my only known option related to studying the mind. Without a mentor or role model to guide me, this whole process of figuring out who I wanted to become was long and tedious.

We are often urged to remember where we came from. I am a proud alumna of Spelman College. My passion for supporting the training of black lives in academia stems from my undergraduate experiences at Spelman College, a historically black college in the southeastern region of the United States. As a Spelman student, I witnessed firsthand the benefits of having a career-related mentor before college entry. I worked at Morehouse School of Medicine during my junior and senior years. I worked with the Benjamin Carson Science Academy, Elementary Science Education Partners, and the Medical Post Program. I have vivid memories of the hands-on science experiments, career fairs, and college tours that I helped facilitate in these programs. Each program involved mentors who encouraged children to dream about becoming scientists, reinforcing the idea that they were capable of joining the ranks of other black scientists.

The purpose of this chapter is to bring awareness to the positive contributions that Historically Black Colleges and Universities (HBCUs) make in preparing K–12 students for college success. This chapter shares the importance of gaining career and college preparatory exposure through mentored experiences at HBCUs. It is organized as a discussion of K–12 academic interventions or culturally enriching communities of practice housed at HBCUs.[1] More specifically, this chapter addresses the ways in which these programs use the master-disciple approach to mentoring to prepare K–12 students for college.

Background

College enrollment disparities exist between black and white students. In 2018, 64 percent of black students who graduated from high school enrolled in postsecondary education compared to 71 percent of white students.[2] Census data also suggests that fewer black students, 54 percent, are persisting through their fourth year of college compared to white students, 71 percent.[3] The largest gender gap for college completion, 10 percentage points, also

1. Byrd and Mason, *Academic Pipeline Project.*
2. *The Journal of Blacks in Higher Education,* "Racial Gap."
3. U.S. Census Bureau, "School Enrollment."

exists among black students. This data suggests a pressing need to reduce educational attainment disparities experienced by black students.

Diversity, equity, and inclusion (DEI) initiatives at US institutions of higher education are growing as a popular strategy to remedy these educational attainment gaps. Marybeth Gasman suggests that DEI initiatives are intertwined with the Black Lives Matter (BLM) movement.[4] The goal of the BLM movement is to create a "world free of anti-blackness, where every black person has the social, economic, and political power to thrive."[5] Started as a way for blacks to gain educational attainment, HBCUs were established and/or accredited prior to 1964 with the sole mission of educating black students.[6]

As Gasman put it, "HBCUs are places where black lives have always mattered."[7] Therefore, it is important to shed light on how HBCUs have succeeded in educating and preparing black and underrepresented minority (URM) youth. Higher education at HBCUs has historically been instrumental in the social mobility for black and URM students. HBCUs have become the leading producers of students who pursue careers in STEM, nursing, and medicine, training nearly one-third of all black STEM PhDs.[8] Moreover, there are twenty-one HBCUs on the National Science Foundation list of top producers of science and engineering doctoral recipients.[9]

What is so special about HBCUs? HBCUs combine cultural experiences and teaching together in a way that students of color gain knowledge from a community of individuals who share similar life experiences and who have navigated the academy successfully. Ivory Toldson outlines three main reasons that HBCUs are successful at training black and URM students:

1. Unique structure of faculty mentors who understand black culture

2. Retention strategies that support lesser prepared students early

3. Culturally relevant teaching practices[10]

---

4. Gasman, "The Black Lives Matter Movement," 1–2.

5. Black Lives Matter, "What We Believe."

6. U.S. Department of Health, Education, and Welfare, "Higher Education Act of 1965."

7. Gasman, "The Black Lives Matter Movement," 1–2.

8. Tyson et al., "Nursing"; Gasman et al., "Black Male Success"; Upton and Tanenbaum, "The Role of Historically Black Colleges and Universities."

9. National Science Foundation, "Survey of Earned Doctorate Recipients."

10. Toldson, "Cultivating STEM Talent."

Claudia Rankins states that "HBCUs embody the best practices for educating students who are marginalized in other learning environments, and it is critical that we look to these schools to learn how to best educate all STEM students."[11] Bringing awareness to the programming offered by HBCUs at the early end of the academic pipeline is a way to expand recruitment and retention of black students into the STEM workforce.

HBCUs naturally link academic preparation within an adopted family of peers and faculty. Oftentimes black and other URM students matriculate through school without the same social capital as their majority peers.[12] Social capital includes the resources tied to networks and relationships. Robert Palmer and Marybeth Gasman identified five themes of HBCUs that contribute to increased social capital for students:

1. Empathy and support through faculty relationships

2. Supportive administrators who go above call of duty

3. Peer support—motivation and encouragement

4. Role models and mentors—illuminating pathways

5. A supportive campus community[13]

Additionally, HBCUs have been described as a source of social capital via their supportive ethos for black males.[14] Understanding the successful components of training programs at HBCUs is fundamental for supporting future black students who are entering the workforce.

K–12 Pipeline Programs

Nationally, K–12 pipeline programs are structured in a variety of formats but have the same broad goal of improving students in academics and more. These programs can have many formats: community outreach programs, curriculum-based active learning experiences, fairs, family and social activities, hands-on exhibits, mentored research projects, scholarship programs, summer bridge programs, test preparation workshops, and tutoring sessions. Pipeline program formats are also implemented across a range of out-of-school times (after school, Saturday, summer, etc.) and a variety of time intervals (single day, weekly, monthly, etc.). The National Research Council

11. Rankins, "HBCUs and Black STEM Student Success."

12. Byrd, "Diversifying the Professoriate."

13. Palmer and Gasman, "'It Takes a Village to Raise a Child.'"

14. Shorette and Palmer, "Historically Black Colleges and Universities."

suggests that productive pipeline programs are characterized by their ability to do the following three things: (1) engage young people intellectually, socially, and emotionally, (2) respond to young people's interests, experiences, and cultural practices, and (3) connect discipline-specific learning out of school, at school, at home, and in other settings.[15]

Many others like myself developed their career interest(s) early with the aid of a K–12 academic pipeline program. The U.S. Naval Academy program followed a common format for K–12 pipeline programs—the summer bridge model. Three types of summer bridge programs service pre-collegiate students transitioning through the pipeline: (1) middle school to high school, (2) high school to first year of college, and (3) orientation prior to college.[16] A national example of a pre-collegiate summer bridge program that targets the high school to first year of college transition is the Meyerhoff Scholars program housed at the University of Maryland Baltimore County. The Meyerhoff Scholars program has served as a model program for training black and URM students for STEM careers for more than thirty years.[17] The program's outcomes are so noteworthy that other institutions like Pennsylvania State University and University of North Carolina-Chapel Hill have replicated its model at their institutions.

Research has shown that summer bridge programs help students overcome barriers that would likely prevent them from succeeding in college. In middle school, exposure to pipeline programming improves problem-solving skills.[18] High school programs have been demonstrated to change misconceptions about health careers and heighten students' motivation towards health careers.[19]

Moreover, summer bridge programs aid in building one's identity and academic success. Pre-college (incoming freshman) students of color experience greater self-efficacy and academic skills after participating in summer bridge programs.[20] Additional research indicates that rates of suc-

---

15. National Research Council et al., *Identifying and Supporting Productive STEM Programs.*

16. Arendale and Lee, "Bridge Programs."

17. Hrabowski, "Broadening Participation."

18. Stohlmann et al., "Middle School Students' Mindsets."

19. Derck et al., "Doctors of Tomorrow"; Porter et al., "Stagnant Perceptions of Nursing"; Katz et al., "Measuring the Success of a Pipeline Program."

20. Salto et al., "Underrepresented Minority High School"; Slade et al., "Getting into the Pipeline."

cess in entry level college courses are higher for summer bridge program participants.[21] They are also more likely to graduate from college.[22]

My own research provides an account of the success of a high school summer bridge program, Upward Bound. Upward Bound offers academic enrichment in reading, science, and mathematics to students who will become first-generation college students or who come from a low-income background. One particular Upward Bound housed at an HBCU was successful at increasing the reading comprehension scores of black high school students due to its emphasis of having a growth mind-set.[23] Adding discussions about growth mind-set had the largest impact on students whose parents only held a high school diploma.[24]

Master-Disciple Mentoring Approach

Survey data from pipeline programs indicates that mentoring is the second ranked approach utilized by K–12 programs at urban universities.[25] Almost three million youth are matched with mentors in the United States yearly.[26] Mentors also serve as role models for the future selves of mentees.

Mentors serve a critical role in socio-emotional, identity, and cognitive development.[27] Mentoring relationships are crucial for persistence in academic spaces as they expand one's understanding of what is needed to be successful. K–12 pipeline programs with a heavy mentoring focus have been successful in propelling black and URM students into STEM careers.[28] An examination of various mentoring research studies revealed that mentored students had slightly higher levels of academic success, motivation, and lower levels of withdrawal or dropout compared to non-mentored students.[29] I think it's necessary to specifically look at the outcomes for students of color at HBCUs since the previously mentioned study did not look at a program's setting, such as being at an HBCU.

21. Wathington et al., "A Good Start?"
22. Salto et al., "Underrepresented Minority High School."
23. Williams et al., "African American High School."
24. Williams et al., "The Relations between Human Capital."
25. Danek and Borrayo, "Urban Universities."
26. Raposa et al., "The Effects of Youth Mentoring Programs."
27. DuBois et al., "How Effective."
28. Mains et al., "Medical Education Resources"; Zaniewski and Reinholz, "Increasing STEM Success."
29. Eby et al., "Does Mentoring Matter?"

Mentoring is viewed as a best practice of HBCUs. Peer and faculty mentoring programs are included in many theoretical frameworks of successful pipeline programs at HBCUs.[30] HBCUs are pioneers in moving students into the STEM workforce by implementing peer mentoring, peer tutoring, and summer bridge programs.[31] What I witnessed at Spelman can be labeled as the master-disciple mentoring approach. The master-disciple approach is one way of describing how identity formation leads to academic achievement through mentoring. The Master-disciple approach describes a situation whereby the mentor guides, teaches, and affirms. Akin to biblical mentoring relationships particularly that of Paul (mentor) and Timothy (mentee), many pipeline programs at HBCUs provide individualized experiences that guide students along their academic paths by teaching them from a strengths-based perspective and affirming their potential for their career goals.

Illuminating K–12 pathway programs

The first step to helping young black lives figure out what they want to be when they grow up is illuminating or identifying academic pipeline programs that can help them. To truly ensure that we reach more black students early, we should continue to promote K–12 pipeline programs in a way that markets both their practicality and their potential for discipleship. HBCU websites are full of summer camp and academic enrichment offerings for elementary, middle, and high school students. Nearly every HBCU sponsors at least one academic pipeline program at the K–12 level.[32]

Jeton McClinton and colleagues recently published a book where all of the chapters refer to the mentoring practices of pipeline programs at HBCUs.[33] However, the focus of their book was only collegiate, graduate, and faculty level programs, not ones at the K–12 level. Eight K–12 academic pipeline programs at HBCUs that are still in existence include mentoring as part of their curricula. They each have evidence-based outcomes from research studies and/or program evaluations. The table below lists and explains each of the programs.

---

30. Doerschuk et al., "Closing the Gaps"; Haggins et al., "Value of Near-Peer Mentorship."

31. Roach, "STEM Success."

32. Byrd and Mason, *Academic Pipeline Project*.

33. McClinton et al., *Mentoring at Minority Serving Institutions*.

Table 1: K–12 Academic Pipeline Programs at HBCUs

Program Name	Description
2 Pathways into STEM (2-Pi STEM) Summer Enrichment Institute Lawson State Community College	Four-week project-based program that includes STEM-related activities (e.g., robotics and computing) and career pathway programming. Peer mentoring is one of the three primary goals of the program. Mentoring is cross-curricular, and the mentoring schedule is designed to improve persistence and self-efficacy in STEM courses.
Aspiring Eagles Academy North Carolina Central University (NCCU)	Five-week pre-college residential summer program that includes gateway courses which continue into the freshman academic year. Mentoring is provided by peers who are upperclass-men or graduate students at NCCU.[34]
Helping Orient Minorities to Engineering (H.O.M.E.) Program North Carolina Agricultural and Technical State University (NC A&T)	Five-and-a-half-week program that provides academic enrichment, professional development activities, and peer mentoring. Peer mentoring sessions include strategies for adjusting to college culture.[35]
NASA Science Engineering Mathematics and Aerospace Academy Morgan State University	Summer and Saturday program that includes hands-on science curriculum that blends parent mentoring with resources from NASA, science centers, museums, local schools, and Morgan State University, including aerospace laboratory simulations.[36]

---

34. Merritt et al., "The Impact of Pre/Post-Enrollment Interventions."
35. Parrish et al., "Helping Orient Minorities."
36. Martinez et al., *The National Evaluation.*

Program Name	Description
Pre-College for Engineering Systems Howard University	Six-week residential program for eleventh- and twelfth-grade students. It exposes students to diverse STEM topics such as electrical engineering and sustainable energy concepts. Howard undergraduate students serve as near-peer mentors by working together with the high school students on their research projects and homework assignments.[37]
Program of Excellence in STEM Florida Agricultural and Mechanical University	Summer and yearlong research and mentorship activities. Typical activities involving mentors include engaging in hands-on laboratory research activities, practicing for public speaking, attending scientific meetings, and touring research labs.[38]
Verizon Innovative Learning Minority Male Program Clark Atlanta University, Jackson State University, Kentucky State University, Morehouse College, Morgan State University, and NC A&T	Serves middle school students by providing a variety of hands-on activities like 3D printing, robotics, mobile app development, and virtual reality. Mentors receive national training from agencies like National Cares Mentoring.[39]
UNC Summer Bridge and Retention Program Elizabeth City State University, Fayetteville State University, NC A&T, NCCU, and Winston Salem State University	Five- or six-week intensive exposure to collegiate mathematics and English instruction supplemented by group activities. Group activities include tutoring, mentoring, social bonding, and co-curricular activities.[40]

There are many other beneficial pipeline programs as well. Organizations like the National Science Foundation's Pathways to Science, the Association of American Medical Colleges, the American Bar Association, and the Academic Pipeline Project offer searchable databases of programs. The Academic Pipeline Project is an especially helpful resource as it is the

37. Momoh, "Outreach Program in Electrical Engineering."
38. Clark, "The Program of Excellence in STEM."
39. Ziker et al., "2016 Verizon Innovative Learning."
40. Wachen et al., "Building College Readiness."

only one that includes the best practices of each program and training outcomes. The databases can be filtered by level of the pipeline and region of the United States. When I reflected on my childhood, and now as a parent, I see the value in being more informed as to how pipeline programs will train my children in academic content areas, inspire them to pursue their career goals, and equip them with building additional networks.

Conclusion

As I have been going through different stages of life as well as working in different diverse workplaces and environments, I recognize the value of career training offered by HBCUs. I still think there is a lot to learn about how HBCUs help prepare young black lives for college readiness and the career workforce. There is a lot to do to make sure we can continue the academic pipeline for future children. Unfortunately, the number of available studies is currently limited in number and in scope, especially for high school STEM, health-related careers, or social and behavioral sciences. Attention is needed for programs that are geared towards increasing the interest of girls in STEM (e.g., Black Girls Code, HBCU Rising) and increasing interest in the social sciences and education. Ongoing research, news reports, and press releases can help to expand public knowledge about career training successes of HBCUs at the K–12 level of the academic pipeline for black youth nationwide.

Chapter 8　**The Church and Community**

—*Lance Lewis*

E ven though it sat a few hundred persons, the hall was packed to standing room only. Though I'd lived in Elk Grove, California, for just over four years, it was the first time I'd seen so many African Americans in one place. The occasion for this gathering was a town hall meeting to address several vile racist incidents directed toward members of the black community of Elk Grove during the summer of 2017. Following a particularly racist note posted on the door of an African American business owner, the city leaders either decided or agreed to have a series of three of these town hall meetings to discuss the racism in our city, finally. The first meeting took place on an early October evening with an agenda to hear from the community about their experiences of racism.

As you might expect, the accounts of racism weren't new. African Americans have experienced this since being dragged to the shores of this land in the seventeenth century. And while the severity of the acts of hatred has of course changed, the sentiment is the same: You're not wanted, you're not welcome, your lives don't matter. Before jumping to judgmental conclusions about my city, let me make it clear that this could have been any city or town in America. I'm thankful that we at least attempted to face it. I'm grateful since many of those who spoke noted our racism was a decades-long sin that will continue to afflict and affect our city should we continue to ignore it. Moreover, though it brought great sadness to hear the multiple accounts of hatred, it was at least comforting for black people to tell of the racism we face to someone other than ourselves. To put it another way, at least for one night black lives mattered.

That's significant since most often, we're essentially told to keep whatever thoughts about the racism we face to ourselves. I'll go further. Whenever we bring up issues of race and racism in this society, we're usually redirected in one of three ways. The first is to deny racism exists in America. The second is to convey that our real issues lie not with racism but with the challenges in our communities to which we should attend. The third is to admit while some racism might exist, it's not all that significant, presents no real barrier to achievement, and besides African Americans should be grateful we get to live in this society.

Tomi Lahren took this approach when asked by Trevor Noah the best way for Colin Kaepernick to carry out his peaceful protest.[1] For several minutes, Noah persisted in asking her what a better way would be for Mr. Kaepernick to voice his concerns. Her only response was to repeatedly state her view against his kneeling during the national anthem. Never once did she offer any kind of alternative way of expression.

One of the main ways to convey to a person or group of people they don't matter is to consistently refuse to hear them and communicate that their concerns are minuscule, petty, and not worth the trouble. Doing so reduces them to little more than an annoying bother you wish would either get with the program or just go away. Perhaps an example will be helpful. Imagine someone close to you (family member, friend, etc.) shared something which had been very hurtful to them. Even though you didn't cause it, they feel it necessary to tell you in the hope of getting some kind of comfort based on your relationship. Now imagine if your response demeaned and dismissed their issue. How would they feel? What would they think of your relationship? More than likely, they'd get the impression that they didn't matter much to you.

In some ways, that's what it feels like as an African American in this society. We hear it when a conservative commentator can't come up with a single alternative to a respectful, peaceful protest. We hear it in the phrase "all lives matter," which some use as a way to nicely tell us to just shut up. And we hear it from conservative evangelicals who make it clear that our concerns aren't "gospel" concerns. That is, they simply don't rise to the level of importance that the living God would be mindful of them even though he told us to cast all our cares on him since he cares for us.

But black lives do indeed matter. If the Christian community is to have a witness to this society that's genuine, relevant, noteworthy, and courageous, it must include active and vocal support for black lives matter. What do I mean by the phrase "black lives matter"? In short, I mean the lives and well-being of black people must be treated with dignity and respect by the people and institutions in this society. Further, the Christian church has a primary responsibility to demonstrate the value of black lives. Black lives matter means this society should press for the time when hundreds of African Americans feel no need to share the pain, anger, and frustration of ongoing racism because our society made it clear that we won't tolerate

---

1. Lahren, "Tomi Lahren Extended Interview."

racism. Moreover, God's church must lead this effort. We should do so because black lives matter to the living God.

By that, I mean the main factor that has been the cause of so much of our trauma and tribulation in America, namely our rich, deep brown skin matters to the living God. Our beautiful black bodies matter to God since he made us in his image. To be more precise, seeing a multitude of deep brown and black-skinned people populate the new heaven and new earth is the living God's expressed and desired will.[2]

Moreover, black lives matter to God in the sense that our history, heritage, culture, and present struggle matter to him. I make this assertion with confidence since, over and over again, the Scriptures declare God's love and concern for the poor, less powerful, marginalized, bruised, and broken-hearted. The living God's care for the lives of black folks flows from his deep concern for minorities.

> For the LORD your God is God of gods and Lord of lords, the great, the mighty, and the awesome God, who is not partial and takes no bribe. He executes justice for the fatherless and the widow, and loves the sojourner, giving him food and clothing. Love the sojourner, therefore, for you were sojourners in the land of Egypt.
>
> —DEUTERONOMY 10:17–19

Tying God's love for black people who live as minorities in this society removes the concept of his love from mere abstraction to concrete action. It says to those who claim to believe in the living God that black people must be loved and valued in the same way the loving God loves and values them. It means we can't whitewash the sentiment behind the phrase "black lives matter" by retorting "all lives matter."

Embracing God's value of black lives might be difficult for some if they persist in relying on ideological models to approach this entire issue. It can be difficult as ideological models tend to focus on American virtues such as strict fairness, individualism, achievement, and individual merit. Ideological approaches can have trouble grasping the truth of Deuteronomy 10 since God's special love for the immigrant could be misinterpreted as a lack of concern for others. When applied to African Americans, certain ideological approaches can recoil from the call to view us as minorities in the biblical sense with the belief that it's not fair to show any kind of special love toward us.

In this instance, we must replace ideological models with redemptive ones. A redemptive model recognizes the wisdom of Deuteronomy 10 with

---

2. Revelation 5–7.

the recognition that dominant groups will always work to ensure their overall well-being in the society they control. Additionally, history shows—especially black history in this society—that dominant groups will work to disadvantage minorities to gain and maintain their dominance and the benefits that flow from it. Deuteronomy 10 calls for God's people to live as a counter-balance to the usual way this country has treated minorities. In so doing, believers who also belong to the dominant group demonstrate their primary allegiance is to the living God and obedience to his word. One of the results of such an approach is a growing unity among believers from dominant and subdominant groups. In our setting, it could mean African American believers and white evangelicals begin to experience the beginnings of true unity, which in time might replace our long-standing divide.

Asserting black lives matter to the living God is also consistent with the character of his one, true, anointed king, the Lord Jesus Christ.

> Give the king your justice, O God, and your righteousness to the royal son! May he judge your people with righteousness, and your poor with justice! Let the mountains bear prosperity for the people, and the hills, in righteousness! May he defend the cause of the poor of the people, give deliverance to the children of the needy, and crush the oppressor!
>
> —Psalm 72:1–4

Our glorious king, the Lord Jesus Christ, knows our historical and present afflictions as black people living in America. Jesus knows exactly how we felt as penned by the Rev. Dr. Martin Luther King, Jr. in his "Letter from a Birmingham Jail": "When you are harried by day and haunted by night by the fact that you are a Negro, living constantly at tiptoe stance, never knowing what to expect next, and plagued with inner fears and outer resentments; when you are forever fighting a degenerating sense of 'nobodyness.'"[3]

To our King Jesus Christ, the cry "black lives matter" is the cry of the afflicted from which he does not ignore or turn away. Though other rulers focus on the rich, connected, insulated, and powerful, this king pays special attention to the afflicted, oppressed, poor, and marginalized. Black lives matter to our Lord Jesus Christ due to his burning thirst for justice. The significance of justice to the rule of the King Jesus Christ is not only stated in Psalm 72 but cast as an essential aspect of God's character.[4] Thus, from our perspective, justice for black people matters to the living God.

3. King Jr., "Letter from a Birmingham Jail."

4. Abundant examples are seen in Psalms 11:7; 33:5; 36:6; 45:7; 89:14; and Jeremiah 9:23–24.

Finally, black lives matter to the living God given the reality of his consistent call for proper action to accompany proper worship. In passage after passage, the living God made it clear that strictly following prescribed elements of worship was in no way a replacement for ignoring the cries, issues, and lives of the afflicted.[5] All of our theology, expository preaching, Bible studies, mission trips, conferences, resolutions, men's, women's, and youth groups count for little if we willfully neglect the call for justice, mercy, and compassion to the vulnerable, minority, and marginalized.

Embracing the reality that black lives matter to the living God puts us in a position to adjust the culture of many of our churches so we can effectively demonstrate God's love to those African Americans in our communities. I'll speak from the perspective of a pastor in a local church since that's my ministry context.

Local churches can highlight the value of black lives in at least three ways. I'll use the town hall meeting as an example of how local churches can respond to those African Americans within their communities to whom they wish to show God's loving concern. While this is a one-time example, I'm convinced it's applicable in most settings and regions that host a black presence. Perhaps the only difference between my context and yours is your community hasn't invited those black people within it to share their stories of racism.

A pastoral response to acknowledge their pain and express sorrow for what happened would serve as a good initial response to the black community. This response would serve notice that black lives matter in the eyes of the pastor and church. Pastors could have done this in one of two ways. First, during the worship service that followed the meeting (perhaps right before having a particular time of prayer for the black community), second by taking to social media to voice empathy, concern, and, of course, welcome to the black community. It would be particularly meaningful for pastors to welcome those in the black community by verbalizing that though some may not want them, they are most welcome in our churches.

Churches wishing to go further in this area can do so by making some adjustments in their regular worship services. Drawing from the rich, deep history of the black church will be of course be of great help in this area. One of the main ways the living God cared for and carried African Americans through our trauma in this land was through our expressive, passionate, and joy-filled Sunday morning worship. It's difficult to describe what God did (and continues to do) through this kind of worship. In so many ways, God

---

5. Abundant examples are seen for example in Isaiah 1; 58; Jeremiah 7; Amos 5; Micah 6; and Zechariah 7.

used our emotive worship to draw us close to him when he was all we had. Passionate, expressive, and joy-filled worship is critical to the psychological well-being of African Americans who get a consistent message from this society that we are not wanted, welcome, or valued. Churches that seek to incorporate a more open and expressive style of worship may find it challenging but not impossible. However, as you might expect it is much more than just singing a few black gospel songs.

It involves the wise and skillful leading of worship, which depends on the presence and power of the Spirit to lead God's people into expressing our heartfelt love for the living God who loves and values us as his own deeply and dearly loved people. One of the distinct aspects of African American worship is its emphasis on the near and active sovereignty of God. The entire worship service presents God as one who is close to his people and ready to help in our time of need. In our worship, it's not just the songs; it's how the songs, those who lead them, and those who respond communicate our gratitude that in God's eyes black lives matter.

Corporate prayer is the next aspect of worship churches can utilize to demonstrate their commitment to showing God's love to black lives. Prayer is not only an expression of our complete dependence on the living God but also strongly signals what or whose lives matter to us. During times of corporate prayer, churches can pray for those issues that affect the African American community. For instance, a church responding to the town hall meeting could have taken the time to consistently pray for God's healing for those who experienced racism as well as pray for the Lord to stop the evil of racism. Praying for those issues that affect African Americans is one of the most effective and tender ways to communicate that black lives matter not just to black people but to the living God.

Preaching is the last aspect of the worship service, where churches can voice their love for black people as a reflection of God's love for us. Preaching works along with prayer in the following way: Whereas in prayer, we voice what's important to us to the Lord, preaching voices to us what the living God considers essential as detailed in his word. And the doctrine of redemptive ethnic unity is one of the key and core aspects of our faith that flows through God's word. Redemptive ethnic unity is simply the visible unity God calls his people in Christ to experience and enjoy as a direct consequence of Christ's redemptive work. It's the kind of unity that should bind believers together to the extent when one part of the body of Christ mourns—such as those African Americans who expressed their grief at the town hall meeting—the whole body mourns. Preaching on the doctrine of redemptive ethnic unity would be a critical component in connecting our conviction that black lives matter to the living God to those black people who live in our community.

Moreover, it communicates God's concerns for the souls and bodies of black folk to the congregation and the wider community. It also sends a strong message that racism will not go unchallenged.

Turning again to the response to our town hall meeting, pastors who wished to welcome the African American community could have given a sermon series on the doctrine of redemptive ethnic unity. A series like this could lead to incorporating the doctrine of redemptive ethnic unity into the regular teaching and discipleship life of the church.

Advocating for issues affecting the black community is another way churches can demonstrate God's commitment to black lives. For example, in response to the town hall meeting, a church could have set up a regular meeting schedule with the African American community and city officials to gauge progress on the issues raised at the meeting.

Will this approach solve all the concerns over racism in our communities? Of course it won't, but we don't engage in redemptive activity because it will completely solve our pressing problems. We do so to follow God's express will, character, and command to love our neighbor as ourselves. Thus, when considering these things, there are at least two crucial questions to ask: How has God called the church to love black people in light of this country's historical and present treatment of them? What's the cost to our witness if we don't?

Following the initial series of town hall meetings, the city set up a community advisory board to work with the police department in hopes of addressing some of the concerns about the police voiced at the meeting. As far as I can recall there wasn't a single response from a Christian church. I don't remember hearing of any church or pastor expressing sorrow and offering any kind of comfort to the city's black community. There was no offer to have a special time of prayer, speak out against the sin of racism, or welcome persons from the African American community into Christian churches.

For all the protestations that "all lives matter" it appears increasingly evident that at least among some, if not many, within the Christian community all lives do not include black lives. Prayerfully, this won't remain the case. Prayerfully, those who so confidently claim to love the living God will begin to express that love toward those he loves. Prayerfully, we'll see a day when those who claim to have faith in Christ see the value of genuinely loving black people. Perhaps in that day, our society will sit up and take notice to a gospel witness that finally begins to matter.

Chapter 9   **Redeemed and Healed for Mission**

—*Anthony B. Bradley*

C ornel West opens chapter 12 on "Wisdom" in the book, *Hope on a Tight Rope*, with this sobering reality, "If you live long enough, a moment of spiritual death is inevitable. The question is: How will you deal with it?"[1] If there is a consensus among Poussaint and the authors of this book, it is this: people in trouble should actively seek help.[2] Because the themes of sin, brokenness, and redemption run through each of our lives, we stand poised to receive desperately needed help. In the black community, however, many are reluctant or unable to obtain the necessary help to heal their weary and wounded souls. For reasons that run the gamut from financial constraints to prideful avoidance, people who need help the most often do not receive it. This lack of help perpetuates a vicious cycle: generation after generation of dysfunctional, broken people. God loves these people; he wants to heal them, to deliver them from despair, and to set them free to be the people he created them to be. God made the world and everything in it. He loves his creation, his people. He wants to redeem them from sin and profoundly change their lives for the better.

Without getting much needed help, the downward spiral of dysfunctional, self-defeating behavior results in curbing black social and economic progress. On December 28, 2008, Rev. E. Dewey Smith, pastor of House of Hope Atlanta in Decatur, Georgia, delivered a powerful sermon from Mark 5. He encouraged God's people to be honest about the inner issues that inhibit them from fully experiencing all the good things that God wants for his people. The unclean spirits—verse 2—plaguing lives in the black community can be purged only if people are willing to be honest about them, submit to God's liberation, and follow God's call for a healed and redeemed people to ally with him in bringing this world into harmony with his will.

1. West, *Hope on a Tight Rope*, 197.
2. Cosby and Poussaint, *Come on People*.

This chapter illustrates God's program for dealing with the complex issues raised by Poussaint using the context of Isaiah 61. God's way of healing is holistic and not an end to itself. Confessing to unclean spirits, opening up to God's healing, and submitting to a new life calling are fundamental steps in accepting God's gift of grace and redemption for his creation.

The passage, Isaiah 61:1–4:

> The Spirit of the LORD God is upon me,
>
> because the LORD has anointed me
>
> to bring good news to the poor;
>
> he has sent me to bind up the brokenhearted,
>
> to proclaim liberty to the captives,
>
> and the opening of the prison to those who are bound;
>
> to proclaim the year of the LORD's favor,
>
> and the day of vengeance of our God;
>
> to comfort all who mourn;
>
> to grant to those who mourn in Zion—
>
> to give them a beautiful headdress instead of ashes,
>
> the oil of gladness instead of mourning,
>
> the garment of praise instead of a faint spirit;
>
> that they may be called oaks of righteousness,
>
> the planting of the LORD, that he may be glorified.
>
> They shall build up the ancient ruins;
>
> they shall raise up the former devastations;
>
> they shall repair the ruined cities,
>
> the devastations of many generations.

Let's Get Real

The prophet Isaiah speaks plainly when addressing Israel about the reality of their situation. Isaiah addresses a people who were enslaved, abused, rejected, ridiculed, segregated, and deeply broken. The words "poor," "brokenhearted," "captives," "bound," "mourn," "ashes," "fainted hearted," and so on, all convey the reality that every life has been devastated and affected by the fall. It is impossible for anyone to live without experiencing struggles, sin, pain, and "spiritual death." Everyone suffers because we live in a world ruled by the "Prince of the Air." The world exists not as it should be. We were born into a world at war. The enemy, the devil, is real and has wreaked havoc on people's lives for centuries. To deny, minimize, or ignore the devil's existence leads to self-deception and the acceptance of sinful, self-destructive behavior. The horrible pathologies mentioned in the Poussaint book reveal the effects of the fall: the black male crisis, out-of-wedlock births, the breakdown of the family and community, bad parenting, substandard education, media consumption without discernment, poor health choices, violence, and poverty. At their roots, these are all moral issues, improved only by the actions of a group radicalized for change by beginning the journey of healing.

Illustration I—Wounded Black Men

Many black men suffer from the dual-edged sword of being over-mothered and under-fathered. God fashioned a child's heart to be radically shaped by the efforts of both parents. Because this is true, unbalanced parenting also contributes to a child's dysfunction. Growing up fatherless may negatively affect developing black males in numerous ways, as Poussaint describes in his book. Fatherless boys never learn about fathering and sadly misunderstand the nature of the vocation. Bell hooks says, "When all black males learn that fatherhood is less about biological creation than about the capacity to nurture the spiritual and emotional growth of a child's life, then they will teach that lesson to the males who come after them."[3] With the absence of many fathers, the lion's share of spiritual and emotional nurturing falls heavily on the shoulders of mothers and grandmothers. As a result, today most black American males grow up in a matriarchy.

In the absence of consistent fathering, most black males are raised in a world dominated by women. Boys socialized by "mama" and "grandmama" through their teen years and early adulthood are often unwittingly emasculated. Black sons often become surrogate emotional husbands or surrogate scapegoats for women who are not being loved well by a strong man. Single mothers then use their sons to meet their emotional needs or as objects of their angry frustration. Bell hooks describes the psychological scars of over-mothering, which requires black males to surrender their childhoods to satisfy their mothers' unmet emotional needs, this way:

> Dysfunctional single mothers and abused married women who have intense rage toward men who have abandoned them often use male children to meet their emotional needs; this is emotional sexual abuse. In some cases, the mother may be lavishing affection on her son while also being verbally abusive about adult black males. She may say, "all men are dogs," that

3. hooks, *We Real Cool*, 114.

they are no "good," or that their penises should be "cut off." This teaches the boy fear and mistrust of adult men. It makes him fear becoming an adult man and as a consequence he may try to emotionally remain a boy forever.[4]

Hooks highlights the long-term and cyclical consequences of people not getting the help they require. The brokenness of emotionally unhealthy mothers negatively affects their sons. Even worse, over-mothering can also turn sons into future misogynists. Boys raised in a matriarchy often grow to resent the constant control of women. At some point in a boy's journey to manhood, he must break free from the world of women and enter into the world of men. When this occurs, some young men may seek to reassert their masculine identity by taking out their over-mothering on female peers. This may explain, in part, why some of the worst misogynistic hip-hop music comes out of matriarchal contexts. Many young men retaliate from over-mothering by reasserting dominance over female peers sexually or through physical violence.

Illustration II—Wounded Black Women

The effects of the fall and the fact of brokenness make life hard for women as well. The absence of good fathers profoundly affects the way in which black women understand their feminine identity. As mentioned earlier, fathers and mothers play a significant role in the formation of their children. If one of these parental influences is missing, greater opportunity for dysfunction exists. Many black women suffer years of sexual violence at the hands of evil fathers, brothers, cousins, uncles, mother's boyfriends, neighbors, strangers, and so on. Many black women shoulder the responsibility of being both father and mother to their children. Black women currently sustain the black church. Many divorced and single moms feel pressured to provide income for themselves and their children with little to no help from the fathers. The many, many demands made on black women create overwhelming stress at times.

When women grow up without fathers, it often creates deep questions about their level of desirability. One of the powerful gifts that fathers give to their daughters is the confidence to know that they are beautiful image bearers of God; they are worthy of spending time with, listening to, and investing in. Women also want to know: does my father delight in me? When that question remains unanswered because of passive or absent fathers or

4. hooks, *We Real Cool*, 124.

answered "no" by violent and abusive fathers, young girls often trade their own dignity by substituting unhealthy relationships with male peers. It is no coincidence that the most sexually active girls are those from homes with absent or abusive fathers. Longing for affirmation, girls attempt to answer the question by giving their bodies to males who do not love them and have not committed their lives to them publicly. Alternatively, many black women self-medicate the effects of abuse or loneliness by overeating. Obesity among black women sometimes signals a woman in distress.

The domino effect of brokenness cannot be overstated: broken men vent their brokenness on women and children; broken women vent their brokenness on men and children. Generations of unhealed sin and brokenness result in generations of dysfunctional people: the cycle has destroyed families and communities for years. Brokenness gives birth to more brokenness, and the cycles of dysfunction continue for future generations. Hurting people hurt others.

The Journey of Healing

The good news is that God provides hope for wounded, broken men and women. Isaiah provides hope for God's people by reminding them that God wants to "bind up," "proclaim liberty," open the prison, proclaim favor, comfort all those who mourn and suffer, and clothe them with "new garments." A new identity. A new name. New hope and invitation to enter into healing. God calls his wounded and broken people toward restoration and healing. God has always wanted his people to be free from lives defined by the reality of their sin and brokenness. Healing wounds and restoring humanity are conditions for becoming the kind of people God created before the effects of the fall.

This explains why the good news is so good. This may explain, in part, why Jesus used this passage as he inaugurated his public ministry.[5] Moving toward what God desires for human life and social restoration involves a necessary process of restoration and healing. The redemption achieved by Jesus Christ is holistic in the sense that it restores the whole creation—especially, broken people. Like those in the time of Isaiah, we regularly look for ways to heal our sin, pain, and brokenness artificially. Long-standing coping methods, using artificial and temporary ways of healing and restoration, do not work. They do not deliver because they cannot fill the deep spiritual void that only the triune God can fill.

5. Luke 4.

High school and college boys who habitually smoke pot, for example, often have poor relationships with their fathers. There is a phrase in counseling known as "acting out." "Acting out" involves self-destructive, self-sabotaging behavior in response to negative or harmful experiences. What many fail to see in the social pathologies that plague many black communities is that self-destructive behavior or activities are not always rebellious, or defiant, but may be simply ways of coping with real pain by acting out, by self-medicating.

Young women act out in response to broken relationships with their fathers by seeking multiple sexual partners. Boys acting out because of fatherlessness respond with violence or try to sooth their real pain with drugs and alcohol. Many adult women self-medicate their pain by overeating. Many young women lacking consistent love will have a child to have someone who finally loves them unconditionally. Men sexually manipulate women to retaliate against matriarchal dominance. Many men try to escape from hopelessness by losing themselves in hours and hours of video games. These are all ways to self-medicate pain. These methods inevitably do not work. These temporary Band-Aids do not heal the pain, and, until people realize this, men and women will never enter the way of freedom and wholeness.

While Poussaint makes valid points regarding social pathologies, a way to overcome and sustain emotional, psychological, and spiritual health is still necessary. The healing to revolutionize the black community to change must come from transformed hearts and minds.

What Doesn't Work

When confronted with the reality of a fallen, imperfect world, people often seek quick fixes. If they just do "this" or "that" and plug into some magic formula, everything will be ok, and life will make sense again. Paul Tripp and Tim Lane write about some of the traps people fall into as they wrestle with the harshness of reality:

> In the book *How People Change*, Timothy Lane and Paul Tripp summarize the false ways people seek change, methods incapable of delivering the internal heart-oriented change really needed. Paraphrased, Lane and Tripp offer this wisdom:
>
> Formalism: The formalist is the one who changes by being a more dutiful Christian. "If I only get more involved in church life, that would grow my faith and make things right again." This person attends church multiple times a week. For them the gospel boils down to participating in the meetings and ministries

of the church. Legalism: The legalist's life centers on a list of do's and don'ts. A legalist's children suffer under the tyranny of performance-oriented conditional love. Being "good" is the goal of the legalist. Mysticism: The mystic becomes a Christian conference junkie longing for the emotional high of an experience in getting closer to God. Following Christ becomes more about emotional experiences than transforming into a different kind of person. The emotional quick fix does not last. Activism: The activist tries to become closer to God and make sense of life by protesting against "liberals" and other non-conservatives. This person falsely believes that religious consistency equals conservative politics and confuses fighting the culture war with healthy spirituality. Biblicism: The Biblicist, or armchair theologian, fills the gap by learning more information about theology and the Bible. Quick to quote dead theologians and to make a sport of arguing theological minutia, the Biblicist believes that the gospel equals a mastery of biblical content and theology. Psychology-ism: These are people who surround themselves with others willing to comfort and pity them for their messed-up lives. The idea is this: "I'll get better if the right people support me and listen to my problems." The church means nothing more than a place to heal brokenness. The right support network will change everything. The gospel simply means healing brokenness. Social-ism: For some people, the gospel simply reduces to a network of fulfilling social relationships. These people may belong to two or three different small groups or constantly need to be with other Christians. As Lane and Tripp explain, a person like this makes fellowship, acceptance, respect, and position in the body of Christ a replacement for communion with Christ.[6]

What is most compelling about this list is that these things can both be right and wrong. Political activism, biblical knowledge, having good friends, etc., do not address the deep needs that only the work of the Holy Spirit can address: to form and shape us according to the reality of the implications of Jesus' death and resurrection. These temporary balms may seem to fill the void, but they can never deliver what they promise. What really creates change is radical reorientation around the truth of redemption.

6. Bradley, "Time for Change?"

What Works

In the book *Broken Down House*, Paul Tripp broadly explains moving forward on the journey toward being a liberated people, free to be fully human through a union with Christ.[7] First, remember that the fallen world wallows in sinful chaos. It is a mess. Television newscasts air stories about war, famine, disasters, unemployment, the disintegration of families, and personal tragedies—all proof of a fallen creation. The Bible's story reminds believers of the fall, that the devil successfully tempted Adam and Eve, resulting in an imperfect, sinful world. The good news? This is not the end of the story. God did not abandon his world to chaos. The solution? God plans to redeem and restore all things to their intended purpose so that all spheres of life reflect his goodness, his grace, and his love.[8] His restored creation will be one in which his people flourish. The flawed, fallen world today offers a distorted, dark view of life; it is all too easy to forget that this world is not the world that is to come—what God intends for his people. Paul Tripp calls this "location amnesia."[9] "Context is your friend," as one professor used to say.

The Bible, however, is honest about the world in its fallen state. As Tripp comments, "The history of your Bible drips with the blood of violence, smells of the stench of human greed, betrayal, and perversion. It is stained with instance after instance of people on the one hand forgetting God, while on the other hand doing their best to take his place. Apart from Christ, none of the people in these stories are moral heroes who always get it right."[10] They did not get it right then, and no one gets it right today. Everyone is in the same boat.

Second, understand what humanity means. It is primarily important to remember that God created human beings in his likeness and image.[11] God gave each human being an identity, a meaning, and a purpose. This view gives each life dignity and worth. God made human beings significantly different from animals, and therefore God gave humans responsible dominion over the lower creatures. Human beings must wisely use everything in God's creation for the glory of God to benefit the world, the community, and the family. Man and woman are part of creation and thus directly involved in its continuous existence, development, and beautification.

7. Tripp, *Broken Down House*, 23–86.

8. 1 Corinthians 1; Romans 8.

9. Tripp, *Broken Down House*, 25.

10. Tripp, *Broken Down House*, 29.

11. Genesis 1:26–28.

Nona Harrison neatly summarizes a Christian's worldview that includes freedom and responsibility; spiritual perception and relationship with God and neighbor; excellence of character and holiness; royal dignity; priesthood in the created world; and creativity, rationality, the arts, and culture as elements of what it means to be made in God's image.[12] As such, human beings may freely make decisions in cooperation and in harmony with God. God created humankind to be in union and community with the holy trinity, the Father, Son, and Holy Spirit. Spiritually, God created humankind for the lifelong process of transformation in order to know and love God and neighbor. This transformation rightly orders our passions, impulses, and reason to excel in moral character to be freely obedient to the will of God. As bearers of God's image, all men and women are endowed with royal dignity. They must use their royal status to rule over and simultaneously develop creation.[13] Human beings have a priestly function in the created world. Christ calls them to cosmic priesthood; this task entails offering the world to God and bestowing God's blessings on the world.[14] Finally, the divine image includes practical reason, which enables all women and men to develop creativity, the arts and sciences, economics, politics, business, and culture.

Third, every man and woman is a sinner. The broken state of the world creates the pain human beings experience because of the sinful actions of others, as well as the broken and sinful responses to these actions. Sin and pain beget more sin and pain; sadly, the cycle repeats itself in every human community, in neighborhoods, and in families. Sin begets sin, but that does not excuse Christians from living responsibly, not in ways contrary to being image bearers of God. God calls Christians to something greater. Again, Tripp reminds us, that "the biblical doctrine of sin confronts each of us with the reality that we are not as good as we imagine we are, and therefore more needy and vulnerable than we typically consider ourselves to be."[15]

Fourth, Christians must know to whom they belong. As followers of Christ, their union with Christ means so much more than they may realize. God's grace works powerfully in each life to show the desperate need for Jesus, his healing, and his restoration. Understanding that God provides a plan for every Christian offers new hope and potential for amazing change and growth. Forgiveness, deliverance, and enablement play key roles in this spiritual transformation.

---

12. Harrison, "The Human Person," 78–90.

13. Van Groningen, *From Creation to Consummation*, 64–65.

14. Harrison, "The Human Person," 86.

15. Tripp, *Broken Down House*, 35.

The grace of forgiveness means forgiving those who inflicted the wounds of abuse, neglect, omission, and absence. Some wounds result from misdirected good intentions that missed the mark. Returning evil for evil out of defensiveness, self-preservation, and/or revenge, however, accomplishes nothing but the creation of more sin and pain. Forgiveness is the beginning of liberation from the prison of living in pain. Forgiving is one of the hardest actions a Christian will ever take. True forgiveness does not mean forgetting or ignoring a sin against oneself; rather, the Christian no longer holds the wrong against the sinner in ways that block his ability to love the sinner. In this way, a believer lives the gospel and treats others in the very same way God treats his people. The true believer walks the walk instead of just talking the talk.

The grace of deliverance is the recognition that God "got you through" and intends on bringing you into the blessed joys of uniting with the Trinity. Paul Tripp says that you are "loved by a dissatisfied redeemer."[16] Jesus is determined to protect each believer from the enemy and transform believers into his image. Through the direct work of the Holy Spirit, God wages war against sin, the flesh, and the devil on the Christian's behalf. Much work must be done in order for the Christian to join God and be with him in glory.

The grace of enablement means that God works his Spirit in every life to empower his followers to become free and live free. God and God alone is the only source of power that can unite believers to his son, deliver them from the power of the evil one, and set them free to be the people he created them to be in Christ. God enables his people to think, act, feel, emote, and live in new and radical ways. The enabling work of the Spirit that "got you over" in the first place is the same grace that actively works to sustain his healing and redemptive work in each life.

Healed for Mission

Verse four of Isaiah 61 depicts the thrilling vision of a broken and weary people pressed by God to be honest about their sin and devastation. Isaiah prophesies the time when God will transform the downtrodden; God will "build up," "raise up", and "repair" his people. These active verbs illustrate how God's liberating act of personal redemption changes individuals and consequently communities. Salvation spills over and affects the world. God uses his people to bless the nations and to serve as redemptive agents. The context of this purpose, identity, and mission are the ruined and devastated spaces in

16. Tripp, *Broken Down House*, 46.

which God's people find themselves joyfully living. Christ presses his claims and the priorities of the kingdom upon these places.

Living in harmony with God as he changes and conforms his believers from the inside out lends a new perspective on family and community. As Poussaint points out, the devastated places in the black community include: the black male crisis, the social pathologies of low-income neighborhoods, the education and moral crisis among black children, media that promotes health-care problems related to bad habits, drug abuse, violence, the criminal justice system, and the lack of economic freedom due to opportunity voids and poor financial management.[17]

Union with Christ means relying on his power and his power alone to live in harmony with God's mission for restoration and reconciliations, to do all things for the glory of God and the flourishing of his creation. However, before beginning the journey of healing, it is important to understand why biblical writers do not limit salvation to the realm of personal issues and problems. God helps his people that they may help others. God uses the redeemed to redeem others. Christians make Christ known to the world by the way they live in their own houses and communities. Understanding then is knowing what God's mission is about, what it means to be in the kingdom, and how the grace given to God's people through the work of the Father, Son, and Holy Spirit empowers Christians to be a blessing to their families and neighbors.

An intimate relationship with God the Father, Son, and Holy Spirit demands that Christians orient themselves to certain facts.[18] First, Christians worship a God with a mission. The God revealed in the Scriptures is personal, purposeful, and goal oriented. He created everything for a reason. God's perfect creation then fell because of original sin, the temptation of Adam and Eve. The Bible's narrative tells the story of God's redemptive purposes unfolding throughout human history, culminating with the eschatological hope of a new creation. Second, if God the creator has a mission and he created human beings in his image, by definition, humankind has a divine calling, a mandate to be fruitful and multiply, to rule, subdue, and cultivate creation. To be human is to have a purposeful role in God's creation. Third, God's people have a specific redemption mission in the history of God redeeming all things. Since Genesis 12, God entrusted his people with the mission to be a blessing to the nations for his sake. God charges his people to move into society's devastated, ruined, and broken spaces for the sake of being blessings in ways that only God will make

17. Cosby and Poussaint, *Come on People*, 1–29.

18. Wright, *The Mission of God*, 61–67.

clear. The mission of God's people to "go" make disciples, to "go" be witnesses means that God's people are to be committed to participate in God's redemption of the whole creation. Finally, Jesus the reigning descendant of Jesse and King David has a mission. The birth, death, and resurrection of Christ fulfills God's promise to his people. The mission of the Davidic heir is both to rule over God's redeemed people and to receive the nations at the ends of the earth as his heritage.[19]

Focusing on the "now what" in the black community touches upon just one aspect of God's redemptive purpose. Being a Christian means that one examines his own holiness in response to God's grace in his personal life, but the Christian also looks at his community in light of:

1. God's purpose for his creation, including the redemption of humanity and the creation of the new heavens and new earth.

2. God's purpose for human life in general and of all that the Bible teaches about human culture, relationships, ethics, and behavior.

3. God's historical election of his people, their identity and role in relationship to the nations, and the demands he made about their worship, social ethics, and total value system.

4. The centrality of Jesus of Nazareth, his messianic identity and mission in relationship to Israel and the nations, his cross and resurrection.

5. God's calling of the church, the community of believing Jews and Gentiles who constitute the extended people of the Abrahamic covenant, to be the agent of God's blessing to the nations in the name of the glory of the Lord Jesus Christ.[20]

The Need for a Kingdom Perspective

Jesus invites us to repent because the kingdom is at hand. He invites Christians to look in the mirror, look at their families, neighborhoods, nations, and the world, and recognize that they live for a greater purpose. In order to heal the black community from the pathologies discussed earlier, to understand and apply a contemporary application of Isaiah's teachings requires that Christians work together for the mission of the kingdom.

Jesus emphasizes the kingdom of God in his teachings and, by extension, so do the apostles. Theological liberalism has emphasized the

19. Psalm 2:8.

20. Wright, *The Mission of God*, 67–68.

kingdom while leaving behind Jesus' mission and call to obedience and discipleship. Many evangelicals, while having great passion for the church and mission, often forsake the forest for the trees. They lose the full impact of the gospel on their local culture. A mission-centered worldview orients all of one's life toward the kingdom and ignites Jesus' followers into radical living here and now.[21]

The kingdom implies more than the salvation of individuals, or the reign of God in people's hearts. It means nothing less than the reign of God over his entire created universe. Colossians 1:9–23 reminds us that Jesus as Lord rescues people from darkness, brings them into the kingdom (verse 13), confirms his Lordship over all creation (verse 15–17), establishes his role as sole head of the church (verse 18), announces his work to reconcile all things in heaven and earth (verse 20), and pronounces victory for his people in the great battle between the kingdom of darkness and the kingdom of God's son (verses 21–23, first announced in Genesis 3:15).

The biblical story describes signs of Christ's Kingdom: the casting out of demons (Matthew 12:28), the fall of Satan (Luke 10:18), the performance of miracles (Matthew 11:4–5), the preaching of the gospel (Luke 10:20; Matthew 5:11), and the forgiveness of sins directly by God in the flesh (Isaiah 33:24; Mark 2:10).

Embracing a kingdom-oriented worldview is also a call to a Spirit-filled mission, orienting all of one's life toward Jesus the King and the Father's purposes for the world. God's people, sent out from the church, bring the kingdom of Jesus to all areas of life mired in sin and brokenness. Jesus' followers act as agents of redemption and restoration for the world.[22] They show the world what it means to live a life reflecting the glory of God in all things: repentance and faith, arts and media, business, education, social life, marriage and family, social justice, caring for the environment, and so on. When confronted with the kingdom responsibilities of being real, healed, and liberated to be what God destined one to be in Christ, it will drive Christians to seek God the Father, the Son, and Holy Spirit.

Conclusion: The Need for Empowering Grace

The same grace that saves and heals us in the name of the Father, the Son, and the Holy Spirit is the same power needed to live kingdom lives in harmony with God's mission. We never stop needing the Holy Spirit. When confronted with the reality of sin and brokenness and a Christian's role in

21. Matthew 6:33.
22. Isaiah 61:1–4.

God's plan to restore creation, Isaiah notes that a Christian's level of spirituality must increase for the following reasons:

1. Christians need a more realistic assessment of who they are in relation to God's mission so that they understand their need of him.

2. Not surprisingly, they will wish they had more power to change things for the good. Having a kingdom perspective reminds them that they seek God's will on earth, as it is in heaven.

3. The craziness of life will tempt Christians to believe that God is not in control of all things.

4. Christians fear other people instead of waiting for God. Christians live in fear instead of trusting in God's sovereign care.

5. A kingdom worldview helps one to trust God's wisdom and love without question even in the most horrible of times. God is working out his plan in his time. God tests and disciplines those he loves in order to build faith and make his people stronger. Just as a loving father disciplines his children, so God disciplines his people.

6. Trusting God means that one may not understand all that he is doing in the world. Following Jesus requires blind faith at times, without much clarity or explanation. This is Job's story.

7. Christians look at other people with greater blessings, and seemingly easier lives and feel envious; they misunderstand that God acts in each individual's life according to his plan for the kingdom. God's providence works in mysterious ways; the Christian must learn to put his faith in the Lord and not in himself or in other people.

As mentioned earlier, a kingdom-oriented vision for healing means that one cannot be passive.[23] If Christians are to be rebuilders of broken places, they cannot idly sit back and let their families or neighborhoods fall into ruins. The Lord desires that Christians become agents of change. Through the power of the Holy Spirit, Christians can become blessings in their families, communities, and the world. God uses his people to make the world the kind of place that functions in harmony with him. This sums up the reason for healing and deliverance: to do the good works that God predestined for each of his people in order for them to live for the kingdom and carry out God's plan to redeem the world.

In the end, the type of help, healing, and mission Isaiah describes explains the importance of the household of faith. It is God's people in

---

23. Tripp, *Broken Down House*, 137.

their mutual union in Christ, working out the mission and calling of the church, that God has chosen to bring about great things for the world. The black community needs to recover a sense of the church's mission to follow Christ in bringing about the redemption of the whole world—people, places, and things. Getting real, getting healed, and being set free is what the church is uniquely equipped to accomplish. Community is vitally important to safely having a context for being honest before God and others about your sin and brokenness, for rightly understanding your purpose in living (encourage each other daily), and living as people of blessing to those around you all for the mission and glory of God. The key to healing and liberating the black community is in the need for revival.

Chapter 10 **The Role of the Church in Impacting Mass Incarceration and Mental Illness in the African American Community**

—*Natalie D. Haslem*

I n May of 2016, not long after being released from a psychiatric hospital, Colby Crawford, a twenty-three-year-old black man, was booked into the Orleans Justice Center. This new $250 million dollar jail had recently replaced the deteriorating structure called the Orleans Parish Prison complex. Ten months later Crawford died. He was diagnosed with multiple mental illnesses, told jail staff he was "hearing voices and seeing spirits," and was moved from a psych ward to the jail's general population as a punishment for minor infractions, a lawsuit claims. Five months after the transfer, the suit says, deputies found Crawford dead in his cell after overdosing on cocaine that another inmate in the general population housing unit smuggled into the jail.[1]

Critics say jail is no place to treat mental illness. The now-defunct Charity Hospital used to be the largest inpatient psychiatric care center in New Orleans. When it closed, jails and prisons became the facilities where inmates with mental illness were housed. The justice system is often faced with the challenge of responding to youth and adults who suffer from mental health problems. This system is failing our youths and adults. However, the black church is responding to the epidemic. The black church is responding by mentoring, tutoring, and supporting at-risk youth and adults, going into prisons and conducting Bible studies, prayer meetings, providing one-on-one support, advocating for victims, educating church leaders about mental illness, seeking opportunities to collaborate and work with community mental health providers, provide depression education and treatment at their facilities, and offering mental health first aid training.

---

1. Chrastil, "Mental Illness Behind Bars."

Background

Mental health issues and illnesses are three times higher among prisoners than the general population. Approximately 18 percent of all US adults experienced a mental health problem in 2014.[2] Among correctional populations, the most recent data estimates the incarcerated are nearly three times as likely to have a mental health problem as the general population. Prisoners with mental health problems are more likely to be repeat offenders and have committed their crimes while under the influence of alcohol or other illicit drugs in comparison to prisoners without any mental health problems.[3]

African Americans represent the largest incarcerated racial group. African Americans make up 35 percent of the prison population, despite comprising only 13 percent of the general population.[4] Research demonstrated that African American males serve longer sentences for similar offenses committed by white males, especially in cases involving drugs.[5] Racial disparities such as these continue after release and create critical barriers to reentry for African American men including disenfranchisement, difficulty in earning and maintaining employment, and health.[6]

Higher rates of mental health problems among the incarcerated population may be due to the use of correctional facilities as a perceived alternative for mental health facilities. This phenomenon was a result of deinstitutionalization or the reduction of state hospital beds, community-based mental health services, lack of access to services to address mental health problems, nonviolent offenses committed by persons with mental health problems, and a reduction in the interest to maintain mental health programs and funding.[7] Originally, "deinstitutionalization" consisted of: (1) the establishment of specialized community treatment services for persons with mental illnesses; (2) the movement of psychiatric hospital patients out of state hospitals into community treatment facilities and services; (3) the diversion of individuals who would have hospitalized to alternative community facilities. In theory, this plan would solve the overwhelming costs of institutionalization. The plan would also allow mental health patients to reintegrate into their communities while decreasing health care costs for committing mentally ill patients. The problem arose when a month after the

2. Substance Abuse and Mental Health Services Administration, "Results from the 2015 National Survey."

3. Baillargeon et al., "Psychiatric Disorders and Repeat Incarcerations."

4. U.S. Census Bureau, "2011–2015 American Community Survey."

5. Mitchell, "A Meta-Analysis."

6. Smith and Hattery, "African American Men."

7. Lamb and Weinberger, "Understanding and Treating Offenders."

act was signed into law, President Kennedy was assassinated, and the Vietnam War needed financing. Without pressure from the executive branch, the placement of community mental health care facilities met resistance in local neighborhoods. As such, plans for the establishment of half-way houses, community residences, outpatient clinics, and other alternatives went largely unfunded. Although these facilities are present today, they are under-funded. Despite mixed efforts to implement the first phase of the deinstitutionalization process, the second phase was implemented. Thousands of patients were released from hospitals. By 1980, fewer than 100,000 patients out of the 559,000 living in state hospitals in 1955 were housed in state hospitals. Many became homeless, were arrested and incarcerated, or died.[8] The deinstitutionalization of the mentally ill caused thousands to be uncared for and thrust them into the streets of America to fend for themselves despite having serious mental health conditions.

Not only were persons suffering from serious mental illness left to care for themselves, but those suffering from mental illness turned to drugs to self-medicate and that ultimately led to incarceration. It is well-known that many people with serious mental illnesses also abuse substances. It happens so regularly that the pairing has come to be called "co-occurring disorders."[9] Those suffering from mental illness and substance abuse are at risk for incarceration. Risk factors for incarceration include prior incarceration, younger age, male gender, racial-ethnic minority groups associated with African Americans and Hispanics, and modifiable risk factors such as co-occurring substance use disorders, lack of Medicaid insurance, untreated schizophrenia, and being homeless.[10] The black community is plagued with poverty, ill heath, violence, and decreased quality of life as incarceration contributes to each.

There has been an unprecedented increase in incarceration among African American males since 1970. In 2009, the incarceration rate among black males was 6.7 times that of white males and 2.6 times that of Hispanic males. Although African Americans represent only 13 percent of the US population, they comprise 35 percent of the jail population. Statistics show that inmate populations for African Americans in federal prisons increased more than 500 percent between 1986 and 2004.[11] Approximately 80 percent of incarcerated adults in the US have a history of involvement with alcohol or illicit drugs. A high prevalence of substance abuse among

8. Gilligan, "The Last Mental Hospital."
9. Slate et al., *The Criminalization of Mental Illness.*
10. Mukku et al., "Overview of Substance Use Disorders."
11. Mauer, "Race, Class, and the Development of Criminal Justice Policy."

the homeless population puts them at a higher risk for committing crimes through arrests for possession of drugs, selling drugs, and public intoxication.[12] Moreover, individuals with co-occurring substance use disorders and mental disorders have a five times greater risk for incarceration in comparison to those without mental illness. In 1983, twelve adults entered prison for a drug offense for every 100,000 adults in the population.[13] However, from 1980 to 2002, the number of persons in state prisons for substance offenses increased from 19,000 to 265,000.[14] This surge of incarceration for drug offenses directly corresponds to the War on Drugs announced by President Ronald Reagan in October 1982.

Defining Serious Mental Illness

Serious mental illness is defined as mental disorders that fall within the categories of schizophrenia, schizoaffective disorder, bipolar disorder, and major depression with psychotic features. Schizophrenia is a severe disorder of thought and perception accompanied by a disturbance in mood and behavior. Schizophrenia is characterized by psychosis or a loss of touch with reality. According to the Diagnostic and Statistical Manual, Fifth Edition (DSM-5), to receive the diagnosis of schizophrenia the patient must present with hallucinations, delusions, or disorganized behavior along with a cluster of negative symptoms or cognitive disorganization. Schizoaffective disorder according to the DSM-5 includes symptoms of schizophrenia and symptoms of bipolar disorder or major depressive disorder. Bipolar disorder is a mood disorder characterized by extreme highs or mania and bouts of depression in emotion over time. Major depression is another mood disorder characterized by extended extreme lows in emotions experienced with episodes of psychosis. Psychosis includes features of hallucinations and delusions.

Prevalence of Mental Illness in African American Inmates

Higher rates of mental health problems among the incarcerated population may be due to the use of correctional facilities as an alternative to treatment in a mental health facility. The high rates of mental health illnesses among

12. Greenberg and Rosenheck, "Jail Incarceration."
13. Iguchi et al., "How Criminal System Racial Disparities."
14. Mukku et al., "Overview of Substance Use Disorders."

youth in the juvenile justice system, compared to the general public, suggest detention facilities and correctional centers for youth are serving as alternative mental health hospitals. More than 20 million Americans are currently or have been incarcerated in the United States. In the US in 2013, there were almost 2.3 million people incarcerated in prisons and jails—one in every 110 adults.[15] The mentally ill are incarcerated two to four times more than the general public in correctional facilities. As a result, there are now ten times more individuals with Serious Mental Illnesses (SMI) in prisons and jails than are in state mental hospitals.[16] Persons with mental illness are disproportionately represented in the criminal justice system. Persons with mental illness have been found to be almost twice as likely as individuals without any known mental illness to be arrested for their behavior in similar situations. Whereas African Americans comprise approximately 13 percent of the total US population, they comprise an estimated 35 percent of incarcerated individuals.[17] In comparison 75 percent of the US population is white, but whites comprise an estimated 40 percent of those incarcerated.[18] African American men are at higher risk of being incarcerated in state or federal prisons at some point in their lifetime, 32 percent, versus 17 percent of Hispanic males and 5.9 percent of white males.[19] The disproportionate incarceration of individuals with SMIs, defined as a diagnosis of schizophrenia and other psychotic disorders, bipolar disorders, major depressive disorders, and dissociative disorders, represents a strain on corrections agencies in the United States. The rate of SMIs in the prison population has remained consistently higher than the general population as mass incarcerations grew over the past four decades.[20] Individuals with SMI comprise approximately 11 percent of the United States prison population, which is more than double the 4.2 percent prevalence rate found in the general population.[21] Some sources state that individuals with SMIs are incarcerated in the United States at a rate five to eight times greater than the percentage of persons with mental illness in society.[22] The prevalence rates for incarcerated youth is even greater. Research estimates that 65 to 70 percent of youth in the juvenile justice system have at least one mental health

---

15. Al-Rousan et al., "Inside the Nation's Largest Mental Health Institution."

16. Al-Rousan et al., "Inside the Nation's Largest Mental Health Institution."

17. Bureau of Justice Statistics, "Prisoners in 2004."

18. U.S. Census Bureau, "Census 2000 Summary File."

19. Bureau of Justice Statistics, "Prisoners in 2004."

20. Frank and Glied, *Better but Not Well.*

21. Frank and Glied, *Better but Not Well.*

22. Slate et al., *The Criminalization of Mental Illness.*

disorder compared to a prevalence rate of 20 percent for the general public of adolescents with mental health problems. Just over 70 percent of youth in twenty-nine programs met criteria for at least one mental health disorder and 79 percent of those had two or more diagnoses.[23] Disturbingly, courts consider youth with multiple and complex problems to be poor candidates for community placements, and thus more youths are entering the criminal justice system at a younger age.[24] African Americans with mental illness were more likely to end up in corrections than in a psychiatric hospital.[25] Similar studies have shown that whites, females, and younger youth were more likely to be involved in the mental health system while minorities tended to be disproportionately represented in the criminal justice system. The rate of SMI in the prison population has consistently remained higher than the general population with time as mass incarceration grew over the past four decades.[26] Many have linked the War on Drugs with the mass incarceration of African American men over the last four decades. The evidence is overwhelming and points to a prejudiced system that has devoted countless hours to incarcerating men and women of color.

Substance Use Disorders and Incarceration of African American Males

Incarceration affects the lives of many African American men and often leads to poverty, poorer health, violence, and a diminished quality of life. Research shows that there has been an unprecedented increase in incarceration among African American males since 1970. In 2009, the incarceration rate among black males was 6.7 times that of white males and 2.6 times that of Hispanic males.[27] It is ironic that although African Americans make up only 14 percent of the US population, they comprise 38 percent of the jail population. Statistics show that the African American inmate population in federal prisons increased more than 500 percent between 1986 and 2004.[28] Of these inmates, 80 percent of the incarcerated adults have a history of involvement with alcohol or illicit drugs. A high prevalence of substance abuse among homeless persons puts them at a higher risk of committing crime through arrests for possession of drugs, selling drugs, and public

23. Shufelt and Cocozza, *Youth with Mental Health Disorders.*
24. Rosenblatt, "Criminal Behavior and Emotional Disorder."
25. Cohen et al., "Characteristics of Children and Adolescents."
26. Frank and Glied, *Better but Not Well.*
27. Mauer, "Race, Class, and the Development of Criminal Justice Policy."
28. Mauer, "Race, Class, and the Development of Criminal Justice Policy."

intoxication.[29] Moreover, individuals with co-occurring substance use disorders and mental disorders have a five times greater risk of incarceration when compared to individuals without co-occurring mental disorders. In 1983, twelve adults entered prison on a drug offense for every 100,000 adults in the population. By 1998, this rate had increased more than sevenfold to eighty-eight per 100,000 adults.[30] There is a direct correlation between the rise in arrests for drug offenses to the War on Drugs. There is also a disparity in the sentencing of African American adults and youths. They are more likely to be referred to the criminal justice system for the criminal offenses related to drugs. They are also more likely to receive longer sentences for similar drug offenses than their white counterparts.

It is not surprising that African Americans make up only a small percentage of crack users, yet they are arrested more for drug related offenses. African Americans constituted over 85 percent of people sentenced for cocaine violations, although they constitute less than 15 percent of all crack users.[31] Statistics show that African American adolescents have lower rates of substance abuse than their white counterparts. Family attitudes and behaviors among black or African American communities discourage drug use among black youth and may explain the low incidences of substance use.[32] According to the 2010 National Survey on Drug Use and Health (NSDUH), black adolescents had lower rates of cigarette use, alcohol use, marijuana use, and non-medical use of prescription-type drugs than other adolescents aged twelve to seventeen. Research shows that young men with substance use disorders have an approximately fourfold greater probability of incarceration for drug related offenses by early adulthood.[33] The question remains: If African American men have lower use of alcohol and illicit drugs, then why do they make up a disproportionate percentage of those incarcerated? The answer rests in Reagan's call for the War on Drugs in the 1980s.

War on Drugs and the Age of Mass Incarceration

Crime and welfare dominated the rhetoric campaign of Ronald Reagan. One of Reagan's favorite and most talked about anecdotes was the story of a Chicago "welfare queen" with "eighty names, thirty addresses, twelve Social

29. Greenberg and Rosenheck, "Jail Incarceration."
30. Iguchi et al., "How Criminal System Racial Disparities."
31. Mukku et al., "Overview of Substance Use Disorders."
32. Mukku et al., "Overview of Substance Use Disorders."
33. Slate et al., *The Criminalization of Mental Illness.*

Security cards, and a tax-free income of over $150,000."[34] Reagan's racially targeted rhetoric was enough to galvanize white America to elect him as president. Once elected, Reagan delivered on his promise to enhance the federal government's role in fighting crime. In October 1982, President Reagan officially announced his administration's War on Drugs. By waging a war on drug dealers and users, Reagan could now crack down on the racially defined "others." In efforts to ensure that his War on Drugs was continuously funded, the Reagan administration launched a media offensive to justify his expansion of the federal government's law enforcement activities. Central to the media campaign was an effort to sensationalize the emergence of crack cocaine in inner-city neighborhoods. These inner-city neighborhoods were communities devastated by deindustrialization and skyrocketing unemployment. The media frenzy created hurt African Americans.

As the drug war was starting in the 1980s, inner-city communities were suffering from economic collapse. The blue-collar factory jobs that had been plentiful in urban areas in the 1950s and 1960s had suddenly disappeared. Prior to 1970, inner-city workers with relatively little formal education could find industrial employment close to home. Globalization, however, changed that. American companies were transferring jobs away from American cities to countries that lacked unions, where workers earn a small fraction of what is considered a fair wage in the United States. The impact of globalization and deindustrialization was felt most strongly in black inner-city communities. As described by William Julius Wilson, the overwhelming majority of African Americans in the 1970s lacked college educations and had attended racially segregated, underfunded schools lacking basic resources. In *When Work Disappears: The World of the New Urban Poor* (1996), he showed how chronic joblessness deprived those in the inner city of skills necessary to obtain and keep jobs. In *More Than Just Race: Being Black and Poor in the Inner City* (2009), Wilson addresses urban poverty among African Americans. Wilson disagreed with the conservative view that African American poverty was due to cultural deficiencies and welfare dependency. He instead argued that the "black underclass" was due to economic changes transferring jobs from the inner city and the lingering effects of past discrimination. Wilson felt like the answer to African Americans' problems could be alleviated by government-funded jobs and social programs that were race neutral, such as universal health care.[35]

The decline in legitimate employment opportunities among inner-city residents increased incentives to sell drugs, particularly crack cocaine. Crack

34. Alexander, *The New Jim Crow.*

35. *Encyclopaedia Britannica,* "William Julius Wilson."

hit the streets in 1985, shortly after Reagan's drug war was announced, leading to a spike in violence as drug markets struggled to stabilize and the frustration associated with increased joblessness rose. Joblessness and crack cocaine swept inner cities at the time that a backlash against the civil rights movement was mounting. The harm caused by crack cocaine left behind unspeakable devastation and suffering for the entire country. Yet, the War on Drugs was even more devastating to African American communities.

Some countries faced with rising drug crime or seemingly intractable rates of drug abuse and drug addiction chose the path of drug treatment, prevention, and education or economic investment in crime-ridden communities. Portugal, for example, decriminalized the possession of all drugs, redirected the money they were using to incarcerate drug users to fund drug treatment and prevention, and decriminalized drug use. Ten years later, Portugal reported rates of drug abuse and addiction had plummeted, as had drug-related crimes.

In September 1986, the drug war would start taking heavily casualties from the African American communities and continues to do so today. In September 1986, the House of Representatives passed legislation that allocated $2 billion to the antidrug crusade, required the participation of the military in narcotics control efforts, allowed for the death penalty for some drug-related crimes, and authorized the admission of illegally obtained evidence in drug trials. Just a month later, President Reagan signed the Anti-Drug Abuse Act of 1986 into law. Among other harsh penalties, the legislation included mandatory minimum sentences for the distribution of cocaine, and more severe punishment for the distribution of crack associated with blacks than powder cocaine, which was associated with whites. In 1988, Congress revisited the drug policy. The resulting legislation authorized public housing authorities to evict any tenant who allowed any form of drug-related criminal activity and eliminated many federal benefits including student loans for anyone convicted of a drug offense. African Americans constituted over 85 percent of people sentenced for cocaine violations, although they constituted less than 15 percent of all crack users. Incarceration, inevitably, affects the lives of many African American men and often leads to poverty, poorer health, violence and, decreased quality of life as legislation is biased and de facto targets the African American community. Because African American men and women experience more psychological distress as a result of substance abuse, mass incarceration, joblessness, discrimination, racial injustice, poverty, and systemically biased legislation targeting minority communities, African Americans typically comprise 38 percent of the jail population—nearly seven times higher than that of white males.

The Role of the Black Church

Certainly it may be argued that the solution to the plight of African Americans rests in legislation being passed that creates equal opportunities for minorities, thus leveling the playing field. Legislation involving drug-related crimes for possession and use need to be repealed and sentences vacated for those serving life sentences for nonviolent drug-related offenses. Mass incarceration has created an underclass or second-class citizen in the African American community, which is also plagued with poverty, unemployment, poor neighborhoods, lack of adequate education and education opportunities, underfunded educational facilities, lack of medical insurance, and lack of social programs. So, despite systemic racism, the black church has taken on the responsibility of improving the mental wellness of the African American community.

The impact of historical adversity which has led to race-based exclusion from health, educational, social, and economic resources cannot be ruled out as the cause of African Americans utilizing mental health services. African Americans utilize mental health services at about half the rate of Caucasian Americans.[36] Many African Americans today still feel the socioeconomic impact of slavery, sharecropping, and Jim Crow. Socioeconomic status is linked to mental health. People that are impoverished, homeless, or incarcerated are a higher risk for poor mental health. Michelle Alexander coined the effects of mass incarceration as "the New Jim Crow."[37] Because African Americans do not utilize the services of mental health organizations, it is not surprising that many rely on their faith and connections to the church.

Literature suggests that African Americans are more likely to rely on their faith as a coping mechanism for dealing with depression, anxiety, or other mental health issues than they are to utilize a mental health professional. One study found that 90.4 percent of African Americans reported use of religious coping in dealing with mental health issues.[38] Because so many rely on their spiritual ties and connections, it is only fitting that the black church have a role in promoting the mental wellness of its congregation.

This is not surprising when the traditional role of the African American church is properly understood. There has always been a connection between faith and the emotional well-being of African Americans. The African American church has traditionally been the gateway into the African American

36. Substance Abuse and Mental Health Services Administration, "Racial/Ethic Difference."

37. Alexander, *The New Jim Crow.*

38. Chatters et al., "Race and Ethnic Differences in Religious Involvement."

community. The African American church serves as an access point to social services, family counseling, and a sense of belonging. African Americans have historically looked to our faith leaders for political guidance and as spokespersons when our communities have needed a voice. Our faith leaders can serve as a pivotal change if African Americans are to move toward improving mental wellness in the African American community.

In order to strengthen the role of the church in promoting mental wellness, African American churches must educate church leaders on mental health, seek opportunities to collaborate and work with community mental health providers, provide depression education and treatment on their campuses, and encourage faith organizations to offer mental health first aid training. Victor Armstrong, the vice president of Behavioral Health, asserts that church leaders must understand that mental health conditions are conditions that warrant medical attention just like physical health conditions.[39] Armstrong also states that the church must seek opportunities to offer mental health services at the local church. Armstrong believes it is important for African American churches to bring in outside mental health professional and community stakeholders to speak to the congregation about mental health issues. He advocates for the church hosting mental health fairs and offering mental health first aid training at their facilities.

The importance of the black church has been documented in four areas of community medicine. The black church has impacted primary care delivery, community mental health, health promotion and disease prevention, and health policy. Studies suggest that churches provide a wide variety of prevention and treatment-oriented programs that assist in the psychological and physical well-being of their congregation.[40]

History has shown that African Americans are more likely to rely on the elders of their churches and their personal spiritual beliefs to cope with psychological distress than reach out to mental health professionals. Rather than seeking help from mental health agencies, African Americans often rely upon churches and other faith-based organizations for support and to help them cope with life's problems.[41] The black church has been a pillar in the African American community for assisting in caring for the mental health needs of its congregation.[42] In the past, black churches have been reluctant to seek the professional help of mental health agencies as these agencies did not address cultural differences and many lack African American

39. Armstrong, "The Role of the Church."
40. Blank et al., "Alternative Mental Health Services."
41. Allen et al., "Being Examples to the Flock."
42. Hardy, "Perceptions of African American Christians' Attitudes."

representation.[43] The interaction between race and attitudes affects an individual's decision to seek mental health care. A client's racial identity has been shown to be a major factor in establishing a positive therapeutic relationship.[44] Racial identity is important because it implies an understanding of the plight of the African American in intrinsic and personal development. Mental health agencies that do not have a diverse ethnic representation struggle to understand the client's worldview or life experiences.[45] Also, a lack of a diverse staff at mental health agencies lends to an error in misdiagnosing African Americans based on stereotypes and media portrayal of blacks.[46] The services offered by the church tend to be free of charge and there is generally a familiarity with the service provider. African Americans who seek support from the church counselor are likely to have a positive experience with the church counselor that may enhance the therapeutic relationship.[47] As one can understand, diversity in mental health agencies and the possible lack of insurance plays a pivotal role in African Americans seeking professional health in the community at traditional mental health agencies, so the black church serves as a viable alternative.

Black Churches Collaborating with Mental Health Agencies

Black churches and mental health agencies working together build a strong collaboration for African Americans to seek mental health care without the stigma generally held in the black community. African Americans face disparities in access to mental health services due to stigma associated with mental illness, cultural mistrust of clinicians, and a general preference of African Americans for mental health support of family members.[48] Black churches and outside agencies have benefited from several successful collaborations.[49] Church-based interventions are a strategy to improve mental health service utilization among African Americans.[50] It is postulated that partnerships between the black church and mental health providers may

43. Whaley, "Clinicians' Competence."

44. Blank et al., "Alternative Mental Health Services." .

45. Allen et al., "Being Examples to the Flock."

46. Parham, *Counseling Persons of African Descent.*

47. Allen et al., "Being Examples to the Flock."

48. Hays and Aranda, "Faith-Based Mental Health Interventions."

49. Austin and Claiborne, "Faith Wellness Collaboration"; Austin and Harris, "Addressing Health Disparities."

50. Hankerson and Weissman, "Church-Based Health Programs."

increase the demand for mental health resources among African Americans by combating stigma, dispelling myths, and developing relationships.[51] Pastors can legitimize the utilization of mental health services by the congregation and serve as gatekeepers to connecting church members to mental health services.[52] There are several successful collaborative initiatives in the community connecting black churches and their congregations to the much-needed mental health services.

Project BRIDGE

Project BRIDGE is a faith-based intervention aimed at reducing substance abuse in African American adolescents. Marcus and colleagues conducted their faith-based intervention program to reduce substance by enlisting sixty-one adolescents.[53] The participants included adolescents who were recruited from two local churches. Project BRIDGE involved risk prevention alternatives and in-depth information about substance abuse.[54] When the program was evaluated, it was found that the control group endorsed significantly more use of marijuana and other drugs than the intervention group. Marcus and his colleagues concluded that the church-based interventions were successful in preventing illicit drug abuse among African American youths. There have been several initiatives that have promoted health and targeted prevention of drug abuse among African American youth and adults. Similarly, a study known as Bridges to the Community was conducted to treat African Americans suffering from cocaine abuse or dependence.

Bridges to the Community

Bridges to the Community is a faith-based intervention that focused on treating African Americans suffering from cocaine abuse to help them abstain from drug use. Stahler and colleagues utilized a coalition of black churches to provide mentors and settings for Bridges to the Community participants.[55] The program enlisted eighteen female study participants who lived at a residential treatment program. The Bridges intervention consisted of interactions with a church mentor and group activities at a nearby church.

51. Hankerson and Weissman, "Church-Based Health Programs."
52. Adkison-Bradley et al., "Forging a Collaborative Relationship."
53. Marcus et al., "Community-Based Participatory Research."
54. Marcus et al., "Community-Based Participatory Research."
55. Stahler et al., "Preventing Relapse."

Compared with women in the control group, women in the intervention group stayed significantly longer in the residential program at both three-month and six-month follow-up assessments. They found that 75 percent of the participants in Bridges and 30 percent of the participants in the control group were drug free at the six-month assessment. The use of black churches to enhance residential drug abuse treatment appears feasible.

INSIGHT Therapy

The INSIGHT therapy was a cognitive behavioral therapy approach designed for women to reduce psychological stress. Mynatt and colleagues conducted a twelve-week long open trial of group psychotherapy at a church aimed at reducing depressive and anxiety symptoms, hopelessness, and loneliness among African American women.[56] The study included women with a mean length of depressive symptoms of ten years. They found that post-treatment scores on the Beck Depression Inventory II and the State Anxiety Inventory were lower than pre-treatment scores. The data was analyzed and showed significant changes in depression. The authors concluded that developing culturally acceptable interventions that reduce risks of anxiety and depression is important.

Educational Support Groups

Similar to INSIGHT therapy, researchers provided educational support on mental disorders to family members of congregation members suffering from mental illness. Pickett-Schenk enlisted twenty-three participants, each of whom had a family member with mental illness.[57] These participants attended support groups at a metropolitan church. No treatment was provided to the participants in the support groups or directly to their family members. Pre-study outreach activities included educational booklets on the causes and treatment of mental illness, a telephone hotline for crisis intervention services, and a half-day workshop on mental illness. At the conclusion of the study, Pickett-Schenk reported that 91 percent of participants increased their understanding of the causes and treatment of mental illnesses. Seventy percent reported an increase in morale as a result of the information received. The author concluded that the faith-based support groups provided families of persons with mental illness with valuable

56. Mynatt et al., "Pilot Study of INSIGHT Therapy."
57. Pickett-Schenk, "Church-Based Support Groups."

knowledge and emotional support. Studies like these continue to provide indisputable evidence for the support of faith-based programs at black churches in helping African Americans deal with and cope with mental illness, substance abuse, and incarceration. There is hope that church visits to prisons by clergy will decrease recidivism or re-entry into the prison system. Expanding prison visitation from faith leaders might also effectively reduce recidivism. A study conducted by the Minnesota Department of Corrections indicated that not only did visitation significantly reduce recidivism, but that visitation from clergy in particular was especially effective.[58] Visits from clergy lowered the rate of re-conviction by 24 percent. Research clearly showed that clergy visitation proved effective in significantly reducing recidivism. There is promise that faith-based programs will continue to address the growing needs of the African American community as related to substance abuse, mental illness, and mass incarceration.

Ideas for Successful Collaborations

Successful collaborations such as the ones mentioned between churches and mental health agencies serve to inform the public that such partnerships are attainable and useful in bridging the gap between under-utilization of mental health services in the African American community. Dempsey, Butler, and Gaither feel that these collaborations benefit churches by providing services to African Americans in underserved communities.[59] They also benefit mental health professionals as it teaches and encourages culturally sensitive approaches geared toward the black church community. Dempsey, Butler, and Gaither also explored some successful methodologies for mental health professionals creating a collaborative relationship with black churches. They listed several best practices for creating a collaborative relationship with black churches:[60]

1. Awareness: The counseling professional must be aware of their ability and skill level as it relates to working with diverse patients. Counselors should explore their personal stereotypes, prejudice, power, and privilege.

2. Assessment: A thorough assessment to understand church culture, etiquette, and protocol to avoid social errors such as calling some church officials by their first name.

58. Bensimon, "Exploring Faith-Based Correctional Programming."
59. Dempsey et al., "Black Churches and Mental Health Professionals."
60. Dempsey et al., "Black Churches and Mental Health Professionals."

3. Seek Approval: It is always appropriate to seek approval from the head pastor. Conversations with the head pastor should include ways to render culturally sensitive and appropriate services to the congregation.

4. Church Health Fairs: A presence at the church provides mental health professionals the opportunity to address the benefits of counseling, accessible resources, confidentiality, and stigmas present in the African American community.

5. Mental Health Training: Provide training for church pastors and leadership regarding the benefits of mental health services and relying on the church for accurate information regarding spirituality, support, and community resources. Conversations should focus on understanding roles, expectations, and limitations in collaborative efforts.

6. Join the Community: Mental health professionals prove to be most successful when they become active members of the community they serve.

7. Conduct Research: Conduct valuable research and follow up with information to dispel myths and decrease mistrust in African American communities.

8. Invite Wisdom: This is accomplished by conducting ongoing educational support groups about the causes and treatment for mental illness. Also, pastors should sit on mental health organizations' advisory boards to provide valuable information about reaching the African American community in a culturally sensitive manner.

These are just some of the recommendations that black churches can utilize to galvanize a positive relationship between the African American community and mental health agencies. The black church serves as a gateway to building long-lasting relationships with the African American community. Hopefully, these liaisons can create an atmosphere of respect and trust for mental health providers and provide an opportunity for clinicians of diverse backgrounds to develop culturally sensitive training when treating members of the African American community. These are just some of the successful methodologies that can be used when fostering a collaborating initiative between mental health professionals and the black church.

Conclusion

A history of racism, misdiagnosis, and a lack of culturally sensitive services have led many in the African American community to under-utilize mental health services, distrust providers, and seek solace from clergy. The black church has a pivotal role in connecting the African American community to the much-needed mental health services to address serious mental illness, substance use disorders, and mass incarceration resulting from mental illness and substance abuse. Serious mental illness, substance use disorders, and racism all play a role in the epidemic of mass incarceration of the African American community. Mass incarceration, spurred by mental illness and substance use disorders, is certainly the "New Jim Crow" in the African American community. It is incumbent of the African Americans leaders to develop initiatives in the black community to inform and educate its population on mental illness, substance abuse, mental health treatment, and decreasing recidivism.

Chapter 11 The Black Church and Orthodoxy

—ANTHONY CARTER

For what does it profit a man to gain the whole world and forfeit his soul?

—MARK 8:36

What is orthodoxy? The English word *orthodoxy* comes from the Greek word *orthodoxia*. It is a combination of the words *orthos,* which means "right," and *doxa,* which means "opinion." Orthodoxy, therefore, means having the right opinion or right belief. Christian orthodoxy, therefore, is holding to and affirming the right beliefs concerning historical and biblical Christianity, as well as the major doctrines that define what Christianity is and thus distinguishes it from all other religions of the world. Every religion has its standard of orthodoxy; in this respect, Christianity is no different.[1]

Christian orthodoxy has always been understood as being rooted in the Bible as the inspired Word of God. Yet, while the Bible is the place of revealed orthodoxy, the church of Jesus Christ has been the guardian and defender of Christian orthodoxy. Therefore, when the church loses its way as guardian and defender of biblical orthodoxy and begins to establish orthodoxy apart from the Bible, the church has abdicated its God-ordained calling and its uniqueness in the world. And rather than being an institution of orthodoxy, it becomes duplicitous in the reign of heresy or heterodoxy.

In *Come on People*, Alvin Poussaint calls African Americans to a kind of social and communal orthodoxy. He has called for a right opinion or belief about ourselves that will lead to a right demonstration of constructive, and not destructive, behavior. This orthodoxy is based upon the universal principles of love, respect, hope, and caring; and it comprehends a concern for the overall welfare of the community. His desire is for a community of people who realize that caring for and respecting each other begins with

---

1. Elwell, ed., *Evangelical Dictionary of Theology,* 808.

caring for and respecting oneself. However, though it begins there, according to Poussaint, it does not stop there. That desire must reach its fulfillment in realizing that the health of one is achieved for the benefit and the health of all. Nevertheless, articulating and guarding orthodoxy typically has been the realm of the church. Thus, even in espousing their views of African American society and offering corrections and solutions, Poussaint frequently refers to the church.

Poussaint does not have a chapter dedicated to the church and its role in a virtuous society. However, throughout the book, it is clear that he envisions a community where places of worship, particularly churches, play a significant role in the articulation, demonstration, and reinforcement of the values Poussaint espouses. According to Poussaint: "The black church has always been a force for black people throughout the worst times in our history. The church is a key player in the black extended family. We would not have much of a village if we didn't have the church and other faith-based organizations."[2]

He speaks of the church as a civic organization—an institution whose primary role is social reform—thus praising the church for its utilitarian purposes. The church is useful in fostering a society where social ills are alleviated. Consequently, the church is called on by Poussaint to get more active in addressing issues of mental health, sexual promiscuity, and disease (including the promotion of condom use), producing healthy food alternatives, speaking out against self-degrading music, promoting and pulling together the family, calling deadbeat dads to assume their responsibilities, and many other socially responsible agendas.[3]

No one can argue with the church's calling to be an institution of change for our society. Taking up the cause of social injustice and seeking to bring health, education, respect, and responsibility to the world is well within the realm and calling of the church in the world. Nevertheless, while it is *a* calling, it is not *the* calling.

The Call of the Church

In Acts 3:1–7, a lame man begging outside the Temple confronts the Apostles Peter and John. He accosts the apostles and asks them for help. Peter looks at the man with compassion and says, "I have no silver and

2. Cosby and Poussaint, *Come on People,* 43.

3. Cosby and Poussaint, *Come on People,* 186, 180, 172, 145, 83–84, and 143 respectively.

gold, but what I do have I give to you. In the name of Jesus Christ of Nazareth, rise up and walk."[4]

Today, the church in America can no longer say, "We have no silver and gold." The coffers of the church are filled. Megachurches abound. High-priced evangelists and self-proclaimed prophets fly across the country—often times in private jets—pawning their latest schemes of health, wealth, and prosperity. American Christianity is awash in consumerism, and the African American church is the most prolific of the consumers.[5] Indeed, the church can no longer say it does not have silver and gold. Unfortunately, neither can it say, "but what I do have I give to you."[6]

What was once the treasure chest of the church, namely the person of Christ and the message of the gospel, has been exchanged for social expediency and financial gain. What have been lost, indeed forfeited, are an uncompromised, orthodox, biblical view of Jesus and the message of the gospel that saves sinners from the death that is due to all of us for our sin. What has been lost is the unique message and calling of the church.

Contrary to popular notions and suggestions, even by Poussaint, the primary purpose of the church is not the healing of social ills or the righting of social injustices. The church was not given the treasure chest that is the gospel of Jesus Christ for the sole purpose of clothing the naked, feeding the hungry, or demonstrating against abortion. All such issues are important and the church should seek to address them in their proper context, yet not at the expense of its primary objective and calling—namely the saving of souls through the proclamation of the gospel.

No other institution is entrusted with so important—even eternally consequential—a message as the church has been. No other institution has the invaluable treasure that is the promise of the forgiveness of sin and eternal life through Jesus Christ. When we forfeit this most precious treasure for political expediency, financial gain, or social reform, we not only surrender our God-given birthright, but also lose any real, unique, everlasting help we can offer the world.

---

4. Acts 3:6.

5. According to researchers George Barna and Harry Jackson, Jr., "There is a higher percentage of large black congregations than there is among white or Hispanic congregations. In fact, while Willow Creek and Saddleback are regularly touted by the media as the biggest churches in North America, there are at least a dozen black churches whose attendance exceeds either of those well known congregations by at least a couple thousand people per week!" Barna and Jackson Jr., *High Impact African-American Churches*, 28.

6. Acts 3:6.

The world is filled with institutions ready and able to feed the hungry. The world is overrun with individuals and organizations desiring to heal the sick, bring justice to the disenfranchised, and education to the illiterate. Yet, there is only one place people can go to hear the message of redemption from sin and eternal life in Jesus Christ. That place is the church. When the church forfeits the uniqueness of the gospel and turns it into a social construction for civic empowerment and political change, it ceases to be the eternal change agent for which Christ gave his life.

Yes, the church is called to engage in the social well-being of society. Every church needs to be doing all it can to minister to the needs of its community. However, it must do so with the understanding that the need that is most uniquely the calling of the church is the salvation of souls from a far worse condition than poverty, hunger, or disease. The church is called to preach salvation from sin and death through Jesus Christ alone. This is her orthodoxy.

Jesus himself asked the all-important, immediately relevant, rhetorical question, "For what does it profit a man to gain the whole world and forfeit his soul?"[7] The obvious answer is "nothing." Orthodoxy serves as a reminder of the mission and message of the church. The mission is the worship of God through Jesus Christ. The message is repentance from sin and faith in Jesus Christ for the redemption of body and soul from hell and unto eternal life. The church is the only place where eternal profits are guaranteed to all who place faith in Jesus Christ. There are infinite ways to lose your soul. There is only one way to save it. The church has the way. It must reclaim it. It is the heart of orthodoxy.

Recovering a Biblical Orthodoxy

What do you believe? Now there is a question that has fallen out of favor in our modern parlance. In our days of subjectivity and the reign of narcissism, the objectivity of truth and its inherent transforming quality is woefully neglected to the detriment of society. The society that seeks to throw off the constraints of objectivity—and by virtue of this casting off declares itself to be free—is actually more in bondage than it ever imagined. Jesus declared unequivocally that it is the truth, objective reality, that sets one free.[8] Then, he declared himself to be that truth—the most objective demonstration of reality the world has ever seen.[9] Therefore, it is the truth, namely Jesus,

7. Mark 8:36.
8. John 8:32.
9. John 14:6.

which sets men and women free. This freedom gives us a higher purpose for which to live and to realize that life is not about me.

On the other hand, the neglecting of truth has led to a plethora of social and emotional woes that have infected American culture in general and African American culture in particular. It has produced a moral vacuum, the vacuum that Poussaint seeks to address. In *Come on People*, he has attempted to address the moral decline of our society and suggest positive societal moorings as the answer. We must commend Poussaint for the courage to address some of our society's sacred cows (i.e., hip hop music, unhealthy foods, television, etc.) and to suggest that all that feels good to us is not good for us. He writes with a confidence and concern that demands our attention.

However, while seeking to posit objective truth, Poussaint failed to establish an identifiable standard for his truth. Alvin Poussaint is a respected psychiatrist, but that does not mean that his opinions on objective standards of morality are true. There must be an objective standard, or everything and everyone becomes his or her own standard of truth.

Ironically, Poussaint understands this and has sought to speak in terms of objective and absolute values, though not declaring the foundations for such assertions. Perhaps it is understood or assumed. Perhaps he knows that there is a long-standing standard of morality that undergirds African American life. Yet, what they assume I want to declare openly: The only standard to which we can call all people and expect conformity is the standard set by a creator God. It is the reality of God and the right beliefs and understandings (orthodoxy) that must follow in order to produce right living. Thus, orthodoxy begins with the Word of God.

The Bible as the Source of Orthodoxy

Orthodoxy is based in the Bible as the Word of God. There is a word from God for our times as there always has been. Orthodox Christians have always understood this to be true. The Bible has long served as the standard of truth for the African American church and society. Those who would teach contrary and lead others to do the same find themselves on the wrong side of God and orthodoxy.

From the beginning of African American history, adherence to authority has been the norm. Among the first religious writers and Christian preachers of African American descent there was the adherence to the objective standard of the Bible as the Word of God. Jupiter Hammon (1711–1806), one of the earliest African American writers, wrote concerning the Bible's authority and standard for living: "The Bible is the word of God and tells you what you must do to please God . . . In the Bible, God had told us everything it is necessary we should know in order to be happy here and hereafter. The Bible is a revelation of the mind and will of God to men."[10]

Christian orthodoxy is a matter of biblical record. The black church in America has historically held to orthodoxy. It has done so through a high view of Scripture—believing the Bible to be the inspired Word of God. One contemporary African American author and historian has made the point:

> Our forefathers understood that the contents of the Scriptures were powerful because they contain the message of God to his people. Reading the Bible was the dying ambition of many slaves. Its words were manna from heaven for a starving soul. *Inerrant* and *inspired* were not common parlance, but the *ideas* these words represent were once commonly held. It was the perspective of our earliest leaders and thinkers.[11]

The African American church used to be a stronghold for biblical orthodoxy.[12] Even during the civil rights era when it was most active in pursuing social reform, the vast majority of predominantly African American churches were orthodox. It was still an institution committed to the message of Jesus Christ and resolute in its belief that the Bible is the inspired and infallible source of that message. Whether the issue was the abolition of slavery or the end of "separate but equal," the black church managed to fulfill its social responsibility while maintaining the highest view of Scripture and its primary message of salvation. Yet, these foundational sentiments and convictions have waned in our day. The tragedy is that the Bible has lost its preeminent place as the source of orthodoxy in many black churches, and we seem to no longer believe that it is sufficient for revealing to us the mind and will of God for our lives together. One contemporary rap group, Christcentric, well captured the loss of the supremacy of Scripture in our time when they wrote:

> Sufficiency of scripture
> How it used to be a fixture,
> Now it's swirled into a world mixture
> Expose the fallacy of this mentality
> Lord, restore your word to its centrality![13]

10. Hammon, *Jupiter Hammon*, 237.

11. Anyabwile, *The Decline of African-American Theology*, 241.

12. For a more comprehensive study of the development of early African American theology and orthodoxy and the nature of the subsequent and unfortunate decline, see Anyabwile, *The Decline of African-American Theology*.

13. Christcentric, "Sufficiency of Scripture."

There is a prophetic word! "Lord, restore your word to its centrality." Unfortunately, as the church became more political, it decided that integrating lunch counters was more important than the integrity of the faith.[14] Don't misunderstand: I am not arguing for an "either/or" understanding of social responsibility and theological integrity. On the contrary, I would argue for a "both/and." The church of Jesus Christ has a calling for both theological integrity and social responsibility. However, biblical orthodoxy must have primacy and direct and correct all social agendas. Unfortunately, this has not been the norm of late. The predominantly black church has sacrificed her theologically orthodox heritage for political expediency and social reform.[15] And when the church moves away from a biblical, humble, objective orthodoxy, it inevitably replaces it with an unbiblical, human-centered, subjective orthodox—which is no orthodoxy at all. Sadly, such has become the case in the black church in America.

Fortunately, it has not always been the case and it need not be the case in the future. The call to social reform among black Americans must also be a call to reform among predominantly black churches. It needs to begin with a return to and reaffirmation of what we believe.

We Believe

The oldest statement and most commonly held affirmation of orthodoxy may be found the Apostles' Creed. The Apostles' Creed is believed to be the earliest ecumenical statement, or set of commonly held Christian beliefs. It is called a "creed" from the Latin word *credo* meaning, "I believe." It is called the *Apostles'* Creed because, though some have erroneously believed that the apostles originally wrote the statement, it claims to be a biblically consistent summation of what the apostles taught.[16] It was written during the first few centuries of the church and today it is the most widely held and commonly agreed upon core doctrine of Christian belief. Therefore, it is safe to say that

14. For all the social good the nonviolent civil rights movement accomplished, it also initiated the mass decline in historic orthodox biblical convictions within the black church. James Washington commented at the time, "The nonviolent movement has added to the evidence that Negro houses of worship are essential as meeting places and that black religion is a source of Negro leadership. But the movement has also declared that every other aspect of Christianity is of limited value and interest." Washington, *Black Religion,* 28.

15. Like Esau in the Bible, we have sold out theological birthright for that which is fleeting and only momentary (see Genesis 25:29–34).

16. Elwell, ed., *Evangelical Dictionary of Theology,* 72.

while not all orthodoxy is contained in the creed, any statement concerning orthodoxy must begin with the Apostles' Creed and its application.

The oldest formal African American denomination is the African Methodist Episcopal Church. Believed to have been founded in 1787, it is the longest enduring denomination of predominantly African American Christians.[17] Today this long-standing church states: "To find the basic foundations of the beliefs of the African Methodist Episcopal Church, you need look no further than The Apostles' Creed."[18] The creed states:

> I believe in God the Father Almighty, Maker of heaven and earth, and in Jesus Christ his only son our Lord who was conceived by the Holy Spirit, born of the Virgin Mary, suffered under Pontius Pilate, was crucified, dead; and buried. The third day he arose from the dead; he ascended into heaven and sitteth at the right hand of God the Father Almighty; from thence he shall come to judge the quick and the dead. I believe in the Holy Spirit, the Church Universal, the communion of saints, the forgiveness of sins, the resurrection of the body and the life everlasting. Amen.[19]

The creed begins where all orthodoxy must begin and where biblical orthodoxy in our day must be reclaimed, namely with belief in God.

We Believe in God

It could and should be argued that the creed of African American culture has always been, "We believe in God." This affirmation has been the common denominator uniting virtually all African Americans and has been the rallying point for most of the major advancements in African American culture. Atheism, while growing in popularity in European culture, has never been a popular philosophy in America. This is even more acutely accurate among African Americans. Those who would dare raise the banner of atheism (or even the more skeptical notion of agnosticism) within the African American community would raise that with very few allies.

Throughout the history of America, the vast majority of those who spoke most eloquently and most powerfully for the cause of African American hopes and dreams have been men and women of faith. From the illiterate black slave organizers to the first black intellectuals, there is a common thread woven throughout their tapestry—an understanding that echoes

---

17. Mitchell, *Black Church Beginnings,* 66.

18. The African Methodist Episcopal Church, "Our Beliefs."

19. The African Methodist Episcopal Church, "Our Beliefs."

with singularity clarity in their voices: "We believe in God the Father Almighty, Maker of heaven and earth."[20]

From Jupiter Hammon to Phyllis Wheatley; from Nat Turner to Frederick Douglass to Booker T. Washington; from Marcus Garvey to Malcolm X and Martin Luther King, Jr.—those who desired to move African Americans forward have done so understanding that there is a God—an almighty creator who is with us and for us. Today is no different. From Russell Simmons and Denzel Washington to Oprah Winfrey and Cornel West to the Congressional Black Caucus and the president of the United States, African American cultural icons still confess overwhelmingly, "We believe in God." Poussaint seems to assume this, but an outright statement of this belief and the necessary accountability inherent in it is foundational to any cultural or moral reformation.

There must be a higher authority, a standard of righteousness to which all men are called, if our proposals for change are going to have validity and substance. That authority must rest in a sovereign creator who holds all people accountable for their actions. A call to morality must always begin with a call to God. The church that recovers this foundational truth and waves the banner of our accountability before God will be a church with relevant orthodoxy.

We Believe in Jesus

At the heart of Christian orthodoxy is the person and work of Jesus Christ. No church can be taken seriously, and no expression of Christianity can have any validity if it does not affirm the centricity of Christ. Therefore, the Apostles' Creed, while beginning with God the Father, speaks loudest when it confesses the truth about Jesus Christ.

No doubt, Jesus Christ is a polarizing figure. He does not suffer fence sitters, or those who see him simply as a good teacher or example but not as Lord.[21] Jesus demands total allegiance.[22] Historically, the church has affirmed this. The church of Jesus Christ has long asserted the uniqueness of Jesus and his lordship, and the church that once unashamedly asserted the uniqueness of Christ needs to do so once again. Orthodoxy demands it and our world needs it.

The church that once declared that there is salvation in no other name than Jesus, needs to declare it still. The church that once held out faith in

20. The African Methodist Episcopal Church, "Our Beliefs."

21. Matthew 10: 37–38; Luke 18:18–30.

22. John 12:23–26.

Jesus Christ as the only means of redemption from sin and as the only hope for the world, must affirm it once again. The world needs the church to be the bastion of orthodoxy it is called to be. The African American community needs it too. At the heart of this orthodoxy is the proclamation of the person and work of Jesus.

Some may suggest that the claims of Christ are not relevant for our times. Yet, the church must not only insist that Christ is relevant but must demonstrate it as well. Orthodoxy demands that we do so. Understood biblically, the death and resurrection of Christ is not only the most significant event in history, but it is at the same time the most relevant. Not only did Christ get out of the grave on Easter morning, but so too did hope.

It should not surprise us that the first African American president should be elected on a platform built around the idea of hope. No matter how prosperous or impoverished people believe themselves to be, hope is what keeps us moving. No institution in the history of America has instilled more hope in more people than the church—and particularly the black church. We are reminded that the song known as the Negro National Anthem states: "Sing a song full of the faith that the dark past has taught us, Sing a song full of the hope that the present has brought us."[23] Hope has always been a hallmark of the black church. But why? Why the emphasis and articulation of hope? Because, at the heart of the gospel message is the good news that God in Jesus Christ has brought love, light, and hope into the world. This hope was perfectly displayed in the resurrection of Jesus Christ.

If we have a generation of people who embody hopelessness and self-destructive despair, their cure is the resurrection of Christ. Poussaint is correct when he asserts that Christianity once offered hope.[24] I assert that when Christianity affirms its God-given orthodoxy it still offers hope—the only real, lasting hope. It is a hope that sin can be forgiven, guilt removed, and shame overcome. The healing of families and communities must begin with the healing of sin-ravaged souls. This is the business of the cross of Christ. Yet, part of the hopelessness that plagues our community is a result of the church abandoning the message of Christ and trading it for a message of financial prosperity and political influence. It is not surprising that the Bible says that such people are to be most pitied in this world, because they have abandoned the one true source of lasting hope.[25] The only hope there is for a seemingly hopeless world is the resurrection of Christ. The faithful orthodoxy embodying church has always affirmed and

23. Johnson, "Lift Every Voice and Sing."

24. Cosby and Poussaint, *Come on People*, 33.

25. 1 Corinthians 15:17–19.

demonstrated this truth. We must do so once again. It is the greatest gift we give to a hopeless world.

We Believe in Life after Death

Perhaps nothing has produced more morally devastating effects than the failure of Americans in general, and African Americans in particular, to seriously consider that this life is not the end. Materialism, hedonism, and narcissism have so infected our age that one is hard pressed to believe that this present generation could survive a day in the world one hundred or even fifty years ago. Poussaint, in his assessment of the moral decay he witnesses, states: "I have seen enough to know that, no matter what people tell you, this mayhem is not a part of our culture the way our music is. This violence is not a part of our culture the way our literature is. And this vulgarity has never been a part of our culture before."[26]

The richest, smartest, healthiest generation of African Americans is also the poorest, sickest, and spiritually weakest generation this world has ever seen. This is largely due to the shortsightedness that has gripped us. We have lost sight of everything except the immediate—what is immediately available to me and how I might indulge myself today. It has been said that the creed of our generation is "Get all you can and can all you get." We desire no satisfaction except that which brings immediate pleasure. Delayed gratification is a cursed idea.

Culpable in this generation's grab for the immediate is a church which has lost its orthodox understanding of heaven and hell and reward and punishment. The emphasis in the most prominent places of worship across the country is a rich and lavish lifestyle. It is a focus on getting financial and physical blessings. Little today is spoken concerning the emphasis in the Bible on tomorrow and eternity. Yet, Jesus himself declared unambiguously: "Do not lay up for yourselves treasures on earth, where moth and rust destroy and where thieves break in and steal, but lay up for yourselves treasures in heaven, where neither moth nor rust destroys and where thieves do not break in and steal. For where your treasure is, there your heart will be also."[27]

This lack of orthodoxy has led to a church that seemingly teaches the very opposite of what Jesus taught. Rather than labor for eternity, churchgoers are told to labor for today. In the one place where the world should hear a message of eternity and delayed gratification, it is hearing a message

26. Cosby and Poussaint, *Come on People*, xvii.

27. Matthew 6:19–21.

of immediate satisfaction. The church would serve the world well if it proclaimed once again the orthodox understanding of heaven and hell and how an eternal perspective needs to trump a temporal perspective.

Jupiter Hammon in writing to his fellow slaves stated that the most important thing is not that they are free, but that they are saved from their sins and the punishments of eternal death. He wrote:

> But this, my dear brethren, is by no means the greatest thing we have to be concerned about. Getting our liberty in this world is nothing to our having the liberty of the children of God. Not the Bible tells us that we are all, by nature, sinners, that we are slaves to sin and Satan, and that unless we are converted, or born again, we must be miserable forever. Christ says that except a man be born again, he cannot see the kingdom of God and all that do not see the kingdom of God must be in the kingdom of darkness. There are but two places where all go after death, white and black, rich and poor: those places are heaven and hell. Heaven is a place made for those who are born again and who love God, and it is a place where they will be happy forever. Hell is a place made for those who hate God and are his enemies and where they will be miserable for all eternity.[28]

Hammon, like most of the African American Christians of his day, had his orthodoxy in order. Being free from slavery was a great concern and one for which Hammon and others were ready to give their lives. But Christian slaves understood that freedom from oppression was not as important as freedom from sin, death, and judgment. This provided the motivation for life and hope for tomorrow.

Today, we need men and women who will say along with Hammon that immediate goals are worthwhile, but they must not be obtained at all cost. The church needs to be a bastion and beacon of eternity in a world that is consumed with the here and now. Our community desperately needs our orthodoxy. The world needs it too.

Only the Church: Reclaiming Orthodoxy

The tragedy of too many predominantly African American churches is that they have gained much of the world, but are losing their souls. Prophetic voices have been sold and silenced for political favors and esteem. For example, a church too closely allied to the Democratic Party in decrying social inequalities and promoting the cause of civil rights can lose its voice in the

---

28. Hammon, *Jupiter Hammon*, 236.

fight against the slaughter of millions of babies through the ungodly abortion industry. Conversely, a church too closely allied with the Republican Party may find a voice to sound forth the evil of abortion, but will find little credibility with those who lack affordable health care and are on the wrong end of economic policies that profit the rich.

The church that has no allegiance except the Lord Jesus Christ and his kingdom can and must speak prophetically and even poetically on the evils of abortion and unjust wars; on the inequitable administration of the death penalty, and on pay inequity for women. The church of Jesus Christ does have social responsibilities. It is responsible for equipping Christians with the message of the gospel so that they can go out into the world and be agents of hope, change, and eternal life. In doing so, the church produces citizens who are good neighbors and friends.

However, when the church loses its message and mission, so too do individual Christians. The call of Poussaint is a call to social reform. Yet, before the church can reform society in a way that honors God, it must first reform itself and reclaim the orthodoxy that gives it power and authority in this world.

How do we accomplish the reclamation of orthodoxy and the centrality of Jesus Christ as mission and message in the church? Others have written well on this subject.[29] Here I offer a few, though not exhaustive, suggestions:

1. *The church needs to recommit itself to the Bible as the Word of God.* For too long, the African American church has let the media, society, politicians, and even its own members set the agenda. We have let self-aggrandizing pastors and bishops decide what is best for the church (and thus themselves) and who have in turn not given Scripture its rightful place in the life of the church. Healthy, biblical orthodoxy begins with understanding that the Bible is the Word of God and speaks infallibly as it sets the agenda for the church and individual Christians as well. The Bible makes this claim for itself: "All Scripture is breathed out by God and profitable for teaching, for reproof, for correction, and for training in righteousness, that the man of God may be competent, equipped for every good work."[30]

2. *The church needs to recommit itself to the uniqueness of its mission and message.* Only the church of Jesus Christ has the message of Jesus as the hope and savior of the world. Only the church has a message that will not only benefit humanity in time, but more importantly in eternity.

29. Anyabwile, *Decline of African-American Theology*, 237–46.

30. 2 Timothy 3: 16–17.

Only the church has the answer for the sin and guilt that plagues individuals and nations. When the church is living out the true calling of its creed, namely the proclamation of Jesus Christ as Savior and Lord, it is being what God called it to be, namely a light to the nations. Orthodoxy reclaimed is the best hope the church has of really offering hope to a hopeless world. Our world is no more needful than was the world of Paul's day, and yet Paul declared,

> For since, in the wisdom of God, the world did not know God through wisdom, it pleased God through the folly of what we preach to save those who believe. For Jews demand signs and Greeks seek wisdom, but we preach Christ crucified, a stumbling block to Jews and folly to Gentiles, but to those who are called, both Jews and Greeks, Christ the power of God and the wisdom of God.[31]

3. *The church needs to once again clarify its doctrinal distinctives.* The life and living of the church are rightly connected to the doctrinal preaching and teaching of the church. A church washed in moral failure can too often trace those failures to a decline in the biblical clarity and the doctrinal integrity of its teaching and preaching. Unfortunately, it is common today to downplay doctrine and to stay away from it because "it may divide." Yet, the nature of truth is to divide. Orthodoxy, by definition, is opinionated and, when necessary, dogmatic. A society morally adrift—where right is too frequently wrong and wrong all too often right—does not need a church unsure of what it believes.[32] The church needs to sound a clear call for truth and moral standards. However, without biblical parameters of truth, the standards of right and wrong are not only lost in our churches but also in our homes and community. Therefore, "Let us hold fast the confession of our hope without wavering, for he who promised is faithful."[33]

4. *The church needs to recover its connection with the history of the Christian church.* Ask the average American churchgoer his understanding of church history and inevitably he will begin reciting the immediate history of the building in which they meet weekly for worship. For most, the history we know is no more than those snippets of information (minus the splits and court battles) shared annually during the weeklong church anniversary. While there is a place for this immediate

---

31. 1 Corinthians 1:21–24.
32. Isaiah 5:20.
33. Hebrews 10:23.

recollection, a more needful understanding is the identification we have with the saints of ages and cultures past. Connecting with the church through the centuries will remind us that we have had an orthodoxy that has been claimed and reclaimed throughout the years and has not only informed the church but sustained her in some of her most trying times. It will remind us that we do not need a new orthodoxy, only new voices and new methods of making historical orthodoxy known. Remember the admonition:

> Therefore, since we are surrounded by so great a cloud of witnesses, let us also lay aside every weight, and sin which clings so closely, and let us run with endurance the race that is set before us, looking to Jesus, the founder and perfecter of our faith, who for the joy that was set before him endured the cross, despising the shame, and is seated at the right hand of the throne of God.[34]

Today, some are calling for a new theology, while others are proclaiming that God is doing a "new thing." On the contrary, we do not need a new theology; we need to recover the orthodoxy that has already been delivered to the church by the Spirit of God.[35] The test of orthodoxy is to place it in differing context and not have it change, but watch as it changes people. It will produce voices unique to its time, decrying the evils of its day, yet never denouncing or denying the source from which it springs, namely the Bible—the inspired, all-sufficient Word of God—or the message and mission of that source, namely Jesus Christ and eternal life through him.

The world is waiting.

34. Hebrews 12:1–2.
35. Isaiah 5:20.

Chapter 12 **The Prosperity Gospel**

—KEN JONES

W here does one begin when addressing the poisonous strand of
American evangelicalism known by such labels as "word faith,"
"name it and claim it," or the "prosperity gospel"? So much has transpired
since Walter Martin (the original *Bible Answer Man* radio host) called attention to this danger lurking on the sidelines of evangelicalism—both on his
radio program and in his classic work, *The Kingdom of The Cults*. Martin's
successor, Hank Hanegraaff, continued to carry the torch on the air and
with two books of his own, *Christianity in Crisis* and *Counterfeit Revival*.
Yet, despite the clarion call of these diligent servants, the prosperity gospel not only flourishes, it has become the norm within the rank and file of
evangelical Christianity. Let me begin by turning to one of the prosperity
gospel proponents for a definition of this school of thought. What follows
are various statements made by Creflo Dollar:

> Poverty is not the will of God for any believer . . . From Genesis
> to Revelation, the Bible proves that poverty goes against every-
> thing God desires for believers. Poverty is a spirit designed to
> keep believers in financial bondage . . . The Bible says that wealth
> is stored up for the righteous (Proverbs 13:22, NAS). However,
> it will remain stored up until you claim it. Therefore claim it
> now! You possess the ability to seize and command wealth and
> riches to come to you (Deuteronomy 8:18). Exercise that power
> by speaking faith filled words daily and taking practical steps to
> eradicate debt. Like God, you can speak spiritual blessings into
> existence (Romans 4:17).[1]

Thankfully, Dollar took down the Facebook post the latter half of those
comments came from twenty-four hours after posting due to immediate
backlash. Perhaps there was always a time when these views emanated from

1. Blair, "Why Creflo Dollar Believes Poverty is Ungodly,"; Dedrick, "Creflo Dollar
Removes Facebook Post."

the fringes of evangelicalism. But on any given Sunday, many of the above quotations can be heard in varying degrees from numerous evangelical churches that don't explicitly espouse the gospel of prosperity. David Van Biema and Jeff Cho illustrate this point in a September 2006 article in *Time* magazine, citing a poll where 61 percent of Christians polled believe that God wants people to be prosperous and 31 percent agreed that if you give your money to God, God will reciprocate.[2] The prosperity gospel's crossover impact is illustrated by the wildly successful little book *The Prayer of Jabez,* written by Bruce Wilkinson, a respected Bible teacher and founder of Walk Thru The Bible Ministries. *The Prayer of Jabez* spread through the evangelical community like wildfire, not because people were appalled at its content, but because they found this book helpful. The subtitle of the book, *Breaking Through to the Blessed Life,* not only indicates the aim of the book but also reflects the evangelical mindset that has allowed aberrant "word-faith" teaching to become normative, if not the new orthodoxy. Wilkinson says in his preface:

> Dear Reader,
>
> I want to teach you how to pray a daring prayer that God always answers. It is brief, only one sentence with four parts, and tucked away in the Bible, but I believe it contains the key to a life of extraordinary favor with God. This petition has radically changed what I expect from God and what I experience every day by His power. In fact, thousands of believers who are applying its truths are seeing miracles happen on a regular basis.[3]

Two things strike me as I reflect on these words. First, I am struck by how removed this respected Bible teacher is from historic Christian teaching on matters like gaining God's favor. But also, I am struck by how much this preface sounds like something straight from a word-faith pulpit. Wilkinson's book was published in 2000; since then prosperity theology has spilled over into the mainstream of American Christianity. I don't know how important it is to question where the teaching originated, although many would posit it began with Pentecostalism. I think the more pressing question is this: how did it find its way into the very heart of orthodox Christian teaching? An early twentieth-century circuit preacher named Samuel Morris angered many churches for interpreting 1 Corinthians 6:19 to mean that an indwelling Holy Spirit imputes human divinity. George Baker, one of Morris's disciples, took this teaching even further,

2. Van Biema and Cho, "Does God Want You To Be Rich?," 15.

3. Wilkinson, *The Prayer of Jabez,* preface.

dubbing himself "Father Divine." Father Divine took his show on the road to the backwoods of Georgia in 1912. But his eccentric claims of divinity alienated the very churches providing him a platform. Father Divine was arrested in Valdosta, Georgia, in 1914 as a public nuisance and considered possibly insane. Yet few even raise an eyebrow when prosperity preacher Kenneth Copeland claims, "You don't have a God living in you; you are one. You are part and parcel of God."[4]

Copeland, of course, is much celebrated, not ejected from the church. Walter Martin and Hank Hanegraaff saw something terribly wrong with these statements, but many professing Christians don't recognize the harm. Again, the question is raised: how did we come to accept the absurdities of the prosperity gospel? The simple answer reflects a seismic shift in Christian thinking, specifically as it relates to man, God, and the Bible. This non-creedal, non-confessional Christianity raises expectations and assumptions about and from the Christian faith that simply fail theological or historic scrutiny. The prosperity gospel simply mirrors that shift.

Notice how Creflo Dollar and Bruce Wilkinson both assume that human success and fulfillment (as defined by them) is what God desires for his people. Furthermore, both are convinced that certain principles in the Bible, when applied and practiced correctly, will bring about God's will of blessings and prosperity. Reformed theologian Michael Horton, a keen observer of this shift in evangelical thought, noted that "a number of theologians have pointed out the striking similarities between this prosperity message and ancient Gnosticism. Like the ancient heresy, the Word of Faith message assumes a sharp dualism between spirit and matter, promising mastery over one's external circumstances by learning the secret principles of the invisible realm."[5]

Two main roads created the intersection and convergence of orthodox teaching and the prosperity movement. On the one hand there is the path blazed by E. W. Kenyon, dubbed by D. R. McConnell as the father of the modern word-faith movement. Kenyon was not a Pentecostal, but traveled in Pentecostal circles and greatly influenced post-World War II Pentecostal faith healers. Among the Pentecostal faith healers influenced by Kenyon's writings were William M. Branham, T. L. Osborn, and Kenneth Hagin.[6] Hagin, the most noteworthy of Kenyon's disciples, gave voice to his teachings. According to McConnell, Hagin's writings, in many instances, virtually quoted Kenyon's books verbatim. McConnell cites Christian Science, New

4. Copeland, "The Force of Love," audio tape.
5. Horton, *Christless Christianity*, 67–68.
6. McConnell, *A Different Gospel*.

Thought, Unity School of Christianity, and Science of the Mind as the major influences on Kenyon's theology.[7]

Hagin dovetailed Kenyon's metaphysical cultic teaching into the faith healing branch of Pentecostal thought, thus becoming the "granddaddy" of that movement. Among those who pay homage to Hagin as their theological mentor are Kenneth Copeland, Benny Hinn, and Fred Price. The popularity of these three prosperity preachers took the teachings of Kenyon through Hagin to dizzying heights, inspiring many preachers in their wake and spawning the growth of Pentecostal and non-Pentecostal churches committed to word-faith doctrine. The prosperity gospel flourished because the seeds had been planted, but it also had preachers like Copeland and Price preaching dramatically with open Bibles. Only through erroneous expositions and Scripture twisting could they make their claims with Biblical support. They claimed man was not merely the *imago Dei* (image of God), but gods in themselves, able to speak words that create or alter circumstances. If one could conceive it and believe it, then one could receive it. Teaching the power of faith and human words represents one road that has led to the acceptance of the prosperity gospel.

The other road hearkens back to the liberal theology of Harry Emmerson Fosdick. Fosdick was ordained as a Baptist minister in 1904 and appointed Professor of Practical Theology in 1908, a post he held until 1948. From 1910 to 1924, Fosdick also served as regular guest minister of the First Presbyterian Church in New York. His preaching, teaching, writing, and radio ministries railed against traditional and orthodox Christianity with its emphasis on evangelism and its uncritical use of the Bible. He emphasized insights drawn from psychology, evolution, and modern political and social movements, accenting the ethical rather than the doctrinal aspects of the Christian faith.

Fosdick was a very effective communicator. His book *Being a Real Person* (1943) stressed the personal peace and power of religion.[8] Norman Vincent Peale, Fosdick's disciple, took things a step further with *A Guide to Confident Living* (1948) and *The Power of Positive Thinking* (1952). Peale's most prominent disciple, Robert Schuller, founded the Crystal Cathedral in Southern California. Although reared and ordained in the Reformed Church of America, Schuller unashamedly draws from the pragmatic pop psychology of Peale and Dale Carnegie in shaping his message heard by millions through his enormously popular television ministry. Among his

7. McConnell, *A Different Gospel*.

8. Elwell, ed., *Evangelical Dictionary of Theology*, 424.

many best-selling books are *Self-Esteem, Self Love,* and *Believe in The God Who Believes in You.*

Joel Osteen seems to be the latest torchbearer of this man-centered distortion of Christian faith where God's will has been morphed into the American Dream. Osteen is the pastor of Houston's Lakewood Church. With a winsome style, he preaches his brand of self-esteem and human potential to millions via his television ministry. Michael Horton has this to say about the message and meteoric rise of Osteen:

> Perhaps no greater example of the church's American captivity can be discerned than in the remarkable success of Joel Osteen. To the extent that it reflects any theology at all, his message represents a convergence of Pelagian self-help and Gnostic self-deification. If a bland moralism from Protestant liberalism became part of the evangelical diet through Schuller, Osteen has achieved the dubious success of making the "name-it-claim-it" philosophy of Kenneth Copeland and Benny Hinn mainstream. Osteen represents a variety of the moralistic, therapeutic deism that in less extreme versions seems to characterize much of popular religion in America today. Basically, God is there for you and your happiness. He has some rules and principles for getting what you want out of life, and if you follow them, you can have what you want.[9]

In Osteen, the two roads intersect—the one trod by Kenyon, Hagin, and Copeland, and the one that flows from Fosdick, Peale, and Schuller. Horton offers another keen insight on the intersection of these seemingly divergent paths in the ministry of Osteen. "There are no television healing lines, blessed prayer clothes, or other eccentricities of yesterday's televangelism. Nevertheless, the key tenets of Word of faith dominate his teaching, although it is communicated in the terms and ambiance that might be difficult to distinguish from most mega-churches and other seeker-driven ministries."[10]

I would like to examine the shifts within evangelicalism that have made Prosperity Theology less threatening and offensive. A good place to begin is the diminishing significance of doctrine among evangelicals. Perhaps a more accurate way of stating it would be the diminishing significance of the doctrines of historic Protestantism among an ever-growing number of evangelicals. As will be demonstrated below, this ever-growing number of evangelicals and Prosperity Theology proponents espouse doctrine, doctrine that is decidedly different from the orthodox Christianity set

9. Horton, *Christless Christianity,* 68.

10. Horton, *Christless Christianity,* 69.

forth in traditional creeds and confessions. In other words, doctrinal agreement between evangelicals and the prosperity gospel is often the result of evangelicals (and even word-faith teachers) departing from their doctrinal standards. This doctrinal departure is one of the steps on the road from liberalism. David Wells writes,

> In the United States this preoccupation with doctrine was one of the consequences of the bitter disputes with liberalism at the beginning of the twentieth century. Liberals said Christianity was about deeds, not creeds. They said it was about life, not doctrine. Their conservative opponents, the fundamentalists, insisted that Christianity was about creeds as well as deeds. It was about doctrine as well as life. They came to define their distinction from liberalism, as they should have, in terms of their creeds and doctrines.[11]

Early twentieth century liberals maintained that dogmatic defense of historic Christian doctrine stifled vibrant Christian living and created unnecessary division between other Bible-believing Christians that held to different doctrines on both primary and secondary issues. In response, evangelicals held firm to certain core fundamentals, such as the inspiration and inerrancy of Scripture, the virgin birth of Christ, the atoning work of the cross, the bodily resurrection from the grave, and the second coming of Christ in final judgment. With these fundamentals at the center, evangelicals were able to reach beyond their denominations to cooperate with others in establishing colleges, conferences, publishing houses, and para-church ministries.

But, as Wells observes, "What happened, though, was that this doctrinal vision began to contract. The goal that diversity in secondary matters would be welcomed quite soon passed over into an attitude that evangelicalism could in fact be reduced simply to its core principles of Scripture and Christ."[12] J. Gresham Machen, who was an early combatant against Christian liberalism, offered this cryptic if not prophetic warning: "The enemy has not really been changed into a friend merely because he has been received within the camp."[13] With the contracting of evangelicalism, many have been welcomed into the evangelical camp. "The unraveling of evangelical truth was signaled initially in an odd series of definitional tags that became evident in the 1980s and 1990s. That was when a whole series of hybrids emerged: "feminist evangelicals, ecumenical evangelicals,

11. Wells, *The Courage to Be Protestant*, 5.

12. Wells, *The Courage to Be Protestant*, 8.

13. Machen, *Christianity and Liberalism*, 23.

liberal evangelicals, liberals who were evangelicals, charismatic evangelicals, catholic evangelicals, evangelicals who were catholic, and so it went."[14] Add to this list prosperity gospel evangelicals. The cover of *Time*'s September 17, 2001 issue featured a picture of T. D. Jakes with the question, "Is this man the next Billy Graham?" Whatever one thinks about the theology of Billy Graham, the point of reference is clear: just as Graham was the face of evangelicalism for at least two generations, Jakes may be the face of evangelicalism for the next two generations.

The reason for such a lofty contemplation is the enormous popularity of Jakes and his successful television ministry, movie credits, best-selling books, entrepreneurial genius, crossover appeal, and community involvement. All of these are commendable, especially the latter. But what about his message? In the November 1996 *Charisma*, he spoke of people who have "failed to appreciate their divinity."[15] He also implied, "during an interview and in his sermons—Jesus was a rich man. He had to have been, in order to have supported his disciples and their families during his ministry."[16] Both of these statements express the distorted (heretical) doctrine of word-faith teachers. Back when doctrine was more important to evangelicals, the fact that Jakes still holds to the modalistic position of his oneness Pentecostal background would have been enough to exclude him from the evangelical camp, but not in today's market.

Like the rest of the super-apostles of the new breed prosperity gospel, Jakes' sermons are emotionally charged pep talks that focus on human empowerment in overcoming life's obstacles while realizing one's destiny and potential. Two critical doctrines of historic Protestantism are undermined by such preaching: the doctrine of God and the doctrine of man. In commenting on the confusion of these two doctrines by the liberals of his day, Machen writes,

> God, therefore, it is said in effect, is not a person distinct from our selves; on the contrary our life is part of his. Thus, the Gospel story of the Incarnation, according to modern liberalism, is sometimes thought of as a symbol of the general truth that man at his best is one with God . . . And modern liberalism, even when it is not consistently pantheistic, is at any rate pantheisizing. It tends everywhere to break down the separation between God and the world, and the sharp distinction between God and man.[17]

14. Wells, *The Courage to Be Protestant*, 16.
15. Walker, "T.D. JAKES."
16. Henry, "Bishop Jakes is ready."
17. Machen, *Christianity and Liberalism*, 63.

This failure to recognize such a "sharp personal distinction between God and man" is at the heart of the prosperity gospel's emphasis on the power of human thoughts and words in changing one's destiny. As Joel Osteen has said previously,

> It's not enough to just read [the Bible], it's not enough to just believe it. You've got to speak it out. Your words have creative power. And one of the primary ways we release our faith is through our words. And there is a divine connection between your declaring God's favor and you seeing God's favor manifest in your life . . . You've got to give life to your faith by speaking it out.[18]

Here's an excerpt from one of Creflo Dollar's sermons in January 2005:

> Words control the body. Oh glory to God! And regardless of what's going on in your physical body, you got to talk to it. I'm telling you I talk to my major organs . . . I speak words to it . . . The tongue in your mouth will control every inch of your physical body! Do not tolerate sickness and disease as long as you got a working tongue that can speak the established word of God![19]

Both of these suave, immensely popular television preachers simply express the "old" doctrines of prosperity gospel. What's clear is that these teachers ascribe to the words of sinful men, a power that belongs only to God. But what may have been frowned upon by evangelicals in an earlier day has found a hearing in our day.

When orthodox doctrine is relaxed or even resented because it is perceived as being divisive (when it is actually serving a defining role), what remains is a religious atmosphere that unites around something other than the truth. One of the long-standing criticisms of old-school doctrinal preaching is its emphasis on sin and human depravity, perceived as negative and defeatist. So instead of human depravity and the need for a law-keeping, guilt-bearing mediator (Christ), prosperity preachers focus on human potential and the need to rise above adverse circumstances. It is precisely in the doctrine of God and of man that the Christian gospel and the prosperity gospel show their differences. If man's biggest problem is his sinful condition (which he can do nothing in his own power to change), then his greatest need is a Savior who can do for him what he is unable to do for himself. The Christian gospel announces what God has done in and through Christ for man's salvation, which is given freely. The doctrine of the substitutionary atonement, reconciliation, and the regenerating and

18. Alnor, "Joel Osteen."
19. Wise, "Creflo Dollar Critique."

illuminating work of the Holy Spirit are the constituent parts of the message. But, the message itself is the announcement of what God has given and done in Christ for the salvation of his people. The prosperity gospel sees man's biggest problem as his temporal circumstances and physical condition, so its message centers on issuing commands to think positive thoughts, speak the right words, and follow the right steps in order to break through. Machen, contrasting Christianity and liberalism, says, "Here is found the most fundamental difference between liberalism and Christianity—Liberalism is altogether in the imperative mood, while Christianity begins with a triumphant indicative; Liberalism appeals to man's will, while Christianity announces, first the gracious act of God."[20]

In the Scripture references above, God the Father and God the Son are the active ones, and people are brought to salvation by passively and humbly receiving through faith the gift of the Father in his Son. But, Osteen says that we have to "grow in favor by declaring it. It's not enough to just read it, it's not enough to just believe it. You've got to speak it out."[21] Here's another Osteen imperative: "Keep a good attitude and do the right thing even when it's hard. When you do that you are passing the test. And God promises you your marked moments are on their way."[22] No matter how exciting the carrot at the end of the stick may be, imperatives are law and not gospel.

Americans in particular seem to be prone to such imperatives because we have enormous confidence in our individual and collective ability to accomplish great things. As Billie Holiday sang, "The difficult I'll do right now. The impossible will take a little while."[23] We are the "can-do" nation with a track record of great accomplishments against great odds. But, when it comes to the things of God we are like all of mankind, impotent and bankrupt, guilty before our Sovereign Lord, Creator, and Judge. What is needed in that situation is a Savior, and the prosperity gospel adherents can only offer a pep talk. It might be claimed that the imperatives of the prosperity gospel are not in relation to salvation but rather to victorious Christian living once a person is saved. However, given the prosperity gospel's conception of man I doubt that is the case. Yet, if it were, it indicates another problem, what Michael Horton has called "assuming the Gospel" or taking the gospel for granted. Horton describes it this way: "The idea

---

20. Machen, *Christianity and Liberalism*, 47.
21. Alnor, "Joel Osteen."
22. Alnor, "Joel Osteen."
23. Holiday, "Crazy He Calls Me."

that The Gospel is necessary for getting saved, but after we sign on, the rest of the Christian life is all the fine print."[24]

The issue of assuming the gospel may cause so many otherwise conservative Bible-believing evangelicals to listen to what the prosperity preachers are saying. Perhaps they are simply disregarding the absurd and spurious, instead clinging to the positive. That might indeed be the call for some, because orthodox doctrinal preaching has long been accused of missing the mark when it comes to the "real issues" of life. This especially seems to be the case in evangelical circles where it is assumed that the gospel is solely evangelistic. If the gospel is only for the lost, then what about the saved?

The Prosperity preachers offer their "you can do it" imperatives as the solution. But, the Apostle Paul takes a decidedly different approach. In his Letter to the Colossians, Paul tackles the system of victorious Christian living offered by certain teachers in Colossae. His exhortation is that the Colossian 1:1–14 believers would be strengthened in the knowledge of what God has given in the gospel of Jesus Christ—there is not one single imperative. He goes on in verses fifteen through twenty-three to expound the excellence of the person and work of Christ. In 2:6–7 he says, "therefore as you received Christ Jesus the Lord, so walk in him, rooted and built up in him and established in the faith, just as you were taught, abounding in thanksgiving."[25] Paul's only imperative is to be rooted and built up in the knowledge of Christ (which is "the faith" alluded to in verse seven). The need to be rooted and built up in the knowledge of Christ is because as life becomes difficult there will always be some teachers who are prepared to take you "captive by philosophy and empty deceit, according to human tradition, according to the elemental spirits of the world, and not according to Christ."[26] The means for spiritual empowerment offered by these teachers consisted in abstaining from certain foods and drinks, observing festivals, worshipping angels, and experiencing visions.[27] Paul says, "these have indeed an appearance of wisdom in promoting self-made religion and asceticism and severity to the body, but they are of no value in stopping the indulgence of the flesh."[28]

It's not a stretch to see the similarity between the troubling doctrines of the teachers in Colossae and the empowerment formulas and principles offered by today's prosperity teachers. In 2:9–10, Paul says, "For in him the

24. Horton, *Christless Christianity*, 120.

25. Colossians 2:6–7.

26. Colossians 2:8.

27. Colossians 2:16–18.

28. Colossians 2:23.

whole fullness of deity dwells bodily, and you have been filled in him, who is the head of all rule and authority."[29] In verses 11–25, Paul expounds on our union with Christ and he makes the point that his victory is our victory. In chapter three, the apostle begins his practical exhortations, which consist in a series of imperatives. Two things should be noted about Paul's imperatives.

First, they follow the gospel indicatives. Paul begins with the announcement of what we have been given in Christ, not with what we ought to do or ought not to do. Second, Paul's imperatives are back-dropped with this reasoning: Because of our union with Christ, we were buried with him, raised with him, and he has cancelled "the record of debt that stood against us with its legal demands . . . he disarmed the rulers and authorities and put them to open shame, by triumphing over them in him."[30] In other words, we do not begin with the gospel for our salvation and then move on to something else for spiritual growth and maturity.

In his interview with Joel Osteen, CBS's Bryan Pitts quoted from one of Osteen's books: "To become a better you, you must be positive towards yourself, develop better relationships, embrace the place where you are." Pitts goes on to say, "Not one mention of God in that. Not one mention of Jesus Christ in that," to which Osteen replied, "That's just my message . . . I'm called to help people . . . how do we work the Christian life? And these are principles that can help you."[31] The problem, as previously stated, is that Osteen's "principles" make assumptions about human ability that simply do not correspond to the reality of our fallen nature. Furthermore these "principles" are not much different from what can be found in pop psychology and the motivational speaking circuit. It is what Horton calls "turning the Good News into good advice."[32]

Prosperity theology's confusion on the doctrines of God and of man is seen not only in their imperative-laden gospel, but also in the broad area of divine providence. Question twenty-seven of The Heidelberg Catechism asks, "What do you understand by the Providence of God?" The answer says, "God's providence is his almighty ever present power, whereby, as with his hand, he still upholds heaven and earth and all creatures, and so governs them that leaf and blade, rain and drought, fruitful and barren years, food and drink, health and sickness, riches and poverty, indeed, all things, come to us not by chance but by his fatherly hand."[33] The follow-up

---

29. Colossians 2:9–10.

30. Colossians 2:14–15.

31. Pitts, "Joel Osteen Answers His Critics."

32. Horton, *Christless Christianity*, 101.

33. Heidelberg Catechism, "Lord's Day 10," 526.

question asks what advantages come from acknowledging God's creation and Providence? The answer: "We can be patient in adversity, thankful in prosperity, and with a view to the future we can have a firm confidence in our faithful God and Father that no creature shall separate us from his love; for all creatures are so completely in his hand that without his will they cannot so much as move."[34]

Prosperity gospel preacher Fred Price espouses a different view,

> Now this is a shocker! But God has to be given *permission* to work in this earth realm on behalf of man . . . Yes! *You are in control!* So if man has control, who no longer has it? God . . . When God gave Adam dominion, that meant God no longer had dominion. So God cannot do anything in this earth unless *we let* Him. And the way we let Him or give Him permission is through prayer."[35]

One of the things about Fred Price and the prosperity teachers of his day is they knowingly and unashamedly defied orthodox evangelical teaching. While the current group attempts to be less abrasive in their undermining of orthodox doctrine, the substance of their teaching is no less an assault on orthodoxy.

One of the things that stands out in the answer to the Heidelberg Catechism question twenty-seven is the acknowledgement that "health and sickness, riches and poverty, indeed, all things, come not by chance, but by his fatherly hand."[36] This might be mistakenly perceived as fatalism by some. If a person stood in the rain for any period of time without proper covering, he will likely catch a cold. If a person spent his paycheck on electronic gadgets instead of paying the rent, he is likely to be evicted. Theologians call this concurrence, which Louis Berkhof defines as:

> *The co-operation of the divine power with all subordinate powers, according to the pre-established laws of their operation, causing them to act and to act precisely as they do* . . . It should be noted at the outset that this doctrine implies two things: 1. That the powers of nature do not work by themselves that is, simply by their own inherent power, but that God is immediately operative in every act of the creature. This must be maintained in opposition to the deistic position. 2. That second causes are real, and not to be regarded simply as the operative power of God. It is only on condition that second causes are real, that we can properly

34. Heidelberg Catechism, "Lord's Day 10," 526.

35. Hanegraaff, *Christianity in Crisis*, 113.

36. Heidelberg Catechism, "Lord's Day 10," 526.

speak of a concurrence or co-operation of the first cause with secondary causes. This should be stressed over against the pantheistic idea that God is the only agent working in this world.[37]

Berkhof describes the deistic position alluded to above by stating, "God's concern with the world is not universal, special and perpetual, but only as a general nature. At the time of creation he imparted to all his creatures certain inalienable properties, placed them under invariable laws and left them to work out their destiny by their own inherent powers."[38] It is clear from this that the prosperity preachers represent a deistic position on divine providence, which is due in part to the Pelagian legacy inherited from Finney. The imperatives offered in the prosperity gospel are "invariable laws" that when exercised will bring about one's destiny.

Price says, "If you keep talking death, that is what you are going to have. If you keep talking sickness and disease, that is what you are going to have, because you are going to create the reality of them with your mouth. That is divine law."[39] In that case, it is the individual that determines the outcome either by speaking words that "create reality" or "release" God's power. You can see how these quotes differ from Berkhof and the Heidelberg Catechism. But, more importantly, these quotes differ from what is set forth in Scripture. In 2 Corinthians 12, Paul prays three times for a thorn to be removed from his flesh and it was not.[40] Instead, Paul is told "my grace is sufficient for you, for my power is made perfect in weakness," to which he responds, "I will boast all the more gladly of my weaknesses, so that the power of Christ may rest upon me."[41] No amount of positive confessions or principles could alter what God clearly intended Paul to bear.

As noted above, there are laws of nature at work that God has ordained in the governing of human history. But, Berkhof reminds us, "the laws of nature should not be represented as powers of nature absolutely controlling all phenomena."[42] It is God at work through these laws and not an inherent power in the laws. Christians should heed the biblical commandments in the ordering of their lives. While some adversity can be the result of wrong and sinful choices, some difficulties and tribulations exist that simply cannot be explained. It is cruel, callous, and unbiblical to assume knowledge for all that a Christian may suffer in this life. It is appalling to think that

---

37. Berkhof, *Systematic Theology*, 169.

38. Berkhof, *Systematic Theology*, 167.

39. Price, *Living in the Realm of Spirit*, 29.

40. 2 Corinthians 12:7–9.

41. 2 Corinthians 12:9.

42. Berkhof, *Systematic Theology*, 169.

we have formulaic, man-made solutions to these very real hurts. The only viable help is to point the hurting soul to the Gospel of Christ in Word and sacrament. It is there that God's covenant faithfulness is reaffirmed—sealed in the blood of his Son. The gospel reinforces the doctrine of providence, reminding believers that suffering does not mean lost favor with God or separation from his love. Consider the words of Paul:

> But we have this treasure in jars of clay, to show that the surpassing power belongs to God and not to us. We are afflicted in every way, but not crushed; perplexed, but not driven to despair; persecuted, but not forsaken; struck down, but not destroyed, always carrying in the body the death of Jesus, so that the life of Jesus may also be manifested in our bodies.[43]

Romans 8:28 clearly expresses divine providence: "We know that for those who love God all things work together for good."[44] This leads the Apostle Paul to explain the reason for such confidence in verses 31–34:

> What then shall we say to these things? If God is for us who can be against us? He who did not spare his own Son but gave him up for us all, how will he not also with him graciously give us all things? Who shall bring any charge against God's elect? It is God who justifies. Who is to condemn? Christ Jesus is the one who died—more than that, who was raised—who is at the right hand of God, who indeed is interceding for us.[45]

Having confidently explained that all things work together for good for the saints, Paul then teases out the implications of his confidence in verses 35–39:

> Who shall separate us from the love of Christ? Shall tribulation, or distress, or persecution or famine, or nakedness, or danger or sword? As it is written "For your sake we are being killed all the day long; we are regarded as sheep to be slaughtered." No, in all things we are more than conquerors through him who loved us. For I am convinced that neither death nor life, nor angels nor rulers, nor things present nor things to come, nor powers, nor height nor depth, nor anything else in all creation, will be able to separate us from the love of God in Christ Jesus our Lord.[46]

---

43. 2 Corinthians 4:7–10.
44. Romans 8:28.
45. Romans 8:31–34.
46. Romans 8:35–39.

This is why saints are exhorted to look with confidence outside of themselves to the person and work of Christ to be assured that their circumstances are governed by a loving, gracious, and faithful Sovereign God. Question one of the Heidelberg Catechism asks, "What is your only comfort in life and in death?" The answer proclaims,

> That I am not my own, but belong with body and soul, both in life and in death, to my faithful Savior Jesus Christ. He has fully paid for all my sin with his precious blood, and has set me free from all the power of the devil. He also preserves me in such a way that without the will of my heavenly Father not a hair can fall from my head; indeed, all things must work together for my salvation. Therefore, by his Holy Spirit he also assures me of eternal life and makes me heartily willing and ready from now on to live for him.[47]

Prosperity theology teaches to trust in one's own ability to change circumstances by applying their principles, which somehow activates God's power and favor. But, biblical Christianity teaches that God's power and favor are at work, and his purposes are being accomplished even in the most trying circumstances. In considering the context of the prosperity gospel, let us be as clear and biblical in our analysis as Machen was in opposing the liberalism of his day. We are dealing with another gospel entirely; American evangelical beliefs have shifted so far that the aberrant gospel of prosperity theology has gained increasing acceptance within our ranks. Having forsaken the standards of historic Protestantism, we have accommodated to the spirit of the age. Consequently, today's Christianity retains some of the terms and forms of orthodoxy, but with the substance of another gospel, i.e., no gospel at all.

So, where do we go from here? Pastors are the first line of defense against the growing prosperity gospel movement. As a pastor, I recognize the many struggles and pressures associated with the office. But, I think it is necessary to don blinders to avoid characterizing our office by the example of super-apostles. The title of one of John Piper's books captures the mentality we should strive for: *Brothers, We Are Not Professionals*. To this I would add, we are also not life coaches, cheerleaders, motivators, entertainers, or CEOs. We are under-shepherds overseeing the flock of the Good Shepherd. We are overseers of redeemed souls. We cannot afford to get distracted by the outward success of those who peddle another gospel and lose sight of what the office we have been called to entails. We have not been called to be successful but rather to be faithful. My concern at this point is not with

47. Heidelberg Catechism, "Lord's Day 1," 519.

those who think that the prosperity gospel is authentic, but with those who embrace the Christian gospel, yet believe that the prosperity gospel offers something. Both the methods and the message of our office have been established for us. Paul encourages Timothy,

> I charge you in the presence of God and of Christ Jesus, who is to judge the living and the dead, and by his appearing and his kingdom: preach the word; be ready in season and out of season; reprove, rebuke, and exhort, with complete patience and teaching. For the time is coming when people will not endure sound teaching, but having itching ears they will accumulate for themselves teachers to suit their own passions.[48]

I'm sure that most of us heard this text preached at our ordination, but the days that Paul says are coming have arrived. Our office as under-shepherds requires us to faithfully carry out the task of preaching Christ clearly and consistently. We are to preach and teach the Word of God with the strength and maturity of the flock in view.[49] I think if we are to stem the present tide, it must begin with pastors committing to preaching Christ and him crucified, who accept the doctrines of orthodoxy, and who are vanguards of the name of Christ, not their own reputations. Brothers, we are neither social reformers nor community organizers nor motivational speakers. Let us heed the word of the Lord to Ezekiel:

> And he said to me, "Son of man, I send you to the people of Israel, to nations of rebels, who have rebelled against me. They and their fathers have transgressed against me to this very day. The descendants also are impudent and stubborn: I send you to them, and you shall say to them, 'Thus says the LORD God.' And whether they hear or refuse to hear (for they are a rebellious house) they will know that a prophet has been among them."[50]

For Christians who are not in ministry, now is the time to do as Paul challenged the Corinthians; "Examine yourselves, to see whether you are in the faith . . ."[51] Examine the claims of the Christian faith as set forth in Scripture and in the creeds, confessions, and catechisms of historic Christianity. Examine what the prosperity teachers profess. But, know what you believe and why you believe it. Don't be fooled by your emotions or by what you see, because emotions can be misleading and the same is true for

48. 2 Timothy 4:1–3.
49. Ephesians 4:11–24.
50. Ezekiel 2:3–5.
51. 2 Corinthians 13:5.

what can be seen. Christianity is a religion of revealed truth. The question is not first whether or not it works, but whether or not it is true. Christianity is true; be strengthened and built up in that truth knowing that God has set his promises in that truth which centers in his Son. Paul says in Ephesians 4:14 that being strengthened in the truth of Scripture is what brings us to maturity "so that we may no longer be children, tossed to and fro by the waves and carried about by every wind of doctrine, by human cunning, by craftiness in deceitful schemes."[52] The best defense against the myriad of false doctrines that pollute the religious landscape (and will continue to pollute it until our Lord returns) is knowing truth, trusting it, savoring it, growing in it, and being thankful for it.

52. Ephesians 4:14.

Bibliography

Adams, Kenneth. *Silently Seduced: When Parents Make Their Children Partners.* Deerfield Beach, FL: Health Communications, 1991.

Adkison-Bradley, Carla, et al. "Forging a Collaborative Relationship Between the Black Church and the Counseling Profession." *Counseling and Values* 49 (2005) 147–54.

African American Policy Forum. "Did You Know? The Plight of Girls & Women in America." https://static1.squarespace.com/static/53f20d90e4b0b80451158d8c/t/5422deoee4b080d53cf82554/1411571214756/Did-You-Know_Plight-of-Black-Women.pdf.

The African Methodist Episcopal Church. "Our Beliefs." Accessed February 19, 2020. https://www.ame-church.com/our-church/our-beliefs/.

Alexander, Michelle. *The New Jim Crow: Mass Incarceration in the Age of Colorblindness.* New York: New, 2012.

Allen, Argie J., et al. "Being Examples to the Flock: The Role of Church Leaders and African American Families Seeking Mental Health Care Services." *Contemporary Family Therapy* 32 (2010) 117–34.

Alnor, Jackie. "Joel Osteen: The Prosperity Gospel's Coverboy." *The Christian Sentinel,* June 2003.

Al-Rousan, Tala, et al. "Inside the Nation's Largest Mental Health Institution: A Prevalence Study in a State Prison System." *BMC Public Health* 17 (2017) 1–9.

Al-Shabazz, Ayesha. "Believing Change is Possible." *Teaching Tolerance* 63 (2019) 11–12.

American Psychology Association. "Increasing Student Success Through Instruction in Self-Determination." July 21, 2004. https://www.apa.org/research/action/success.

Anderson, Elijah. *Code of the Street: Decency, Violence, and the Moral Life.* New York: W. W. Norton, 1999.

Anyabwile, Thabiti. *The Decline of African-American Theology.* Downers Grove, IL: InterVarsity, 2007.

Arendale, David R., and Nue Lor Lee. "Bridge Programs." In *Handbook of College Reading and Study Strategy Research,* 3rd ed., edited by R. F. Flippo and T. W. Bean, 1–35. New York: Routledge, 2017.

Armstrong, Victor. "The Role of the Church in Improving Mental Wellness in the African American Community." American Foundation for Suicide Prevention, July 23, 2019. https://afsp.org/the-role-of-the-church-in-improving-mental-wellness-in-the-african-american-community/.

Arroyo, A. T., and M. Gasman. "An HBCU-Based Educational Approach for Black College Student Success: Toward a Framework with Implications for All Institutions, American." *Journal of Education* 121 (2014) 57–85.

Augustine. *The Confessions*. Translated by Maria Boulding. Hyde Park, NY: New City, 1997.

Austin, Sandra A., and Nancy Claiborne. "Faith Wellness Collaboration: A Community-Based Approach to Address Type II Diabetes Disparities in an African-American Community." *Social Work in Health Care* 50 (2011) 360–75.

Austin, Sandra, and Gertrude Harris. "Addressing Health Disparities: The Role of an African American Health Ministry Committee." *Social Work in Public Health* 26 (2011) 123–35.

Baillargeon, Jacques, et al. "Psychiatric Disorders and Repeat Incarcerations: The Revolving Prison Door." *American Journal of Psychiatry* 166 (2009) 103–9.

Barna, George, and Harry Jackson Jr. *High Impact African-American Churches*. Ventura, CA: Regal, 2004.

Bensimon, B. "Exploring Faith-Based Correctional Programming." Right on Crime, March 31, 2017. http://rightoncrime.com/2017/03/exploring-faith-based-correct ional-programming/.

Berkhof, Louis. *Systematic Theology*. Grand Rapids: Eerdmans, 1993.

Bhargaw, Sanika. "Community Meeting Discusses Issues Facing Students of Color." WMTV Wisconsin, February 23, 2019. https://www.nbc15.com/content/news/Community-meeting-discusses-issues-facing-students-of-color-506276421.html.

Bir, Beth, and Mondrail Myrick. "Summer bridge's effects on college student success." *Journal of Developmental Education* 39 (2015) 22–30.

Black Genocide. "Abortion and the Black Community." Accessed February 19, 2020. http://www.blackgenocide.org/black.html.

Black Lives Matter. "What We Believe." Accessed February 20, 2020. https://black livesmatter.com/what-we-believe/.

Blair, Leonardo. "Why Creflo Dollar Believes Poverty is Ungodly and Christians Should Claim Their 'Inheritance of Wealth and Riches.'" *The Christian Post*, March 23, 2015. https://www.christianpost.com/news/why-creflo-dollar-believes-poverty-is-ungodly-and-christians-should-claim-their-inheritance-of-wealth-and-riches.html.

Blank, Michael B., et al. "Alternative Mental Health Services: The Role of the Black Church in the South." *American Journal of Public Health* 92 (2002) 1668–72. https://doi.org/10.2105/ajph.92.10.1668.

Bond, M. Jermane, and Allan A. Herman. "Lagging Life Expectancy for Black Men: A Public Health Imperative." *AJPH Perspectives*, 106 (2016) 1167–69.

Bradley, Anthony B. "Inner-city Education Fails without the Church." The Acton Institute, June 8, 2011. https://acton.org/pub/commentary/2011/06/08/inner-city -education-fails-without-church.

———. *Something Seems Strange: Critical Essays on Christianity, Public Policy, and Contemporary Culture*. Eugene, OR: Wipf and Stock, 2016.

———. "Time for Change? Now What?" *World*, December 9, 2009. https://world.wng. org/2009/12/time_for_change_now_what.

Brown, Tamara, and Baruti Kopano, eds. *Soul Thieves: The Appropriation and Misrepresentation of African American Popular Culture*. Contemporary Black History. London: Palgrave MacMillian, 2014.

Bureau of Justice Statistics. "Prisoners in 2004." U.S. Department of Justice. October 23, 2005. https://www.bjs.gov/index.cfm?ty=pbdetail&iid=915.

Burleigh, J. H. S., ed. *Augustine: Earlier Writings*. Philadelphia: Westminster, 1953.

Burrell, Tom. "Negative Images 'Brainwash' African Americans." *Talk of the Nation.* NPR, March 18, 2010. https://www.npr.org/templates/story/story.php?storyId= 124828546.

Byrd, Curtis D. "Diversifying the Professoriate." PhD diss., University of Georgia, 2016.

Byrd, Curtis D., and Rihana S. Mason. *Academic Pipeline Project: Diversifying Pathways from the Bachelors to the Professoriate.* Amherst, MA: Lever, in press.

Cagle, N. L., et al. "K–12 Diversity Pathway Programs in the E-STEM Fields: A Review of Existing Programs and Summary of Perceived Unmet Needs." *Journal of STEM Education,* 19 (2018) 12–181.

Carson, D. A. *Matthew: The Expositor's Bible Commentary.* Grand Rapids: Zondervan, 1995.

Center for Law and Social Policy. "Young Women of Color and Exposure to Violence." Focus group. CLASP Report. 2017. https://www.clasp.org/sites/default/files/publications/2018/12/2018_exposuretoviolence.pdf.

Chatters, Linda M., et al. "Race and Ethnic Differences in Religious Involvement: African Americans, Caribbean Blacks and Non-Hispanic Whites." *Ethnic and Racial Studies* 32 (2009) 1143–63. https://doi.org/10.1080/01419870802334531.

Chrastil, Nicholas. "Mental Illness Behind Bars: The Hard Lessons of Orleans Parish." *The Lens,* November 26, 2019. https://thelensnola.org/2019/11/26/mental-illness-behind-bars-the-hard-lessons-of-orleans-parish/.

Christcentric. "Sufficiency of Scripture." Track 4 on *Reformation.* Christcentric Records, 2004. Compact disc.

Clark, C. J., et al. "The Program of Excellence in STEM: Involvement of Traditionally Underrepresented Students in STEM Education through Research and Mentoring at Florida A&M University." Paper presented at 2015 IEEE Integrated STEM Education Conference, Princeton, NJ, March 7, 2015.

Cohen R., et al. "Characteristics of Children and Adolescents in a Psychiatric Hospital and a Corrections Facility." *Journal of the American Academy of Child & Adolescent Psychiatry* 29 (1990) 909–13.

Copeland, Kenneth. "The Force of Love." February 5, 1986. PTC Broadcast (TBN). Audio tape.

Corbett, D., et al. *Effort and Excellence in Urban Classrooms: Expecting and Getting Success with All Students.* New York: Teachers College Press, 2002.

Cosby, Bill, and Alvin Poussaint. *Come on People: On the Path from Victims to Victors.* Nashville: Thomas Nelson, 2007.

Council of the Greater City Schools. "Annual Report: 2010–2011, A Year in Review." 2010. https://www.cgcs.org/cms/lib/DC00001581/Centricity/Domain/16/Annual_Report10_11_Website.pdf

Crenshaw, Kimberlee Williams, et al. "Black Girls Matter: Pushed Out, Over Policed and Under Protected." Columbia Law School, Center for Intersectionality and Social Policy Studies, and African American Policy Forum. February 4, 2015. https://www.law.columbia.edu/sites/default/files/legacy/files/public_affairs/2015/february_2015/black_girls_matter_report_2.4.15.pdf

Danek, Jennifer, and Evelin Borrayo. "Urban Universities: Developing a Health Workforce that Meets Community Needs." *Coalition of Urban Serving Universities* (2012) 1–36.

Dedrick, Carrie. "Creflo Dollar Removes Facebook Post Endorsing Prosperity Gospel." *Christian Headlines,* October 9, 2015. https://www.christianheadlines.com/blog/creflo-dollar-removes-facebook-post-endorsing-prosperity-gospel.html.

Dempsey, Keith, S., et al. "Black Churches and Mental Health Professionals: Can This Collaboration Work?" *Journal of Black Studies* 47 (2016) 73–87. https://doi.org/10.1177/0021934715613588.

Derck, Jordan, et al. "Doctors of Tomorrow: An Innovative Curriculum Connecting Underrepresented Minority High School Students to Medical School." *Educational Health* 29 (2016) 259–65.

Dillard, Coshandra. "Black Minds Matter: Interrupting School Practices that Disregard the Mental Health of Black Youth." *Teaching Tolerance* 63 (2019) 45–48.

Doerschuk, Peggy, et al. "Closing the Gaps and Filling the STEM Pipeline: A Multidisciplinary Approach." *Journal of Science Education Technology* 25 (2016) 682–95.

Douglas, Bruce, et al. "The Impact of White Teachers on the Academic Achievement of Black Students: An Exploratory Qualitative Analysis." *Educational Foundations* 22 (2008) 47–62.

DuBois, David L., et al. "How Effective are Mentoring Programs for Youth? A Systematic Assessment of the Evidence." *Psychological Science in the Public Interest* 12 (2011) 57–91.

Dyson, Michael Eric. *Know What I Mean? Reflections on Hip Hop.* New York: Basic Civitas, 2007.

Eby, Lillian T., et al. "Does Mentoring Matter? A Multidisciplinary Meta-Analysis Comparing Mentored and Non-Mentored Individuals." *Journal of Vocational Behavior* 72 (2008) 254–67.

Encyclopaedia Britannica. "William Julius Wilson." December 16, 2019. https://www.britannica.com/biography/William-Julius-Wilson.

Elias, Maurice. "Social-Emotional Skills Can Boost Common Core Implementation." *Phi Delta Kappan* 96 (2014) 58–62.

Elwell, Walter A., ed. *Evangelical Dictionary of Theology.* Grand Rapids: Baker, 1994.

Episcopal Diocese of Chicago. "Harvard Professor Jonathan Walton to Speak at Absalom Jones Celebration." February 6, 2017. https://episcopalchicago.org/harvard-professor-jonathan-walton-to-speak-at-absalom-jones-celebration/.

Equal Justice Initiative. "Sexual Exploitation of Black Women." August 8, 2016. https://eji.org/history-racial-injustice-sexual-exploitation-black-women.

Erickson, Millard J. *Christian Theology.* 2d ed. Grand Rapids: Baker, 1998.

Frank, R. G., and S. A. Glied. *Better but Not Well: Mental Health Policy in the United States Since 1950.* Baltimore: Johns Hopkins University Press, 2006.

Franklin, John Hope, and Alfred A. Moss Jr. *From Slavery to Freedom: A History of African Americans.* 8th ed. Boston: McGraw-Hill, 2000.

Frazier, E. Franklin. *Black Bourgeoisie: The Book That Brought the Shock of Self-Revelation to Middle-Class Blacks in America.* New York: Free, 1997.

Frazier, E. Franklin, and C. Eric Lincoln. *The Negro Church in America/The Black Church Since Frazier.* New York: Schocken, 1974.

Gaines, Joel, R. "Marked 'Urgent': Unity within Diversity in our Christian Schools." ACSI. Republished January 13, 2020. https://blog.acsi.org/three-steps-unity-through-diversity.

Gasman, Marybeth. "The Black Lives Matter Movement and Historically Black Colleges and Universities." *Penn GSE Perspectives on Urban Education* 14 (2017) 1–2.

Gasman, Marybeth, et al. "Black Male Success in STEM: A Case Study of Morehouse College." *Journal of Diversity in Higher Education* 10 (2017) 181–200.

Gilligan, J. "The Last Mental Hospital." *Psychiatric Quarterly* 72 (2001) 45–77.

Glaude, Eddie S., Jr. *In a Shade of Blue: Pragmatism and the Politics of Black America.* Chicago: University of Chicago Press, 2007.

Goss Graves, Fatima. "How We Can Help Black Female Students." *Education Week.* November 12, 2014. https://www.edweek.org/ew/articles/2014/11/12/12graves.h34 .html.

Greenberg, Greg A., and Robert A. Rosenheck. "Jail Incarceration, Homelessness, and Mental Health: A National Study." *Psychiatric Services* 59 (2008) 170–77. https:// doi.org/10.1176/ps.2008.59.2.170.

Grissom, Jason A., and Christopher Redding. "Discretion and Disproportionality: Explaining the Underrepresentation of High-Achieving Students of Color in Gifted Programs." *AERA* 2 (2016) 1–25.

Haberman, Martin. "The Pedagogy of Poverty vs. Good Teaching." *Phi Delta Kappan* 92 (2010) 290–94. https://www.researchgate.net/publication/240322311_The_ Pedagogy_of_Poverty_versus_Good_Teaching.

Haggins, Adrianne, et al. "Value of Near-Peer Mentorship from Protégé and Mentor perspectives: A Strategy to Increase Physician Workforce Diversity." *Journal of the National Medical Association* 110 (2018) 399–406.

Hammon, Jupiter. *Jupiter Hammon and the Biblical Beginnings of African-American Literature.* Edited by Sondra O'Neale. Metuchen, NJ: Scarecrow, 1993.

Hanegraaff, Hank. *Christianity in Crisis: The 21st Century.* Nashville: Thomas Nelson, 2012.

Hankerson, Sidney H., and Myrna M. Weissman. "Church-Based Health Programs for Mental Disorders Among African Americans: A Review." *Psychiatric Services* 63 (2012) 243–49. https://doi.org/10.1176/appi.ps.201100216.

Hardy, Kimberly M. "Perceptions of African American Christians' Attitudes Toward Religious Help-Seeking: Results of an Exploratory Study." *Journal of Religion & Spirituality in Social Work: Social Thought* 31 (2012) 209–25. https://doi.org/10.1 080/15426432.2012.679838.

Harrison, Nona Verna. "The Human Person and the Image and Likeness of God." In *The Cambridge Companion to Orthodox Christian Theology*, edited by Mary B. Cunningham and Elizabeth Theokritoff, 78–90. Cambridge: Cambridge University Press, 2008.

Hays, K., & M. P. Aranda. "Faith-Based Mental Health Interventions with African Americans." *Research on Social Work Practice,* 26 (2016) 777–789. doi: 10.1177 /1049731515569356.

Headley, Anthony J. *Created for Responsibility.* Anderson, IN: Bristol House, 2006.

Heidelberg Catechism. "Lord's Days." http://www.heidelberg-catechism.com/pdf/lords -days/Heidelberg-Catechism.pdf.

Henry, Kaylois. "Bishop Jakes is Ready. Are You?" *Dallas Observer,* June 20, 1996. https://www.dallasobserver.com/news/bishop-jakes-is-ready-are-you-6406265.

Hernandez-Sheets, Rosa. *Diversity Pedagogy: Examining the Role of Culture in the Teaching-Learning Process* London: Pearson, 2005.

Hing, Julianne. "New Report Details Barriers to Black Girls' Success." *Color Lines,* September 25, 2014. https://www.colorlines.com/article/new-report-details-barriers -black-girls-success.

Hoekema, Anthony A. *Created in God's Image*. Grand Rapids: Eerdmans, 1986.

Holiday, Billie. "Crazy He Calls Me." Track 4 on *Lover Man*. Decca, 1951. Vinyl record.

hooks, bell. *We Real Cool: Black Men and Masculinity*. New York: Routledge, 2004.

Hopson, Darlene Powell, and Derek S. Hopson. *Different and Wonderful: Raising Black Children in a Race-Conscious Society*. New York: Simon and Schuster, 1993.

Horton, Michael. *Christless Christianity*. Grand Rapids: Baker, 2008.

Howard, Tyrone C. *Why Race and Culture Matter in Schools*. New York: Teachers College Press, 2010.

Hrabowski, Freedman A. "Broadening Participation in American Higher Education: A Special Focus on the Underrepresentation of African Americans in STEM Disciplines." *Journal of Negro Education* 87 (2018) 99.

Hutchinson, Earl Ofari. "Come on People, No, Come on Cosby." *The Huffington Post*. Updated May 25, 2011. http://www.huffingtonpost.com/earl-ofari-hutchinson/come-on-people-no-come-on_b_68990.html.

Hymowitz, Kay S. "The Black Family: 40 Years of Lies." *City Journal*, Summer 2005. https://www.city-journal.org/html/black-family-40-years-lies-12872.html.

Ice Cube. "Gangsta Rap Made Me Do It." Track 4 on *Raw Footage*. Lench Mob, 2008. Compact disc.

———. "Child Support." Track 5 on *Laugh Now, Cry Later*. Lench Mob, 2006. Compact disc.

———. "Thank God." Track 10 on *Raw Footage*. Lench Mob, 2008. Compact disc.

———. "The N**** Trap." Track 11 on *Laugh Now, Cry Later*. Lench Mob, 2006. Compact disc.

Iguchi, M. Y., et al. "How Criminal System Racial Disparities May Translate into Health Disparities." *Journal of Health Care for the Poor and Underserved* 16 (2005) 48–56. https://doi.org/10.1353/hpu.2005.0081.

Iloabugichukwu, Arah. "Not Every Black Girl Survives Private Schools." *The Weekly Challenger*, December 10, 2018. http://theweeklychallenger.com/not-every-black-girl-survives-private-school/.

Jay-Z. "Jay-Z: Conversations in Hip Hope Part 1." Fuse. November 9, 2009. https://www.youtube.com/watch?V=7z5uitvrrLY.

Johnson, James Weldon. "Lift Every Voice and Sing." Poetry Foundation. https://www.poetryfoundation.org/poems/46549/lift-every-voice-and-sing.

Johnson, Lyndon B. "The Great Society." Speech at University of Michigan Commencement, Ann Arbor, MI, May 22, 1964.

Jones, Joy. "Marriage Is for White People." *Washington Post*, March 26, 2006. https://www.washingtonpost.com/wp-dyn/content/article/2006/03/25/AR2006032500029.html.

The Journal of Blacks in Higher Education. "Racial Gap in College Participation Rates in the United States." December 16, 2019. https://www.jbhe.com/2019/12/the-racial-gap-in-college-participation-rates-in-the-united-states/.

Katz, Janet R., et al. "Measuring the Success of a Pipeline Program to Increase Nursing Workforce Diversity." *Journal of Professional Nursing* 32 (2016) 6–14.

Keener, Craig S. *Matthew*. Downers Grove, IL: InterVarsity, 1997.

King, Natalie S. "When Teachers Get It Right: Voices of Black Girls' Informal STEM Learning Experiences." *Journal of Multicultural Affairs* 2 (2017) 1–15. https://pdfs.semanticscholar.org/03dc/8512f4efaa2facfe4df69368a85d42de2e84.pdf.

King, Martin Luther, Jr. "Letter from a Birmingham Jail." April 16, 1963.

———. *Where Do We Go from Here: Chaos or Community?* Boston: Beacon, 1967.

Kozol, Jonathan. *Amazing Grace: The Lives of Children and the Conscience of a Nation.* New York: Broadway, 2012.

———. *The Shame of the Nation: The Restoration of Apartheid Schooling in America.* New York: Broadway, 2006.

Kwon, Lillian. "Churches Unveil Plan to Ease Plight of Black Men." *The Christian Post,* March 4, 2010. https://www.christianpost.com/news/churches-unveil-plan-to-ease -plight-of-black-men.html.

Lahren, Tomi. "Tomi Lahren Extended Interview." By Trevor Noah. *The Daily Show,* November 30, 2016.

Lamb, H. Richard, and Linda E. Weinberger. "Understanding and Treating Offenders with Serious Mental Illness in Public Sector Mental Health." *Behavioral Sciences & the Law* 35 (2017) 303–18. https://doi.org/10.1002/bsl.2292.

Lesaux, Nonie K., and Sky H. Marietta. *Making Assessment Matter: Using Test Results to Differentiate Reading Instruction.* New York: Guilford, 2011.

Lewis, Robert. *The Quest for Authentic Manhood.* Nashville: LifeWay, 2005.

Lincoln, C. Eric, and Lawrence H. Mamiya. *The Black Church in African American Experience.* Durham, NC: Duke University Press, 1990.

Machen, J. Gresham. *Christianity and Liberalism.* Grand Rapids: Eerdmans, 1997.

Mains, Tyler E., et al. "Medical Education Resources Initiative for Teens Program in Baltimore: A Model Pipeline Program Built on Four Pillars." *Education for Health* 29 (2016) 47–50.

Marcus, Marianne, et al. "Community-Based Participatory Research to Prevent Substance Abuse and HIV/AIDS in African-American Adolescents." *Journal of Interprofessional Care* 18 (2004) 347–59. https://doi.org/10.1080/13561820400011776.

Martinez, A., et al. *The National Evaluation of NASA's Science, Engineering, Mathematics, and Aerospace Academy (SEMAA) Program.* Bethesda, MD: About Associates, 2010.

Masci, David. "5 Facts About the Religious Lives of African Americans." Pew Research. org, February 7, 2018. https://www.pewresearch.org/fact-tank/2018/02/07/5-facts-about-the-religious-lives-of-african-americans/.

Mauer, M. "Race, Class, and the Development of Criminal Justice Policy." *Rev. Policy Research* 21 (2004) 79–92.

McClinton, Jeton, et al. *Mentoring at Minority Serving Institutions (MSIs): Theory, Design, and Practice.* Charlotte, NC: Information Age, 2018.

McConnell, D. R. *A Different Gospel.* Peabody, MA: Hendrickson, 1998.

McConville, J. Gordon. *Deuteronomy.* Downers Grove, IL: InterVarsity, 2002.

McMickle, Marvin. *Where Have All the Prophets Gone? Reclaiming Prophetic Preaching in America.* Cleveland: Pilgrim, 2006.

Merritt, B., et al. "The Impact of Pre/Post-Enrollment Interventions on Campus Success for First-Generation College Students." *Journal of Higher Education Management* 32 (2017) 227–42.

Miller, John W. *Proverbs.* Scottdale, PA: Herald, 2004.

Mitchell, Henry H. *Black Church Beginnings: The Long-hidden Realities of the First Years.* Grand Rapids: Eerdmans, 2004.

Mitchell, Ojmarrh. "A Meta-Analysis of Race and Sentencing Research: Explaining the Inconsistencies." *Journal of Quantitative Criminology* 21 (2005) 439–66. https://doi.org/10.1007/s10940-005-7362-7.

Momoh, J. A. "Outreach Program in Electrical Engineering: Pre-College for Engineering Systems (PCES)." *IEEE Transactions on Power Systems* 29 (2014) 1880–87.

Morgan, Joan. *When Chickenheads Come Home to Roost: My Life as a Hip Hop Feminist.* New York: Simon & Schuster, 1999.

Moynihan, Daniel Patrick. "The Negro Family: The Case for National Action." United States Department of Labor Report, Washington, DC, 1965.

Mukku, Venkata K., et al. "Overview of Substance Use Disorders and Incarceration of African American Males." *Frontiers in Psychiatry* 3 (2012) 1–5. https://doi. org/10.3389/fpsyt.2012.00098.

Muhammad, Gholnecsar E., and Sherell A. McArthur. "Styled by Their Perceptions: Black Adolescent Girls Interpret Representations of Black Females in Popular Culture." *Multicultural Perspectives* 17 (2015) 133–40.

Mynatt, Sarah, et al. "Pilot Study of INSIGHT Therapy in African American Women." *Archives of Psychiatric Nursing* 22 (2008) 364–74. https://doi.org/10.1016/j.apnu .2007.10.007.

National Center for Education Statistics. "Digest of Education Statistics: 2017." 2018. https://nces.ed.gov/programs/digest/d17/.

National Criminal Justice Reference Service. "Report of the National Advisory Commission on Civil Disorders." U.S. Department of Justice, 1967.

National Education Association. "Race Against Time: Educating Black Boys." February 2011. http://www.nea.org/assets/docs/educatingblackboys11rev.pdf.

National Organization for Women. "Black Women and Sexual Violence." February 2018. https://now.org/wp-content/uploads/2018/02/Black-Women-and-Sexual-Violence-6.pdf.

National Partnership for Women and Families. "America's Women and the Wage Gap." September 2019. https://www.nationalpartnership.org/our-work/resources/economic -justice/fair-pay/americas-women-and-the-wage-gap.pdf.

National Research Council, et al. *Identifying and Supporting Productive STEM Programs in Out-of-School Settings.* Washington, DC: The National Academies, 2015.

National Science Foundation. "Survey of Earned Doctorate Recipients from U.S. Universities." National Center for Science and Engineering Statistics Directorate for Social, Behavioral and Economic Sciences. December 2019. https://ncses.nsf. gov/pubs/nsf20301/.

National Women's Law Center. "Unlocking Opportunities for Black Girls: A Call to Action for Educational Equity." 2014. https://nwlc.org/wpcontent/uploads/2015/08/ unlocking_opportunity_for_african_american_girls_report.pdf.

Nelson, Raina. "Still Separate, Still Unequal: The Role of Black Women and Girls in the Legacy of *Brown v. Board of Education.*" *AAUW*, May 17, 2018. https://www.aauw. org/2018/05/17/still-separate-still-unequal/.

Northside Achievement Zone. "NAZ Results Summary: A Game Changing Approach That Is Working." 2017. https://northsideachievement.org/wp-content/uploads/ NAZ-Results-Summary_onlinelayout.pdf.

The Notorious B.I.G. "Things Done Changed." Track 2 on *Ready to Die.* Bad Boy, 1994. Compact disc.

NWA. "Straight Outta Compton." Track 1 on *Straight Outta Compton.* Ruthless, 1988. Compact disc.

Obgar, Jeffrey Ogbonna Green. *Black Power: Radical Politics and African American Identity.* Baltimore: John Hopkins University Press, 2004.

Ohikuare, Judith. "When Minority Students Attend Elite Private Schools." *The Atlantic*. December 17, 2013. https://www.theatlantic.com/education/archive/2013/12/when -minority-students-attend-elite-private-schools/282416/.

Palmer, Robert T., and Marybeth Gasman. "'It Takes a Village to Raise a Child': The Role of Social Capital in Promoting Academic Success for African American Men at a Black College." *Journal of College Student Development* 49 (2008) 52–70.

Parham, Thomas A. *Counseling Persons of African Descent: Raising the Bar of Practitioner Competence*. Thousand Oaks, CA: Sage, 2002.

Parrish, L. L., et al. "Helping Orient Minorities to Engineering (HOME) Program: A Pre-College Summer Bridge Program." Paper presented at American Society for Engineering Education, Session W1A. Daytona Beach, FL, August 6–8, 2017.

Payne, Daniel Alexander. "Welcome to the Ransomed." In *African American Religious History: A Documentary Witness*, edited by Milton C. Sernett, 232–44. Durham, NC: Duke University Press, 2001.

Pew Research Center. "Religious Composition of Blacks." February 7, 2018. https:// www.pewforum.org/religious-landscape-study/racial-and-ethnic-composition/ black/.

Pickett-Schenk, Susan A. "Church-Based Support Groups for Families Coping with Mental Illness: Outreach and Outcomes." *Psychiatric Rehabilitation Journal* 26 (2002) 173–80. https://doi.org/10.2975/26.2002.173.180.

Pitts, Byron. "Joel Osteen Answers His Critics." CBS News, October 11, 2007. https:// www.cbsnews.com/news/joel-osteen-answers-his-critics/2/.

Porter, Gloria, et al. "Stagnant Perceptions of Nursing among High School Students: Results of a Shadowing Intervention Study." *Journal of Professional Nursing* 25 (2009) 227–33.

Price, Fredrick K. C. *Living in the Realm of Spirit*. Tulsa: Harrison House, 1989.

Quinn, Eithne. *Nuthin' but a "G" Thang: The Culture and Commerce of Gangsta Rap*. New York: Columbia University Press, 2004.

Race Forward. "What is Systemic Racism? [Videos]" The Center for Racial Justice Innovation. April 20, 2015. https://www.raceforward.org/videos/systemic-racism.

Rankins, Claudia. "HBCUs and Black STEM Student Success." *Peer Review* 21 (2019) 50–51.

Raposa, Elizabeth B., et al. "The Effects of Youth Mentoring Programs: A Meta-analysis of Outcome Studies." *Journal of Youth Adolescence* 48 (2019) 423–43.

RB-Banks, Yvonne, and Joseph Meyer. "Childhood Trauma in Today's Urban Classroom: Moving Beyond the Therapist's Office." *Journal of Educational Foundations* 30 (2017) 63–75.

Richardson, Willie. *Reclaiming the Urban Family: How to Mobilize the Church as a Family Training Center*. Grand Rapids: Zondervan, 1996.

Ricks, Shawn A. "Falling through the Cracks: Black Girls in Education." *Interdisciplinary Journal of Teaching and Learning* 4 (2014) 10–18.

Roach, Ronald. "STEM Success." *Diverse: Issues in Higher Education* 32 (2015) 15–23.

Rosenblatt, Jennifer A., et al. "Criminal Behavior and Emotional Disorder: Comparing Youth Served by the Mental Health and Juvenile Justice Systems." *The Journal of Behavioral Health Services & Research* 27 (2000) 227–37. https://doi.org/10.1007/ bf02287315.

Salto, Lorena M., et al. "Underrepresented Minority High School and College Students Report STEM-pipeline Sustaining Gains after Participating in the Loma Linda University Summer Health Disparities Research Program." *PLOS One* 9 (2014). https://doi.org/10.1371/journal.pone.0108497.

Scazzero, Peter. *Emotionally Healthy Spirituality: Unleash the Power of Life in Christ.* Grand Rapids: Zondervan, 2006.

Science Education Resource Center. "How to Engage and Support Urban Students." *Pedagogy in Action.* Accessed February 23, 2020. https://serc.carleton.edu/sp/library/urban/how.html.

Scott-Jones, Diane, and Maxine L. Clark. "The School Experiences of Black Girls: The Interaction of Gender, Race and Socioeconomic Status." *Phi Delta Kappan* 67 (1986) 520–26.

Serwer, Adam. "Our Racial Interior: Review of *Whistling Vivaldi: And Other Clues to How Stereotypes Affect Us (Issues of Our Time).* *The American Prospect,* April 9, 2010. https://prospect.org/culture/racial-interior/.

Sherlock, Charles. *The Doctrine of Humanity.* Downers Grove, IL: InterVarsity, 1996.

Shorette, R. C., and R. T. Palmer. "Historically Black Colleges and Universities (HBCUS): Critical Facilitators of Non-Cognitive Skills for Black Males." *Western Journal of Black Studies* 39 (2015) 18–29.

Shufelt, Jennie L., and Joseph J. Cocozza. *Youth with Mental Health Disorders in the Juvenile Justice System: Results from a Multi-State Prevalence Study.* Delmar, NY: National Center for Mental Health and Juvenile Justice, 2006.

Slade, John, et al. "Getting into the Pipeline: Summer Bridge as a Pathway to College Success." *Journal of Negro Education* 84 (2015) 125–38.

Slate, Risdon N., et al. *The Criminalization of Mental Illness: Crisis and Opportunity for the Justice System.* Durham, NC: Carolina Academic, 2013.

Smith, E., and A. J. Hattery. "African American Men and the Prison Industrial Complex." *Western Journal of Black Studies* 34 (2010) 237–98.

Smith, Jesse C. *Black Firsts: 4000 Ground-Breaking and Pioneering Historical Events.* Detroit: Visible Ink, 2012.

Snoop Dogg. "Gin & Juice." Track 3 on *Doggystyle.* Death Row, 1993. Compact disc.

Sorrels, Barbara. "Reaching and Teaching Children Exposed to Trauma." Presentation at RT Elementary, October 16, 2018. Gryphon House. https://www.earlychildhoodwebinars.com/wp-content/uploads/2018/10/Slides-3-per-page_Trauma-Informed-Care-in-ECE_10_17_2018.pdf.

Stahler, Gerald J., et al. "Preventing Relapse Among Crack-Using Homeless Women with Children: Building Bridges to the Community." *Journal of Prevention & Intervention in the Community* 15 (1997) 53–66.

Stohlmann, M., et al. "Middle School Students' Mindsets Before and After Open-Ended Problems." *Journal of Mathematics Education at Teachers College* 9 (2018) 27–36.

Strauss, Lilo T. "Abortion Surveillance—United States, 2003." November 24, 2006. Surveillance Summary for the Centers for Disease Control and Prevention, Washington, DC.

Substance Abuse and Mental Health Services Administration. "Racial/Ethnic Difference in Mental Health Service Use Among Adults." Department of Health and Human Services. Accessed December 5, 2019. https://www.samhsa.gov/data/sites/default/files/MHServicesUseAmongAdults/MHServicesUseAmongAdults.pdf.

———. "Results from the 2015 National Survey on Drug Use and Health: Detailed Tables." September 8, 2016. https://www.samhsa.gov/data/sites/default/files/NSDUH-DetTabs-2015/NSDUH-DetTabs-2015/NSDUH-DetTabs-2015.pdf.

Thiong'o, Ngugi wa. *Decolonising the Mind: the Politics of Language in African Literature.* London: James Currey, 1986.

Thomas, Angie. *The Hate U Give.* New York: Balzer + Bray, 2017.

Thompson, Gail L. *Through Ebony Eyes: What Teachers Need to Know But Are Afraid to Ask About African American Students*. San Francisco: Jossey Bass, 2004.

Toldson, Ivory A. "Cultivating STEM Talent at Minority Serving Institutions: Challenges and Opportunities to Broaden Participation in STEM at Historically Black Colleges and Universities." In *Growing Diverse STEM Communities: Methodology, Impact, and Evidence*, 1–8. Washington, DC: American Chemical Society, 2019.

Tripp, Paul. *Broken Down House*. Wapwallopen, PA: Shepherd's, 2009.

Tyson, Teresa, et al. "Nursing at Historically Black Colleges and Universities." *Journal of Professional Nursing* 34 (2018) 167–70.

Upton, Rachel, and Courtney Tanenbaum. "The Role of Historically Black Colleges and Universities as Pathway Providers: Institutional Pathways to the STEM Ph.D. Among Black Students." American Institutes for Research, 2014. https://www.air.org/resource/role-historically-black-colleges-and-universities-pathway-providers-institutional-pathways.

U.S. Census Bureau. "2011–2015 American Community Survey 5-year Estimates." 2015. Accessed December 20, 2019. https://factfinder.census.gov/faces/tableservices/jsf/pages/productview.xhtml?src=bkmk.

———. "Census 2000 Summary File." December 2000. https://factfinder.census.gov/faces/tableservices/jsf/pages/productview.xhtml?src=bkmk.

———. "School Enrollment in the United States: October 2018—Detailed Tables." https://www.census.gov/data/tables/2018/demo/school-enrollment/2018-cps.html.

U.S. Department of Health, Education, and Welfare. "Higher Education Act of 1965 Section-by-Section Analysis." Washington, DC: Office of Education, 1965.

Van Biema, David, and Jeff Chu. "Does God Want You To Be Rich?" *Time*, September 10, 2006. http://content.time.com/time/magazine/article/0,9171,1533448,00.html.

Van Groningen, Gerard. *From Creation to Consummation*, vol. I. Dordt, IA: Dordt College Press, 1996.

Vollman, Alexandra. "Health Professions Schools: Bridging the Gap for Underrepresented Minorities." Insights into Diversity, April 8, 2015. https://www.insightintodiversity.com/health-professions-schools-bridging-the-gap-for-underrepresented-minorities/

Wachen, J., et al. "Building College Readiness: Exploring the Effectiveness of the UNC Academic Summer Bridge Program." *Journal of College Student Retention: Research, Theory & Practice* 20 (2018) 116–38.

Wacquant, Loïc J. D. "The Cost of Racial and Class Exclusion in the Inner City." In *The Ghetto Underclass: Social Science Perspectives*, edited by William Julius Wilson, 25–26. Newbury Park, CA: SAGE, 1993.

Walker, Ken. "T.D. JAKES: Like Thunder From Heaven." *Charisma*, November 1996. http://www.charismamag.com/anniversary/pages-from-our-past/24162-t-d-jakes-like-thunder-from-heaven.

Warren G. "I Want It All." Track 5 on *I Want It All*. Restless Records, 1999. Compact disc.

Washington, James. *Black Religion: The True Negro and Christianity in the United States*. Boston: Beacon, 1964.

Wathington, Heather, et al. "A Good Start? The Impact of Texas's Developmental Summer Bridge Program on Student Success." *The Journal of Higher Education* 87 (2016) 150–77.

Weiner, Lois. *Preparing Teachers for Urban Schools: Lessons from Thirty Years of School Reform*. New York: Teachers College Press, 1993.

Wells, David F. *The Courage to Be Protestant*. Grand Rapids: Eerdmans, 2008.

West, Carolyn M., and Kamilah Johnson. "Sexual Violence in the Lives of African American Women: Risk, Response, and Resilience." VAWnet, March 2013. https://vawnet.org/material/sexual-violence-lives-african-american-women-risk-response-and-resilience.

West, Cornel. *Hope on a Tight Rope*. Carlsbad, CA: Hay House, 2008.

Whaley, Arthur L. "Clinicians' Competence in Assessing Cultural Mistrust Among African American Psychiatric Patients." *Journal of Black Psychology* 37 (2011) 387–406. https://doi.org/10.1177/0095798410387133.

White, Bianca A. "The Invisible Victims of the School-to-Prison Pipeline: Understanding Black Girls, School Push-Out, and the Impact of the Every Student Succeeds Act." *William and Mary Journal of Race, Gender, and Social Justice* 24 (2018) 641–63.

Wilkinson, Bruce. *The Prayer of Jabez*. Colorado Springs: Multnomah, 2000.

Williams, Rihana S., et al. "African American High School Students' Reading Comprehension Performance as a Function of Academic Enrichment Program Exposure." In "Black in America: A Scholarly Response to the CNN Documentary—Policy Brief Series 2010" by Center for African American Research and Policy. 2010.

———. "The Relations Between Human Capital, Implicit Views of Intelligence, and Literacy Performance: Implications for the Obama Education Era." *Urban Education* 46 (2011) 563–87. doi:10.1177/0042085910377514.

Williamson, Marianne. *Healing the Soul of America*. New York: Simon & Schuster, 2000.

Willingham, D. T. "Do Visual, Auditory, and Kinesthetic Learners Need Visual, Auditory, and Kinesthetic Instruction?" *American Educator* 29 (2005) 31–44.

Wilson, Amos. *The Developmental Psychology of the Black Child*. 2d ed. Brooklyn: Afrikan World InfoSystems, 2014.

Wilson, William J. *When Work Disappears*. New York: Vintage, 1996.

Wise, Reverend Robert. "Creflo Dollar Critique." Forgotten Word Ministries. Accessed February 19, 2020. http://www.forgottenword.org/dollar.html.

Wright, Christopher. *The Mission of God: Unlocking the Bible's Grand Narrative*. Downers Grove, IL: InterVarsity, 2006.

Zaniewski, A. M., and D. Reinholz. "Increasing STEM Success: A Near-Peer Mentoring Program in the Physical Sciences." *International Journal of STEM Education* 3 (2016) 2–12.

Zeichner, Kenneth M., and Liston, Daniel. *Reflective Teaching: An Introduction*. Reflective Teaching and the Social Conditions of Schooling Series. 2d ed. London: Routledge, 1996.

Ziker, C., et al. "2016 Verizon Innovative Learning Minority Male Program: Summer Program Evaluation Executive Summary." Paper presented at SRI International, Menlo Park, CA, November 1, 2016.

Index